NEW TIDES
IN THE
PACIFIC

RECENT TITLES IN
CONTRIBUTIONS IN POLITICAL SCIENCE
Series Editor: Bernard K. Johnpoll

NEW TIDES
IN THE
PACIFIC

Pacific Basin Cooperation and the Big Four (Japan, PRC, USA, USSR)

EDITED BY Roy Kim *and* Hilary Conroy

Contributions in Political Science, Number 188

GREENWOOD PRESS
New York · Westport, Connecticut · London

LIBRARY OF CONGRESS CATALOGING-IN-PUBLICATION DATA

New tides in the Pacific.

(Contributions in political science, ISSN 0147-1066 ;
no. 188)
Bibliography: p.
Includes index.
1. Pacific Area—Economic integration. 2. Pacific
Area cooperation. 3. Pacific Area—National security.
I. Kim, Roy U. T. II. Conroy, Hilary, 1919–
III. Series.
HC681.N48 1987   337.1′9   87-8406
ISBN 0-313-25625-X (lib. bdg. : alk. paper)

Library of Congress Catalog Card Number: 87-8406
ISBN: 0-313-25625-X
ISSN: 0147-1066

First published in 1987

Greenwood Press, Inc.
88 Post Road West, Westport, Connecticut 06881

Printed in the United States of America

∞

The paper used in this book complies with the
Permanent Paper Standard issued by the National
Information Standards Organization (Z39.48-1984).

10 9 8 7 6 5 4 3 2 1

The Editors jointly dedicate this book to their dear friends,
Louis and Josephine Klein, founders of
the Interchange for Pacific Scholarship

Roy Kim dedicates it to his father, Won-il Kim

The spirit of commerce has a tendency to soften the manners of men and to extinguish those inflammable humors which so often have kindled into wars.

Alexander Hamilton, 1787

Contents

Foreword

The idea of a "Pacific Community" has been one of the most stimulating—yet misunderstood—concepts addressed in recent years by foreign policy analysts throughout the world. In some instances, even its origins are debated as if it were necessary to establish its pedigree and ultimately its legitimacy as a topic worthy of intellectual discussion.

In now appears that theory is being overtaken by events. With few exceptions, senior officials in Pacific Basin nations have begun to examine the idea of closer cooperation on a multilateral basis with serious, albeit cautious, interest. The United States has for some years gently encouraged the development of wider Pacific institutions, and Japan has provided important intellectual stimulus.

More recently, the other two major Pacific powers—China and the Soviet Union—have indicated an unequivocal interest in exploring avenues of regional economic cooperation. The entry of China into the Asian Development Bank, for example, and its discussions with the Pacific Economic Cooperation Conference underscore Chinese desires to demonstrate a more positive and outward-looking approach in their regional relations. Of equal significance, perhaps, is Mikhail Gorbachev's Vladivostok initiative on July 28, 1986. In calling for a new era of cooperation with the Asian-Pacific region, this speech and the positions taken in the Soviet government statement on April 23, 1986, raise new questions about the aspirations and activities of the Soviet Union in the Pacific Basin. Significantly for the contents of this volume, Western reporting and analysis has overlooked an important dimension of the Vladivostok speech: that portion concerned with the idea of a "Pacific Community." This is a term that has become for the Soviets a kind of epithet for "imperialist" aspirations in the region. Yet Gorbachev has seized upon a change in nomenclature by the new regional grouping—the Pacific Economic Cooperation Conference—as the pretext for a new Soviet approach to regional dialogues, one that challenges other countries to include the USSR in their deliberations.

A mere announcement of a change in attitude, however, does not constitute a basis for participation by the Soviets in the kind of highly substantive discussions that are progressing among the Pacific market economies. Instead, there remain to be established certain concrete initiatives by the Soviet Union to increase its credibility as a serious economic partner alongside these dynamic and highly competitive nations, and simultaneously to reduce its excessive military presence in Asia. To suggest this is not, as Gorbachev indicates, yet another saber-rattling effort aimed at depicting a "Soviet threat" in East Asia, but is based on a practical assessment of the current Soviet economic and political involvement in the entire Pacific Basin in comparison to other parts of the world.

In any event, these developments—along with a more forthcoming attitude toward regional cooperation by most of the ASEAN nations—suggest the need for a wider examination of the economic and geopolitical forces driving the so-called Pacific Cooperation Movement. This volume takes an important step in that direction not only by providing perspectives from the United States and Japan, but also be examining Soviet and Chinese interests in Pacific Basin developments.

During my tenure as the Republican leader of the United States Senate, it was my privilege to discuss broad global issues with leaders in each of the four major Pacific powers considered herein. At that time, a genuine regional movement in the Pacific Basin was only a gleam in the eyes of a few visionaries. Today, as these same nations confront the dramatic transformations occurring in the Pacific and the new challenges they present, there is clearly a need for a wider framework for regional consultation and cooperation. Pacific economic and political interdependence makes such questions unavoidable. Volumes such as this, it is to be hoped, make them easier to understand.

The Honorable Hugh Scott
Chairman, United States Committee
for Pacific Economic Cooperation

Acknowledgments

This volume is a collective endeavor, and we want to express our sincere appreciation to those who made it possible. Our thanks for the assistance of the International Studies Association, which provided financial support for the international scholars to participate in two special panels on "Pacific Basin Cooperation" at its 1981 annual convention in Philadelphia. Mrs. Charlotte Conroy and Mrs. Sharlie C. Ushioda contributed invaluable technical assistance in the preparation of the manuscript. Michele Breslauer assisted with the index. The Interchange for Pacific Scholarship (IPS) has sponsored its preparation for publication.

We wish to thank all of the authors. In the course of writing their contributions, they reworked their separate chapters several times. As a rule, we encouraged them to express their own viewpoints without any specific guidelines.

The Ford Foundation and the International Research & Exchanges Board provided research grants for Roy Kim to travel several times to China, Japan, and the Soviet Union. He was also assisted by Dean Thomas Canavan, College of Humanities & Social Sciences, Drexel University, with reduced teaching loads. Vivian Hianos, Bridgett Kuharik, and Nadine Matthew of Drexel University assisted Roy Kim for this volume.

Finally, we want to express our gratitude to the staff of Greenwood Press for their patient assistance, encouragement, and support.

Introduction

ROY KIM
with HILARY CONROY

In many ways the development of this volume, like that of the Pacific Basin Movement itself, has been slow but steady. The concept of Pacific Basin cooperation was first brought to prominence in 1979 by Japanese Prime Minister Masayoshi Ohira when he appointed a study group. Made up primarily of scholars, the group submitted a report on the theoretical basis and practical implications of the concept in 1980. Largely based on the report, Ohira discussed the concept with Australian Prime Minister Malcolm Fraser in the same year when he visited Australia. With the support of these two Pacific leaders, an international seminar, attended by representatives of business, governments, and scholars from fifteen Pacific countries, was held at the Australian National University in Canberra. Since then, follow-up conferences, with varied names but at times known as the Pacific Economic Cooperation Conference (PECC), have been held annually. The spring 1985 conference was held in Seoul, and Canada hosted one in November 1986.

The editors of this volume initially organized two panels on the Pacific Community Movement at the annual convention of the International Studies Association held in Philadelphia in 1981. Based on the potential quality of papers presented by prominent Pacific scholars and a substantial degree of interest from the audience, we then decided to look into the possibility of writing this volume. Using our experience as catalyst, we selected only quality and relevant papers, which were later completely revised and updated. To these we have added, in order to focus on the four major Pacific powers, several original papers by prominent scholars in the field—Professor James Morley (director of the East Asian Institute of Columbia University), Academician Yevgeny Primakov (director of the Soviet Institute of World Economy and International Relations), and Professor John Stephan (director of the Soviet Union in Pacific and Asian Region of the University of Hawaii).

The Pacific Basin region is vastly diversified. Population figures in 1985, for instance, range from the world's smallest independent state, Nauru, in the South Pacific, with an area of eight square miles and a population of 8,000, to the world's largest, China, with an area of almost four million square miles and over one billion people. Economic sizes also range from oil-rich Brunei, with a per capita GNP of nearly $18,000, to some of the island nations with a per capita GNP of less than $350. Culturally and religiously, the basin varies from Confucianism and Buddhism to Islam and Christianity. Yet human resources with a relatively high degree of education abound, and literacy—estimated at 75 percent in the developing Pacific Basin—is well ahead of other regions. Countries of the region owe less than 20 percent of the world's developing-country debt, compared with over 50 percent in Latin America. Their debt-to-service ratio is the lowest of any region—under 16 percent—and their debt-to-export ratio, nearly 80 percent, was the best in the world in 1985.[1]

The region's growing importance is well recognized by the four major Pacific powers. Citing President Theodore Roosevelt at the turn of the century—"the Atlantic is the ocean of the present and the Pacific is the ocean of the future"—President Ronald Reagan stated, at a White House reception welcoming the formation of the U.S. National Committee for Pacific Economic Cooperation in 1984, that "as a Californian, I've long recognized the importance of the Pacific region and I am pleased that during this administration we've been able to expand and deepen our ties with the countries of the Pacific Basin."[2]

Japanese Prime Minister Yasuhiro Nakasone has also recognized the new Asian-Pacific era by observing, in his summer

1983 *Journal of International Affairs* essay, that civilizations have extended their frontiers from the Mediterranean to the Atlantic and from the Atlantic now to the Pacific.[3] In regard to China, it is well for us to remember what the late Chou En-lai once said: "Do not listen to what we say; but watch what we do." Without much rhetoric Beijing today benefits from active economic relations with most of the Pacific region.

Soviet General Secretary Mikhail Gorbachev has also expressed lofty ideals. Speaking from "the Window to the East," Vladivostok, in July 1986, he proclaimed that "the Soviet Union is also an Asian and a Pacific country." Asia, he observed, "which woke up to a new life in the twentieth century, has enriched world progress with its diversified and unique experience in the fight for freedom and independence. This is not only history. This is a living legacy that makes up one of the important fundamentals of the current political realities in this part of the world."[4]

Historically, of course, Russia has long been a Pacific power, especially since the founding of Vladivostok in 1860. Yet Russia's Pacific expansion was effectively checked by a hostile Japan—backed by Britain through the 1902 Anglo-Japanese Alliance. This blocked Russia from acquiring warm-water ports in Manchuria, China proper, and Korea. Soviet Far Eastern occupation by the Western Allies and Japan during and after the Revolution, 1917–22, certainly stressed the region's geostrategic importance to the newly established Bolshevik regime. Some observers have even speculated on some kind of a "Soviet manifest destiny" for Soviet involvement in the Pacific. Whether this will be hostile and upsetting to the region's economic prosperity and political stability, or can be constructive and mutually beneficial to the entire emerging "Pacific Community," is one of the principal questions which this volume addresses.

Long before Russia and other Western powers appeared on the scene, perhaps the most successful regional system on the Pacific—if we are to judge by longevity—was that of Chinese Confucianism. Systematically analyzed by M. Frederick Nelson in his now classic *Korea and the Old Orders in Eastern Asia*, this so-called Chinese tributary system did succeed remarkably well in maintaining stability in the East Asian region over two thousand years of turbulent history. Still, the pretensions of superiority maintained therein by China had rendered it an anachronism by the nineteenth century.

Then, with China and its Confucian system in shambles and at the mercy of European imperialism, a condition which John Fairbank describes as "synarchy" in his *Trade and Diplomacy on the China Coast*, came the Open Door Policy. Articulated by U.S. Secretary of State John Hay in 1899 and 1900, this was not so much a system as a balancing act by which the United States—weak militarily but with enlarging commercial interests—sought to obtain the assent of the European powers and Japan to a self-denying arrangement for the common good, also presumably to China's advantage. It never worked well, but it enjoyed a very good press, especially in the United States, and it had a few moments of glory, as at the Washington Conference in 1921–22, when it was discussed as if it were international law. Yet in the 1930's the Open Door was shut by the Japanese, and although it may be that the Pacific War was—in part, at least—a "war for the Open Door" from the American perspective, that system, such as it was, had by 1941 been preempted by Japan's Greater East Asia Co-Prosperity Sphere (Daitōa Kyōeiken) as a regional system.

This was certainly the worst—meaning the least workable and the least acceptable—of history's three East Asian regional systems. Japan's military was far too insular and crude to become an acceptable leadership, and time for transition to something better did not materialize. Hence, when Japan went down to defeat, there was nothing but a spreading cold war, which became hot in Korea and Vietnam, to replace Japan's "co-prosperity"; and it is only now in the 1980's, over thirty years after its collapse and a decade beyond Vietnam, that the pieces are falling into possible position for a new and better, meaning mutually profitable, useful, and acceptable, regional arrangement. Hence this attempt to perceive and elucidate whatever opportunities there may be for consensus on the construction of a Pacific Basin Economic Cooperation (PBEC) movement is herewith presented.

While the initial official Soviet positions as stated may seem somewhat negative, the new direction expressed by Mikhail

Gorbachev in July 1986 to join in the movement would seem to belie this, as does the analysis by Hiroshi Kimura. The Soviet Union, for the first time, sent an observer to the Fifth Pacific Economic Cooperation Conference (PECC), Vancouver, Canada, in November 1986. Also the People's Republic of China's negativism seems to be giving way. Since the PRC adopted a more "independent foreign policy" beginning in the 1980's, Beijing has appeared to seek a limited detente with Moscow while continuing to improve relations with Washington primarily for internal modernization. In fact, both Beijing and Taipei joined the PECC in November 1986. A. Doak Barnett, in his fall 1986 *Foreign Affairs* essay, suggests that a moderate, reformist, modernizing China should be viewed as a stablizing factor in regional and global perspectives.[5] France Conroy, who twice visited the PRC in 1979 and 1985 and was a participant in a 1981 seminar at Nakhodka, USSR, takes up the Chinese view in his chapter.

Perhaps mindful of Japan's bitter historical experience, Yasuhiro Nakasone, in promoting the movement, has stressed that such cooperation should not assume a military or political character, nor should it be perceived as encouraging the establishment of an exclusive regional bloc for the pursuit of narrow national interests. During his 1985 visit to Canberra, he expressed the hope that cooperation between the Atlantic and the Pacific, and indeed among all countries everywhere, will bring mankind in the 21st century to new heights of achievement.

Centered on the broad theme of *New Tides in the Pacific*, this volume is a collection of original essays by several well-known scholars from different countries who have been keenly interested in the subject for some time. Reflecting on the slow but steady growth of the movement, this book emphasizes the gradually emerging framework of the region's economic cooperation. Careful and systematic attention is given to the complicated and conflicting elements in the process of development.

In our first chapter James Morley reviews the genesis of the Pacific community idea and discusses its particularly close association with Japanese concerns and projections. He persuasively argues from the experience of these formative stages that if the movement is to eventuate, the governments concerned should undertake a more active role than in the past. Leadership from the four major Pacific countries, particularly from Japan and the United States, he suggests, will be essential, but there may be a price to pay.

Chapter 2 is contributed by Academician Evgeny M. Primakov of the Soviet Union. His essay analyzes serious problems of peace and security of the Pacific as an integral component of the global situation. Systematically elaborating what he perceives as contradictory "centripetal and centrifigual" processes taking place throughout the Pacific Basin, he discusses how they could conceivably solve numerous Pacific problems of a global nature. While recognizing their indigenous and regional characteristics and rejecting Soviet-American condominium, he still regards Soviet-American roles as basic prerequisites in solving these problems.

Chapters 3 and 4 further elaborate the Soviet perspective. Using Dimitry Petrov's study of Japan in world politics as a background, Prof. Hiroshi Kimura of Hokkaido University analyzes Soviet objections to Japanese—U.S. concepts of "Pacific Basin Cooperation" on the grounds that it would be exclusivistic. Though called "open" and "free" by former Japanese Prime Minister Ohira and other advocates, it would be, in the Soviet view, "double-faced" (*dboist-vennyi*, literally meaning two-faced). This is in the sense that the community is to be designed to operate among capitalist nations, and while this might be fine for Japan, Taiwan, South Korea, and ANZUS countries (Australian, New Zealand, and the United States), it is incompatible with socialist states. What the United States wants, claim its Soviet critics, is a replica of the (Western) European Economic Community, with a Pacific NATO to back it up.

Dr. Ivanov's essay, initially presented to the 7th International Pacific Nakhodka Seminar in 1983 but subsequently revised to reflect Mr. Gorbachev's new Vladivostok initiatives toward the Pacific, systematically presents potential positive benefits and serious obstacles toward forming a Pacific Economic Cooperation regime perceived by the USSR. Yet, as a trained economist (at the Institute of Oriental Studies where he served as the Academic Secretary before moving to the Institute of World Economy and International Relations), his observations are still quite comprehensive and analytical.

If we were viewing the situation in 1970 instead of in the 1980's, such criticism might indeed be well founded. But since that time, the United States has normalized relations with China, and Japan has undertaken large trade involvement with the USSR. Since all four elements of this quadrant want and need trade—although in varying degrees, to be sure—may ways be found for socialist-capitalist trade in the emerging system?

Chapters 5 and 6 broaden the perspective to America and China. In his essay, John Stephan clearly demonstrates the American penchant for not regarding the Soviet Union as an actor in the Pacific area, as a positive or even negative force. The Pacific has been an American lake, for a time menaced by Japan but since the Pacific war back to its normal (American) environment. Chapter 6 brings China into the Pacific Community setting. Its author France Conroy analyzes, from somewhat philosophical perspectives, the fundamental Chinese posture between Washington and Moscow, and suggests the possible extent of Chinese involvement in the movement.

In chapter 7 Mark Borthwick reviews the U.S. government's position on "Pacific Community" with great care and precision. He shows how and why Washington has been unwilling—perhaps also unable—to take the lead in its development, despite its potential. Leaving the initiative to business and academic circles has been Washington's general approach, and even the mild initiatives proposed by the Senate's Subcommittee on East Asian and Pacific Affairs, headed by John Glenn, were tabled after Glenn left the chairmanship in 1981. However, President Reagan and Secretary of State George Shultz have given, since 1984, indications of special interest in the Pacific region; and as Borthwick indicates, the smaller nations of the region seem to be prodding them.

Chapter 8, by Norman Palmer, takes up the security issue with sense and sensitivity. He shows that it is not just a matter of the United States matching the USSR missile for missile or vice versa, but that each nation and "half-nation" has its own worries, needs, and problems. And he gives more than lip service to the Japanese concept of "Comprehensive National Security," which although it may have been invented by Japanese leaders wishing to escape the pressure for arms buildup and for sharing more of the costs of the defense commitments now paid for by the United States, is nonetheless a sensible idea. It considers not only military preparation and weaponry as factors in national defense, but geographical, economic, and even cultural factors as well.

In the final essay on "Problems and Prospects," I reconsider the Japanese-American relationship in the light of its potential for positive as well as negative prospects for the movement.

Finally, a fundamental question has to be raised. Are the four major Pacific powers prepared to meet the challenges of the new tides in the Pacific? While this problem has been analyzed in all of the essays in this volume—that is our central focus—it still deserves further attention. For the establishment of Pacific Basin Economic Cooperation will certainly require at a minimum their multilateral coordination—unilateral and bilateral approaches are completely inadequate. In this regard, we conclude this volume with a systematic analysis of Gorbachev's surprising Vladivostok initiatives.

We are hopeful that, by identifying the key problems and addressing them from a variety of perspectives, this volume may clarify the issues for scholars, government officials, and journalists with a special interest in this increasingly important region of the world, and that it will give the general reader a sense of the unfolding drama.

Finally, a word on terminology. Gunnar Myrdal, in his now dated but still useful study, *Asian Drama*, devotes an introductory chapter to what he calls "diplomacy by terminology." He is referring mainly to the upgrading of former colonies little by little through the use of words like "underdeveloped," "third-world," "developing," or "new" nations. Likewise, *New Tides in the Pacific* has a problem of "diplomacy" in its terminology. "Pacific Basin Movement" (PBM) may be described as the fairly neutral term for our subject matter, and "Pacific Community" or "Pacific Community Movement" has been preferred and utilized by the West. Yet the Soviet Union has denounced the use of the term "Community," claiming that it masks an American intent to dominate the Pacific and keep Socialist countries out of the movement. Recently, however, Soviets have been using the terms "Pacific Basin Cooperation" and "Pacific Cooperation Movement" in a favorable light. The acronym PCM could lean either way. In this volume the editors have tried to use the terms in ways that take appropriate account of this problem.

Regarding East Asian nations, since most Japanese with international contacts now use the Western order of given name first and family name last, we have done so for all Japanese names, thus Saburo Okita. But with Chinese names it is the opposite, hence Deng Xiaoping.

NOTES

1. Address by Secretary of State George Shultz (excerpt) before U.S. National Committee for Pacific Economic Cooperation, San Francisco, February 21, 1985, in Foreign Press Center, *Statements and Opinions on Pacific Community* (Tokyo: Foreign Press Center, 1985), pp. 45–52.

2. Ronald Reagan, cited in *Pacific Community Newsletter* (Fall 1984), p. 2.

3. Yasuhiro Nakasone, "Foreign Policy and Constitutional Views," *Journal of International Affairs* (Summer 1983), pp. 1–4.

4. The complete text of the speech is found in *Pravda*, July 29, 1986.

5. A. Doak Barnett, "Ten Years after Mao," *Foreign Affairs* (Fall 1986), p. 65.

1

The Genesis of the Pacific Basin Movement and Japan

JAMES WILLIAM MORLEY

A new tide is running in the Pacific: the tide of interdependence. It is gathering strength from the profound surge of the Japanese economy; the increasing thirst for capital, markets, and more advanced technology of the newly industrializing countries of Southeast Asia and Korea; the determined new Asian orientation of Australia; and the epochal shift to Asia and the Pacific of the center of gravity of the foreign trade of the United States. These changes are challenging the countries of the Asian-Pacific region with unprecedented opportunities for mutual gain. At the same time, they are drawing them into such intimate and complex relationships with each other that many thoughtful observers believe that only a new form of regional cooperation can ease the vulnerabilities and relieve competitive strains to which each is being subjected. The new tide is bearing on its crest, therefore, a "Pacific Basin Movement" which, while not yet an effective political force, may well portend a future development of truly historic importance.

Pan-Asia, after all, is an age-old dream. There have been many efforts to draw together the widely scattered parts of the Far Eastern segment of the globe. Some, like the 2,000-year-long expansions of the Chinese or the short-lived Greater East Asia Co-Prosperity Sphere of the Japanese, sought to absorb the lands of East Asia and the western Pacific into indigenous empires. Others, like the 400-year-long colonialism of the West and the competing Soviet, Chinese, and American security treaty networks of our own time, have tried to tie the more accessible peoples of this vast region to power centers far away.

But the Pacific Basin Movement now underway is not calling for a revival of past empires or an expansion of current alliance systems. It differs from the inspiration of these earlier drives in that none of its activists is advocating any kind of arrangement—vague and differing though their proposals are—that would bring the participating countries together on other than a voluntary basis of national equality. It differs from this earlier regionalism also in being stimulated, if not exclusively, at least primarily and overtly by an economic concern: to ease the international tensions generated by the increasing and unprecedented interdependence of the market economies. It should not be surprising, then, that it was in Japan, the strongest of the market economies, that the movement found its first and strongest supporters.

THE SUPPORTERS OF THE MOVEMENT

The movement began in the early 1960's in Tokyo. After a century of struggle Japan had finally emerged as one of the world's great economic powers, only to be awakened from its dream of an ever-widening global market by the formation of the European Community and the threat of protectionism in the United States. The buoyant mood dissolved in an atmosphere of impending international economic crisis. In these circumstances more and more Japanese leaders in business, government, and academia began to look around for additional partners with whom to share their economic future. Some came to believe that they had found such partners in the vast region of the Pacific, where the newly industrializing countries were just then getting underway. Here the vision began to unfold of a new dynamic center of economic development, capable when rationalized of bringing about a profound change in the world balance of power.

This view was conceptualized and advanced particularly by a group of economists associated with Saburo Okita. Okita, who was later to become president of Japan's Overseas Economic

Cooperation Fund, then foreign minister under Prime Minister Ohira, and later president of the United Nations University of Japan in Tokyo, was already in the sixties one of the leading economic planners of postwar Japan. In 1965 he had only recently left his post in the Economic Planning Agency to set up a new macro-economic think tank, the Japan Economic Research Center. It was at one of the center's first conferences, held on November 10–13 of that year, that Professors Kiyoshi Kojima and Hiroshi Kurimoto, both of Hitotsubashi University, launched the idea of a Pacific Free Trade Area (PAFTA) as Japan's response to the EEC. In a paper that was widely distributed, Kojima argued that if the five advanced countries in the Pacific—Japan, the United States, Canada, Australia, and New Zealand—were to form a free trade area among themselves, and then welcome as associated members with preferential treatment such developing countries in Asia and Latin America as wished to join, the result would be a vast Pacific trade expansion.[1] Prime Minister Takeo Miki found it an intriguing concept and urged that it be carefully studied.[2] The Ministry of Foreign Affairs offered financial support for such an investigation, and in February 1968, at its first Pacific Free Trade and Development (PAFTAD) Conference, the center laid the proposition before a group of largely academic economists from countries throughout the region. The benefits to be derived from increased economic cooperation in the Pacific attracted the participants enormously.

So did the vision which underlay Kojima's tables and charts, that of the Pacific Basin not as a narrow rim of disparate countries separated by a great ocean, but as a coherent region with enormous underdeveloped wealth awaiting only the devising of rational formulae and the marshalling of governmental and private energies for its potential to be realized. The PAFTAD economists, as we may call them, quickly formed one of the core groups of the Pacific Basin Movement. Nevertheless, coming from many different countries with different perspectives, these economists found it hard to accept Kojima's specific proposal. The globalists from the advanced countries did not want to see the world market broken up into regional trading blocs. Most economists from overseas did not believe the countries would benefit equally. Manufactured goods exporters like the Japanese were seen to be advantaged far more than primary goods exporters like the Australians, and these academic views seem to have reflected the views held by government economists as well.[3]

More study was required. PAFTA itself was shelved, but plans were made immediately for a series of PAFTAD conferences, which have been held annually ever since, sponsored by an organization or organizations in a different host Pacific country each year. Meanwhile, in Japan in 1970 the Japan Institute of International Affairs (JIIA), a Foreign Ministry–related research organization, commissioned Okita and Kojima to head a project on the Asian-Pacific region, where the prospects for greater cooperation could be carefully assessed. Five senior economists from universities, government, and research organs joined them, and a volume of papers was published in 1971.[4] In the same year the Institute of Developing Economies (IDE), the think tank related to the Ministry of International Trade and Industry (MITI), published *Studies on a Pacific Economic Region*, edited by Seiya Yano.

Moves were made also on the international front. At the first Ministerial Conference between Australia and Japan, held in Canberra in October 1972, the two governments agreed to finance a three-year project (later extended) to be conducted jointly by the Japan Economic Research Center (JERC) in Tokyo and the Research School of Pacific Studies of the Australian National University to look carefully into the economic relations between Australia and Japan in the context of the region. Named the Australia-Japan Economic Relations Research Project, it was headed by Okita and Sir John Crawford, chancellor of the university and former head of the Australian government's Department of Trade and Industry. It was given research direction in Tokyo by Kojima and in Canberra by Peter Drysdale, reader in the Economics Department of ANU. By 1980 the project had drawn together more than 150 economists and by its voluminous reports, and particularly three comprehensive assessments to the two governments, had given a powerful thrust to the Pacific Basin Movement.[5]

By the late 1970's these expanding research efforts had produced an influential interlocking international interest group of professional economists, centering in Japan and Australia, but with participants from most of the other countries of the western Pacific and North America. They were impressed by the dynamism of the region and the growing interdependence among its market economies. They had made a number of technical studies of particular problem areas they felt needed attention, such as trade, investment, industrial structure, and resources, and they had pretty well reached a consensus that some new kind of institutional arrangement was needed.

The PAFTAD group had recommended in 1971 that a policy research organ be established by the governments of the five advanced countries.[6] Kojima continued to believe that PAFTA was the most desirable engine for moving the Pacific economies forward, but he recognized that his colleagues were not ready to accept it. An alternative began to take shape in conversations with his Australian counterpart, Peter Drysdale. It was that of an Organization for Pacific Trade and Development (OPTAD), envisaged as a looser structure, possibly along the lines of the Organization for Economic Cooperation and Development (OECD). Kojima at first thought of this as a halfway house to PAFTA and envisaged it as having powers to enforce certain codes of investment and trade conduct on the constituent nations; but, as the discussions continued and more and more views were accommodated, OPTAD came to be formulated as a kind of forum, not just among the advanced countries, but on a basinwide level. It was conceived as having no regulatory powers, but providing simply an institutional arrangement for identifying issues, exchanging information, and facilitating intergovernmental negotiations on specific functional problems.[7]

In 1976 Crawford and Okita recommended OPTAD to their respective governments.[8] In 1979 Drysdale and Hugh Patrick, then professor of Far Eastern Economics at Yale University but now at Columbia University, an active member of the PAFTAD Conference from the beginning, recommended it to the U.S. Senate Committee on Foreign Relations.[9] While OPTAD had been commented on in many papers by many scholars in the course of the decade, the Drysdale-Patrick paper sets it forth in its most complete, operational form. The authors drew on the research of both the PAFTAD conferences and the Australia-Japan Project and presented the western Pacific as the "fastest growing" region in the world. They pointed out that the thrust of the American economy is also toward the western Pacific, but argued that the potential benefits of this new orientation cannot be realized without the establishment of a new and broader framework for the relationship. OPTAD was then recommended with an initial membership of the market economies of the western Pacific, together with the United States and Canada.

Meanwhile, a second group caught the Pacific fever: the international businessmen associated with the Pacific Basin Economic Council, known as PBEC. Conceived as a meeting of the Japan-Australia Joint Economic Committee, PBEC was organized in 1967 as a private organization with five national committees: Australia, Canada, Japan, New Zealand, and the United States. It was enlarged in 1974 with a Pacific Regional Committee, so that by the end of the 1970's it came to embrace more than 300 influential businessmen throughout the Pacific Basin. Since they were drawn together by a common belief in the potentiality of the region and a common concern for the problems of interdependence, as were the international economists, it is not surprising that when Philip Thompson of the University of Singapore spoke to the PBEC General Meeting in Manila in 1978 about the Pacific Economic Community concept, he struck a responsive chord.

The concept was immediately taken up by the PBEC's new leader, Noboru Gotoh, who had succeeded to the chairmanship of the Japan National Committee and was elected at that meeting as PBEC's international president as well. The energetic chairman and president of the Tokyu Corporation, which owns railways, hotels, and other properties in Japan and throughout the Pacific Basin, Gotoh has been backed by one of Japan's most respected business strategists, Ryuzo Sejima, chairman of C. Itoh and Company, then serving as vice chairman of the Japan National Committee and one of PBEC's international counselors. Former U.S. ambassador to Japan James Hodgson, later chairman of Pathfinder Mines, and Sir James Vernon, chairman of CSR Limited (Australia) and the succeeding international president of PBEC, were particularly enthusiastic. Follow-up discussions were carried on within the constituent committees, particularly the Japan National Committee, and at the General Meeting in Los Angeles in 1979, where Gotoh delivered an especially telling speech on "The Significance of the Pacific Basin and the Role of PBEC in the 1980's."[10] As a consequence, when PBEC met in Sydney on May 5–8, 1980, it had before it a draft proposal for a Pacific Economic Community (PEC) which the Japan National Committee had drawn up, presented for discussion to the Steering Committee the previous October and revised to accommodate the views of other member committees to which it had been circulated.[11]

The PEC was envisaged as embracing the same countries as in the OPTAD conception plus the Pacific coastal nations of Latin America. Eventually it would need "a forum for true cooperation at an international 'inter-governmental' level." As for PBEC itself, it should organize a standing subcommittee to advance the general cause.[12] (The Standing Committee consisted of Vernon, Gotoh, Jose B. Fernandez, chairman of the Far East Bank and Trust Company [Philippines] and chairman of the PBEC Pacific Regional Committee, and PBEC's international director, Weldon Gibson of the Stanford Research Institute.) But it was not prepared to commit itself to any particular organizational formula for the PEC, either PAFTA, OPTAD, or any other, and in fact did not reach a consensus on whether the coordinating mechanism should be at the governmental level at all.

The Stanford Research Institute in California, which provided the staff support for the U.S. National Committee and for PBEC's international activities, was not the only think tank or research center that was drawn into the movement. In Japan, in addition to JERC, JIIA, and IDE already referred to, the Nomura Research Institute began to involve itself. In September 1978 Kiichi Saeki, president of the institute, completed a report for the Japanese government on future national priorities.[13] While reserved in tone and refraining from specifically endorsing the OPTAD proposal, Saeki placed great emphasis on the need for increased economic cooperation in the Pacific region. He proposed the establishment of a $20 billion Pacific Cooperation Fund, an expanded program of personnel exchanges, and a regular series of ministerial or summit conferences.[14] Later that same year on a more popular level the executive vice president of No-

mura and columnist for the Pacific edition of *Newsweek*, Jiro
Tokuyama, published a widely read book in which he heralded
the coming of what he called "the Pacific Century." He not only
championed passionately the formation of a free trade area among
the advanced countries of the Pacific as in Kojima's original
scheme, but called for the creation of a grander Pacific Economic Sphere based on a vision of a Pacific Community tran-
scending differences of economy, culture, and national identity,
and including the less developed countries (LDC's) and particularly the PRC.[15]

In Australia a number of the regional economics specialists at
the Research School of Pacific Studies at the Australian National University and from other universities became involved.
Lawrence Krause at the Brookings Institution, and other individuals at the Asia Society, the Hudson Institute, the Pacific
Forum, the East-West Center, and various universities, including California, Columbia, and Washington, took part. In other
countries of the western Pacific, the Center for Strategic and
International Studies in Jakarta, the Institute of Southeast Asian
Studies in Singapore, the National Institute of Public Administration in Malaysia, the Institute for Far Eastern Studies at
Kyungnam University in Korea, and others began to show interest. In the late 1970's academic conferences proliferated. Articles began to appear, first in *Asia Pacific Community*, then in
other English-language media like the *New York Times*, *Asian
Wall Street Journal*, *Far Eastern Economic Review*, *Foreign Affairs*, and *The Economist*, and in vernacular newspapers and
magazines throughout the region.[16]

It is hardly surprising that by 1978 and 1979 the Pacific Basin
Movement began to impinge on the consciousness of policymakers throughout the region. One particularly important locus
of that consciousness was the select international group of establishment leaders, drawn from the free market countries in
the western Pacific and Northeast Asia, who had been participating in the "Williamsburg Meetings," inaugurated by John D.
Rockefeller III and the Asia Society of New York and Washington as unofficial, informal gatherings designed to strengthen the
sense of community in the Pacific and held annually since 1971.

By the end of the decade more than 400 government officials, business executives, bankers, editors, scholars, and other professional people from all over the region had had the experience of sharing privately and frankly their views on the region's problems and possibilities.

Inevitably the group returned again and again to the question of whether new institutional arrangements for the region were desirable. It was on the agenda of the very first meeting. In 1976 Okita, who had become a co-sponsor of the meetings, reported the gist of the OPTAD proposal which that year he and Sir John Crawford were recommending to their respective governments. Kojima followed up this presentation. So did Thanat Kohman, former foreign minister of Thailand, and Soedjatmoko, former Indonesian ambassador to the United States and the UN, both of whom spoke in November 1977 of the need for some kind of intergovernmental Pacific forum. While no consensus was sought, it is reasonable to believe that by the end of the decade many of the Williamsburgers had seriously considered the arguments for a new regional framework, had reached some conclusion of their own about the various proposals, and had probably shared their views on the subject with other influential persons outside the group.

Thus by the late 1970's four international interest groups were pushing for a new framework of economic cooperation in the Pacific Basin: economists centered around the PAFTAD conferences and the Australia-Japan Project; businesses involved in PBEC; consultants and scholars drawn in by the think tanks and university research centers; and establishment leaders in various fields who had been participating in or were influenced by the Williamsburg Meetings. The movement was particularly strong in Japan. In the United States, Congressman Lester Wolff, with the support of Assistant Secretary of State Richard Holbrooke, had begun pressing for an Asian and Pacific Parliamentary Assembly, and Senator John Glenn was requesting the Congressional Research Service study on the Pacific Basin concept.[17] In Australia, the movement had had even greater success: leaders, both in the government and out, had already given their support.[18]

THE CANBERRA SEMINAR

The strength and breadth of the movement help to explain how it was that in the fall of 1978, when Masayoshi Ohira began his final struggle for the prime ministership of Japan, he picked up the Pacific Basin Cooperation concept as one of the bold new ideas his administration would champion. No doubt he saw in the concept some of the same possibilities that Eisaku Sato had seen five years earlier in the proposal to establish the Asia Development Bank: the opportunity for Japan to pursue a more autonomous course, thereby showing its capacity for leadership and reaping at little cost the benefits of international prestige.[19] The problem was that no consensus had yet emerged within the movement as to the structure needed to facilitate this cooperation or the process for getting it into place. While OPTAD was being pushed hard by a number of the economists, other concerned Japanese believed that they detected a strong reluctance among Southeast Asians to accept OPTAD or indeed any other new Pacific-wide structure at the governmental level. In any event, among many of the Japanese activists there was a strong feeling that in view of the debacle of the Greater East Asia Co-Prosperity Sphere a generation earlier, too-active sponsorship by Japan of any Pacific-wide action might be damaging to the cause.

To seek a way out, on March 6, 1979, shortly after the formation of his cabinet,[20] Ohira appointed as one of his personal policy-advisory task forces the Pacific Basin Cooperation Study Group. Headed first by Okita and from November (when Okita was appointed foreign minister) by Tsuneo Iida, professor of economics at Nagoya University, the study group was made up of vigorous young university professors and officials from relevant government agencies. Senior activists like Gotoh, Kojima, Sejima and Tokuyama served in an advisory capacity.

On November 14, 1979, the group submitted its preliminary report.[21] It recommended that haste be made slowly. The idea of greater cooperation was attractive and important, and government officials should be thinking about these matters. On the other hand, the concept of building some kind of geographical sphere seemed too political; it would be better to proceed along more functional lines, and before the Japanese government adopted or advocated a specific organizational formula, consensus should be sought among the Pacific countries. The group urged that an international symposium be held—preferably sponsored by some country other than Japan—to which would be invited respected individuals from the public as well as the private sectors of each interested country to discuss the issues involved. A cautious initiative, but an initiative nevertheless.

Ohira accepted the group's recommendation and in January 1980, on his visit to Canberra, suggested to Prime Minister Sir Malcolm Fraser that Australia would make a very welcome host. Thus it was that invitations went out from Sir John Crawford, chancellor of the Australian National University, usually to one governmental official and two other persons drawn from among academics or businessmen in each of the market economies of the western Pacific (excluding Hong Kong and Taiwan), and to Canada and the United States in the eastern Pacific to meet in their private capacities as an international advisory group on September 15–18 to consider the desirability of establishing a new framework for economic cooperation in the Pacific.

These developments, low-keyed though they were, stimulated a wave of preparatory activity throughout the region. Prime Minister Fraser confirmed his personal support for the concept on several occasions, notably in May 1979 when he met Ohira at the UNCTAD V meeting in Manila.[22] That summer in Washington Congressman Wolff, as chairman of the House Subcommittee on Asia-Pacific Affairs, held a series of hearings on the Pacific Community idea.[23] Senator William Roth of the Joint Economic Committee began speaking out on the issue. In the fall the State Department sent Deputy Assistant Secretary Erland Heginbotham and Professor Donald Zagoria to the Asian-Pacific countries to gather opinions. And in Tokyo the prime minister's study group made its final report on May 19, 1980.[24]

The final report was eloquent in its praise of the benefits that would flow from greater cooperation in the basin. But to the surprise of those who had been impressed by the support for OPTAD and even bolder initiatives within Japan and were aware of the recommendation in the Foreign Ministry's own think tank that OPTAD should be advanced,[25] the final report urged only that the prime minister should continue along the cautious line of its preliminary report. The possibilities of cooperation could only be realized in the twenty-first century, it said, recommending that for the present governments should limit themselves to backing the appointment of a "private consultative committee" of fifteen to twenty prominent persons, whose function would be to "manage a series of international conferences" and direct the activities of various "working groups of specialists" for the purpose of identifying regional problems and working out solutions which the relevant governments might then wish to consider.

The subject was taken up in many other forums, including, for example, ongoing dialogue groups like the regional roundtables begun in 1974 by the MITI-affiliated, business-supported Asian Club in Tokyo; the Asian Dialogues begun in 1977 by the Japanese Center for Intellectual Interchange; the Japan-ASEAN Symposia inaugurated in 1978 by the *Mainichi Shimbun* and its related Asian Affairs Research Council and overseas counterpart groups; the Japan-Indonesia Conferences held annually since 1973 by the Japan Institute of International Affairs and the Center for Strategic and International Studies; and the bilateral businessmen's conferences sponsored by the Chamber of Commerce in the appropriate Pacific states. The subject surfaced at the First Indonesia-Korea Conference sponsored by the Indonesian Centre for Strategic and International Studies and the Institute for Far Eastern Studies, Kyungnam University, in October 1979; and again at the travelling symposium on "The United States and ASEAN" administered by the Asia Society of New York and Washington in November of that year.

It could not help but attract attention at the international conferences called primarily to explore regional security questions, such as the "Conference on New Foundations for Asian and Pacific Security" held in December 1979 in Pataya, Thailand, by the Institute of Southeast Asian Studies (ISEAS) (Singapore) and the National Security Information Center (New York); the "Seminar on the Changing Postures of the Great Powers and Their Implications" in Kuala Lumpur in March 1980; the "Conference on Regional Security Developments and Stability in Southeast Asia" held in Singapore in March 1980 by the ISEAS in cooperation with the International Institute for Strategic Studies, Chulaluongkorn University; and the "International Conference on the Development of Strategic Thinking in the 1970's: Prospects for the 1980's" held by the Strategic and Defense Studies Centre of the Australian National University in Canberra in August 1980.

But it was at the ad hoc international conferences called specifically for that purpose that the Pacific economic cooperation question got its most thorough preliminary examination. Such conferences, called by various research bodies and involving participants from government, academia, and the media, included, for example, the conference on "Future Economic and Security Cooperation in the Pacific Region" held by the Pacific Forum (United States) in December 1978. In October 1979 the University of Chile held a conference at Easter Island on the theme, "The Pacific Community: Towards a Role for Latin America"; in January 1980 the Indonesian Centre for Strategic and International Studies (CSIS), in conjunction with the American, Australian, and Thai organizations, held a conference in Bali on "Asia-Pacific in the 1980's: Toward Greater Symmetry in Economic Interdependence"; in March 1980 a "Seminar on Pacific Basin Cooperation—What It Means for New Zealand" was held in Wellington; and in May 1980 a "Forum on the Pacific Basin" was held in Taiwan.

By this time it was becoming clear that not everyone favored the movement, and those who did were divided into three camps on the question of organization. At one extreme were those who believed it was time to set up an intergovernmental structure, possibly the OPTAD, a somewhat weaker organization on the OECD model, or a series of ministerial-level or summit conferences as Saeki proposed. At the other extreme were those like Takeshi Watanabe, chairman of the Japan section of the Trilateral Commission, Narongchai Akrasenee, a development economist with ESCAP in Bangkok, and William Watts, president of the Potomac Associates in Washington, who favored a purely private body to coordinate the work of other private bodies—a conception based on the Trilateral Commission and prewar IPR models.[26] In between were those like the members of the Japanese prime minister's study group who, either for reasons of tactics or conviction, favored a structure that was essentially private, but with government support and access.

At Canberra every effort was made to embrace all views and respect the sensibilities that the convenors were so far aware of.[27] Each of the major activist constituencies was represented—the PAFTAD economists, the PBEC businessmen, the Williamsburgers, and the research center–public forum cluster. Representation was provided to each of the countries that were most prominently involved in the movement to date: the five advanced countries (Australia, Canada, Japan, New Zealand, and the United States); the five ASEAN states (Indonesia, Malaysia, the Philippines, Singapore, and Thailand); the Republic of Korea and the southwest Pacific island nations (Papua, New Guinea, Suva Fiji, and Tonga)—in short, the market economies of the western Pacific and North America. Government officials were drawn in, but with no prior agreement on whether governments themselves should or should not be involved, officials were invited only in their private capacities.

The agenda consisted of a set of general questions for informal discussion: What is the "Pacific Community?" What are the issues? Which countries are interested in participating and in what form? What steps should be taken? For background material a set of papers was provided which included speeches and articles covering a broad range of viewpoints. No governmentally authorized views were presented. One can hardly imagine a more inoffensive, open-ended format. After three days of discussion, Sir John Crawford announced publicly that the seminar had confirmed the convenors' conviction that "a new forum for consultation on major regional policy issues" was needed. He said that support seemed to be coalescing around the idea of a regional standing committee, possibly to be called the Pacific Cooperation Committee (PCC), designed "to coordinate an expansion of exchanges of information within the region and to set up task forces to undertake major studies of a number of issues for regional cooperation." Trade, direct investment, energy, marine resources, and international services were among the issues identified.

This was hardly the intergovernmental level the PAFTAD economists desired. Nor was it the Pacific Economic Community called for by the PBEC. It resembles the most cautious suggestion of the Japan study group, but even that was watered down. Clearly the convenors' hopes that the seminar could raise the issue to governmental agendas had been disappointed. The seminar did not move to do so. Sir John said that he would personally report the new PCC concept to the various governments and seek their support and advice. But when Ambassador Luz del Mundo rose in the concluding public forum to express with some force her continuing reservations, the outlook for Southeast Asian government support at least in the near future seemed quite unpromising.[28] The tide that had borne the Pacific cooperation concept to Canberra seemed to be ebbing.

No ASEAN government responded to Sir John's report. Indeed, no government at all did. Washington remained interested, but uncommitted. The staff of the State Department appeared too engrossed with the Soviet problem to put this on their agenda. Even in Tokyo, where his predecessor had come up with the Canberra idea, Prime Minister Suzuki put it on hold. Why?

WHY WAS IT ABORTIVE?

Following the Canberra seminar, I had an opportunity to visit each of the ASEAN capitals in turn and talk with various persons about the Pacific Basin Movement. Those individuals who had been caught up in the movement network before were as enthusiastic as ever, but others, particularly in official positions, who were hearing the ideas more or less for the first time, expressed great uneasiness. They seemed overwhelmed with the size and complexity of their daily problems and frustrated by the weakness of the structures available to deal with them. Yes, economic interdependence was growing, or, for most, continuing from colonial days, but the issue they were struggling with was how to get some leverage on their advanced-country partners, and this they were already working out in the Group of 77, the UNCTAD conferences, and above all ASEAN. From these organizations they derived cohesion and bargaining power, particularly vis-à-vis Japan and the United States. What would the Southeast Asian sages get, they asked, from participation in the

proposed Pacific Cooperation Community, or even the milder
Pacific Economic Community or the PAFTAD or OPTAD except
to be pulled into a den of the economic lions, and once there,
cut off from their LDC cohorts, to be eaten one by one? The
experiences of Western colonialism and the Greater East Asia
Co-Prosperity Sphere were too much alive to overcome the suspicion that the vagueness of Japan's proposal and the indeci-
siveness of the American response in the studies hid hegemon-
ial objectives of greater danger.

The insistence by all at the Canberra seminar, and indeed in
the preparatory meetings, that the movement was purely economic in character and had no interest or relevance to issues of
regional military security was probably necessary if the meeting
was to take place, but perversely enough, it also served to deepen
the uneasiness. For it is clear to most thinking people in Southeast Asia that military power rests in large part on economic
power. The enhancing of economic interdependence among one
set of states, therefore, must have the effect, intended or not, of
exacerbating their relations with excluded states. The Soviet
Union soon expressed its suspicions.[29]

This might not have been such a serious issue if the South-
east Asian states had agreed on their external security needs,
but they did not. Thailand and Singapore, for example, saw
Vietnam backed by the USSR as the principal security threat.
Indonesia and Malaysia saw China as the principal danger and
Vietnam as the power to be wooed.

While each ASEAN state was inclined politically and economically toward the West, and each seemed to want the United
States in its corner if worse came to worst, none, with the possible exception of Singapore, wanted the United States there too
visibly. None wanted to antagonize either the Chinese or the
Russian giants.

Understanding the complexities of these attitudes, the advocates of a new Pacific regional structure generally tried to ignore or deny the inevitable security implications of their economic regionalism. They also tried to be as vague as possible
about the membership they had in mind. Some talked of a basin
including the entire group of Pacific coast countries of North
and South America, together with China; some entertained the

possibility of the eventual inclusion of the USSR. At the other end of the spectrum were those who would limit consideration to the market economies invited to Canberra—presumably the choice of the Japanese and Australian governments, but leaving open the possibility of later adding the PRC and possibly the Pacific states of Latin America, though hardly the Soviet Union. But there was no real decision at Canberra on membership; and on this question too Southeast Asians came away suspicious that the United States and Japan had more in mind than they were revealing. The Southeast Asian states worried that, wherever the membership line was drawn, it ran the danger of antagonizing those excluded and threatening ASEAN with serious diversions and confrontations.

These initial reactions seemed to suggest that the Pacific Basin Movement was not likely to succeed in breaking the barrier to intergovernmental formulation until the Southeast Asian states felt reassured that there would be no significant negative consequences—that is, it would not cause dangerous antagonisms within ASEAN and other developing nations. At the same time, the Southeast Asian states wanted to be reassured that there would be sufficient positive benefits, particularly in the form of greater concessions from the advanced countries to their security requirements. In short, a Pacific-wide structure could be made attractive only in the context of broader, more supportive policies toward the region than either Japan, the United States, or any of the other advanced countries had so far articulated.

This being so, how can one explain the Ohira government's action in proposing the Canberra seminar? After all, Japan is renowned for the thoroughness of its preparatory studies and preliminary soundings—its *nemawashi*. How could it have taken up the Pacific Basin so prematurely?

The answer seems to be found in the excessive zeal of Prime Minister Ohira to make his mark as a dynamic statesman. Like most Japanese prime ministers before him, he wanted to be remembered not only as a master politician, a man who held his party together, brought it to victory at the polls, and kept himself in office, but also a man of vision who advanced his country to a significant new position in the world. That position would have to be, he felt, in close association with the West. Economic

flows, cultural interchange, and security requirements all drew
it there. But geographically and emotionally, Japan was centered in Asia, and its unique role, he felt, would have to be found
in a new relationship to the lands of Asia and the Pacific. How
to formulate this against the backdrop of Japan's imperialist history and the contemporary environment of vast economic dis-
parity was an issue nearly every prime minister had worked over
in the postwar period. In 1977 his predecessor and archrival,
Fukuda, had launched the Manila Doctrine, a statement of Pacific concern for the countries of Southeast Asia. Although heralded by the Fukuda administration as the first and historic step
in Japan's assertion of a new regional role, the doctrine in fact
defined no role except in terms of aid and goodwill. The field
was open, Ohira believed, for a more dramatic formulation.

At the same time he had had enough personal experience in
the Ministry of Finance and in a number of cabinet posts not to
expect such a formulation to come from the bureaucracy. Most
officials, he knew, focused their attention on day-to-day problems. New ideas took a very long time to percolate up through
the bureaucracy, and when they did, most were so compro-
mised into blandness as to lose their political appeal. He went,
therefore, outside the bureaucracy to an imaginative old friend,
Saburo Okita, and invited him to organize a study group of the
brightest young minds he could find. It would appear that Ohira
was influenced by the success of Watanabe and his private colleagues in devising plans for the Asian Development Bank and
possibly of other elite groups of policy-oriented individuals who
had played significant parts in proposing a variety of domestic
policies.[30]

Unfortunately for Ohira, once the ideas were roughed out by
the study group, they were not picked up as had occurred in the
earlier successful examples by the relevant government agencies, where they could be reexamined and refined into workable
government policy. The Ministry of Foreign Affairs, for example, was committed to trying to see things as ASEAN saw them
and was reluctant to take up a cause the ASEAN states were
not championing. MITI could not see that a new Pacific structure would do anything but give the LDCs an enlarged forum

for making greater demands on Japan. The main policy lines of the ministries were set, and no bureau within these ministries was so hungry for new activity as to see advantage in bucking these lines; nor did any entrepreneurial leader step forward to try to devise the concrete policy and build the consensus that substantial bureaucratic support would have required.

Okita was apparently identified for the entrepreneurial role. He was a person of wide experience in policy initiation, but in the early stages of the issue's life cycle he was out of government, and in the final stages he was removed from active leadership by being appointed foreign minister. This may seem to have placed him in an extraordinary strategy position from which to manage the agenda-setting process. Perhaps so, but it seems to have worked the other way around. He did, after all, come to the post from the outside and had little bureaucratic base within the ministry from which to operate. In any event, his attention thereafter was given to a host of other issues.

One other force might conceivably have stirred the bureaucracy to action: the media. The various communities of policy professionals engaged in the Pacific Movement did indeed generate a flood of papers and conferences, thereby giving a vigorous shake to the growing policy network. They did begin to attract media attention, particularly with books like Tokuyama's which heralded *The Pacific Century*, but a full-scale media "boom," sufficient to compel government action, failed to occur.

Thus, when the issue was brought to Prime Minister Ohira's attention, it could hardly be said to have reached the "national agenda." The media and the public were not clamoring for action, and the officials not only were not pushing it, they had not yet decided it was a good thing. This failure to enlist the bureaucracy's support and expertise goes a long way in explaining how it was that the Japanese government's proposal for a Canberra seminar was so vaguely stated. The prime minister wanted something to happen. The bureaucracy did not know what or why. It only knew it did not want Japan to be out in front. Small wonder that the seminar was confused by the Japanese stand. If the leading co-sponsor did not know what it wanted, why were the others there?

THE OUTLOOK

Since the Canberra meeting and the subsequent formation of a number of national committees for exploring or advancing the cause, a series of regionwide conferences have been held—Bangkok in 1982, Bali in 1983, Seoul in 1985, and Vancouver in 1986. They have drawn record participation and have initiated a number of policy-related economic studies. But no government seems yet to share the initial enthusiasm of the Australians for solidifying official commitments.

The experience of these formative stages would seem to indicate that if the tide of interdependence is to sweep the governments of the region into new and effective regionwide arrangements by which, to use Ernst Haas' phrase, new "norms, rules, and procedures" are laid down for the negotiation of a wide range of economic issues, certain conditions will have to be met:

Each country in the basin will have to be convinced that a significant number of the economic issues which trouble it can better be handled in a multilateral context than by the bilateral or bloc negotiations which are currently favored. The supporters of the movement so far have been able to identify a number of such issues theoretically, but have been less successful in persuading their governments to commit themselves to multilateral solutions practically.

Either the United States or Japan, or preferably both, will have to be prepared to make a disproportionate share of the new concessions which greater interdependence may require. The consequences of the behavior of one or another of the smaller states, after all, will be regionally marginal. Conscious of this, these states are inclined to hang back—to accept benefits offered, but not to volunteer to make sacrifices themselves. In short, if the movement is to advance, leadership from the great economic powers, Japan and the United States, will be essential, and those who lead will have to be prepared to pay the price.

The uneasiness about the security implications of the movement will have to be resolved. There persists a fear in the minds of some participants that a movement involving only the market economies, however true it may be that these economies have the most pressing and specific business to transact with each other, may be seen as having security implications and therefore exacerbate relations of each with the Communist powers. The issue of China has been at least temporarily solved by the more open and cooperative policy the PRC has adopted toward its neighbors and its willingness to have a national committee participate alongside another national committee from Taiwan.

With the Soviet Union, North Korea, and the Communist states of Indochina, the economic relations of the Pacific market economies are too low to make any participant groups feel that membership in the Pacific Basin Movement is imperative. At the same time, the apprehension of a security threat from the Soviet Union is too high to make most participants feel that membership is even desirable. On the other hand, no one wants to offend the Soviet Union unnecessarily. The result is a dampening of activity, which presumably can only be overcome by a change in the common sense of "threat," either a heightening, which would intensify a felt need to take action regardless of Soviet attitudes, or a lowering, which would free members to proceed with more confidence.

NOTES

1. First published in English in Kiyoshi Kojima, "Economic Community and Asian Developing Countries," *Hitotsubashi Journal of Economics*, vol. 7, no. 1 (June 1966), pp. 17–37. It has appeared in many forms in Japanese. In English it has been republished in *Measures for Trade Expansion of Developing Countries* (Tokyo: Japan Economic Research Center, 1966), pp. 93–124; revised and expanded in Kojima, *Japan and a Pacific Free Trade Area* (London: Macmillan, 1971), chs. 3 and 7; published again in Kojima, "A Pacific Free Trade Area Proposed," *Pacific Community*, vol. 2, no. 4 (July 1971), pp. 721–731; and critiqued in Kojima, *Japan and a New World Economic Order* (Tokyo: Charles E. Tuttle, 1977), ch. 8.

2. Speech by Takeo Miki on May 22, 1967, in the Assembly Hall of the Yukaigin Biru, published by the Japan Committee for Economic Development (Keizai Doyukai). See also "Aiji-Taiheiyo-ken Koso to Miki gaiko" (The Asian-Pacific sphere conception and the Miki foreign policy), *Asahi janaru*, July 9, 1967.

3. See, for example, the adverse judgment in Parliament of Australia, *Japan: Report from Senate Standing Committee on Foreign Affairs and Defense* (Canberra: Australian Government Printing Service,

1973), ch. 5, excerpted in "Selected Papers and Extracts," distributed at the Pacific Community Seminar, Australian National University, September 15–18, 1980, pp. 321–323.

4. Saburo Okita and Kiyoshi Kojima, eds., *Ajia-Taiheiyo Kyoryoku e no tembo* (Outlook for cooperation in the Asia-Pacific region) (Tokyo: JIIA, 1971). Okita and Kojima edited a second volume to which additional specialists contributed under the title *Ajia-Taiheiyo Keizaiken* (The Asia-Pacific economic sphere) (Tokyo: JIIA, 1973).

5. The first assessment, known as the "Crawford-Okita Report," was published under the co-editorship of Sir John Crawford and Saburo Okita as *Australia, Japan, and Western Pacific Economic Relations* (1976); the second, edited by Peter Drysdale and Kiyoshi Kojima, was entitled *Australia-Japan Economic Relations in the International Context: Recent Experience and Prospects Ahead* (1978); and the third, edited by Crawford and Okita, was entitled *Australia and Japan: Issues in the Economic Relationship* (1980). For an annotated list of publications of the project, see Crawford and Okita, eds., *Raw Materials and Pacific Economic Integration* (Vancouver: University of British Columbia Press, 1978), pp. 312–327.

6. H. E. English and Keith Hay, eds., *Obstacles to Trade in the Pacific Area* (Ottawa: Carleton University Press, 1972), pp. iv–vi.

7. Peter Drysdale, "Pacific Economic Integration, an Australian View," in *Pacific Trade and Development*, ed., Kiyoshi Kojima (Tokyo: JERC, 1968), pp. 208–209; and Kojima, "Japan's Interest in Pacific Trade Expansion," ibid., p. 177. For the evolution in Kojima's thinking, see, for example, "An Organization for Pacific Trade Aid and Development: A Proposal" (Canberra, Australia: ANU, September 1976 mimeo), and Kojima, *Economic Cooperation in a Pacific Community* (Tokyo: JIIA, 1980).

8. Crawford and Okita, *Australia, Japan, and Western Pacific Economic Relations*, pp. 128–129, 138–139.

9. Congressional Research Service, Library of Congress, *An Asian-Pacific Regional Economic Organization: An Exploratory Concept Paper*, prepared for the U.S. Senate Committee on Foreign Relations (Washington, D.C.: U.S. Government Printing Office, 1979).

10. Gotoh's speech is summarized in Japan Center for International Exchange, "Taiheiyo saidan setsuritsu jimbi no tame no chosa-kenkyu hokoku" (Background data preparatory to the establishment of a Pacific Foundation) (Tokyo: JCIE, 1980).

11. Japan National Committee, Pacific Basin Economic Council, "The Concept of a Pacific Economic Community: A Synthesis of the Views of Individual Member Committees" (n.d.), mimeo.

12. *PBEC Report: Sydney Meeting, 1980*, p. 27.

13. The Search for Japan's Comprehensive Policy Guidelines in the Changing World: National Priorities for the 21st Century" (Kamakura: Nomura Research Institute, 1978).

14. From the "Basic Posture and Proposals" section as excerpted in "Selected Papers and Abstracts," distributed among the "Background Papers" by the Australian National University, Canberra, at the Pacific Community Seminar, September 15–18, 1980 (hereafter cited as Canberra Seminar Background Papers).

15. Jiro Tokuyama, *Taiheiyo no seiki: Nihon keiai no katsuro wo motomete* (The Pacific century: in search of a course for Japan's economy) (Tokyo: Diayamondosha, 1978), pp. 57–75.

16. See "Bibliography on the Pacific Community Concept," in Canberra Seminar Background Papers, pp. 359–373.

17. Charles E. Morrison, "American Interest in the Pacific Community Concept," in *The Pacific Community Concept*, comp. Japan Center for International Exchange (Tokyo: JCIE, 1970), p. 38.

18. See, for example, Parliament of Australia, *Japan: Report from Senate Standing Committee on Foreign Affairs and Defense*, ch. 5.

19. For Sato's role in the establishment of the ADB, see Dennis Yasutomo, "Japan and the Asian Development Bank: A New Dimension in Foreign Policy, 1962–1977" (Ph.D. diss., Columbia University, 1981).

20. The Ohira cabinet was formed on December 7.

21. Pacific Basin Cooperation Study Group, *Interim Report on the Pacific Basin Cooperation Concept* (translation), November 14, 1979.

22. Pan Eng Fong, "The Concept of a Pan-Pacific Community and ASEAN: A View from Singapore," in *The Pacific Community Concept*, comp. Japan Center for International Exchange, p. 81.

23. Charles E. Morrison, "American Interest in the Pacific Community Concept," pp. 38–39; and Mark Borthwick, "US Governmental Responses to the Pacific Community Idea," paper presented at the annual convention of the International Studies Association in Philadelphia, March 17–20, 1981, p. 12.

24. Pacific Basin Cooperation Study Group, *Report on the Pacific Basin Cooperation Concept* (translation), May 19, 1980.

25. See the report by Kiyoshi Kojima, "Economic Cooperation in a Pacific Community," (translation), which was accepted by the Japan Institute of International Affairs for inclusion in its commissioned report to the Ministry of Foreign Affairs in October 1979 and was published separately in English by the institute in September 1980 and in Japanese in Nihon kokusai mondai kenkyusho, comp., 1980 nendai:

Nihon gaiko no shinro (Tokyo: Nihon kokusai mondai kenkyusho, 1980), pp. 168–205.

26. Views are summarized in Japan Center for International Exchange, "Taiheiyo saidan . . . ," pp. 40–42.

27. "Agenda, Notes to the Agenda, Selected Papers and Extracts, Bibliography, List of Participants and List of Observers," in Canberra Seminar Background Papers.

28. Ambassador del Mundo was Deputy Director-General, Office of Political Affairs, Ministry of Foreign Affairs of the Philippines.

29. Hiroshi Kimura, "The Japanese Concept of Pacific Basin Cooperation from the Soviet Perspective," paper presented at the annual convention of the International Studies Association in Philadelphia, March 17–20, 1981.

30. For Watanabe's role in the ADB, see Yasutomo, "Japan and the Asian Development Bank"; for a theoretical formulation of the "elite idea process model" which is used here to critique Ohira's decision to call for the Canberra seminar, see John Creighton Campbell, "Old People Problem: The Career of an Issue," paper presented to the Columbia University Seminar on Modern Japan, February 13, 1981 (cited by permission).

2

Problems of Peace and Security in Asia

YEVGENY M. PRIMAKOV

It appears that the current international situation in the Asian continent should not be considered out of context—i.e., without analyzing the situation in the world in general. It is important to note that lately the global dynamics have been directly and, perhaps, increasingly affecting the events in Asia.

The current international situation may be characterized by high degrees of tension. The threat of a nuclear war has increased immeasurably and the arms race has entered a new, extremely dangerous round. A serious threat to mankind is presented by the plan of "star wars" announced by Washington which practically points to the U.S. desire to shift the arms race into space. Implementation of the plan would inevitably trigger an unchecked arms race in all fields. It would make it impossible to limit and more than that to reduce strategic offensive weapons and would sharply increase the danger of a nuclear war.

It is natural that the above aspects directly affect the situation in Asia. The time has long passed when an aggravation of tension or a military conflict in one particular area, for instance in Europe, will not affect or influence in practical terms the situation in other parts of the world. If it is allowed to break out, a future nuclear war would put an end to human civilization. This raises a general human problem which also concerns Asian people, the problem of preventing the danger of nuclear war.

Existing social and political forces at many levels direct their efforts toward the prevention of nuclear war. This objective is pursued by large-scale peace initiatives proposed by the USSR and other socialist countries. Of these, I should mention such an important historical unilateral step as the Soviet refusal to be the first to use nuclear weapons and the calls to freeze nuclear arsenals, to stop any further development of medium-range missiles in Europe with the simultaneous ending of the reciprocal Soviet buildup, and to end completely nuclear weapons testing. That is why the Soviet Union attaches such importance to Soviet-American talks on the entire range of nuclear and space armaments started on March 12, 1985, in Geneva, which present a real hope for a possible deflection of the danger of nuclear war. In order to create favorable conditions for the talks, the USSR again demonstrated its goodwill and decided to announce a unilateral moratorium on the development of its medium-range missiles and to suspend other reciprocal measures in Europe until November 1985.

The subsequent Soviet decision will depend on whether the United States stops the development of its medium-range missiles in Europe. In addition to that, the Soviet Union announced a moratorium on all tests of nuclear weapons starting from August 6, 1985—the fortieth anniversary of the atomic bombing of Hiroshima—and expressed its readiness to immediately resume talks on the complete prohibition of nuclear weapons tests. It continued this moratorium unilaterally until 1987, when Gorbachev announced that it would end only after the first U.S. test.

It should be noted that the Soviet position reflects a wide international consensus on the question of ending the arms race on the planet and its prevention in space. For example, this is testified by the Delhi Declaration of six states on the prevention of a nuclear war adopted in January 1985. The authors of the declaration—heads of states and governments of Argentina, Greece, India, Mexico, Tanzania, and Sweden—made an appeal to take every effort for ending the arms race. They attached special importance to prevention of the militarization of space and halting nuclear weapons tests.

The extensive peaceful proposals made by the Soviet Union

are consonant with the UN decisions. As is well known, the twenty-ninth session of the UN General Assembly adopted a resolution on prevention of the arms race in space.

Along with the decisive struggle against the most dangerous arms race, the Soviet Union and other socialist countries take specific steps designed to reduce the scale of confrontation between the Warsaw Treaty nations and NATO. All this is immediately important for Asia, Africa, and Latin America, as it is aimed at reducing tension and stabilizing the situation in these regions. In this connection, we may recall the Soviet proposal made in April 1984 on the mutual limitation of the activity of the Soviet and U.S. navies as well as on the withdrawal of patrol submarines and the limitation of their zone of action to agreed borders. It is well known that the USSR conducted talks with the United States on the demilitarization of the Indian Ocean. When the two sides approached a concrete agreement, the American delegation interrupted the talks.

The USSR is in favor of creating non-nuclear zones of peace and the adoption of various confidence-building measures which would facilitate the relaxation of international tensions. In their political declaration (1983), the Warsaw Treaty members appealed to the NATO countries to renounce proliferation of their alliance's influence to any part of the world, and to the Persian Gulf in particular. At the same time, the Warsaw Treaty members stressed that they did not have any intention of expanding the zone of influence of their alliance.

Very urgent and important for the developing societies are also the concrete proposals addressed by the Warsaw Treaty countries to the NATO states on the reduction of military spending. They emphasized that the funds saved as a result of reducing military spending might be utilized in the interests of economic and social development, with aid to developing countries included.

The proposals and actions of the USSR and its allies serve to stabilize the international situation both on the global and regional levels. Therefore, great importance is given by many socialist countries to the settlement of acute international conflicts in the world and in Asia in particular. Together with the Soviet Union, the socialist countries of Indochina persistently search for the settlement of the situation in Southeast Asia. They seek to establish an active dialogue with the countries of the ASEAN and to reach mutually acceptable agreement with them which can meet the interests of the peoples in the region as well as of security in Asia and in the world at large. They are prepared to establish good-neighbor relations with the People's Republic of China. This was all recognized by the documents of the tenth conference of foreign ministers of Vietnam, Laos, and Kampuchea held in Ho Chi Minh City, January 1984.

The objective of improving the situation in the Far East is pursued by proposals made by the Democratic People's Republic of Korea on ending the confrontation on the Korean peninsula, replacing the armistice by a treaty of friendship between North and South Korea, adopting the declaration of non-aggression between the two countries, the withdrawal of American troops from South Korea and dismantling the U.S. military bases there, prohibiting the stationing of nuclear weapons in the South, mutual reduction of the armies in the North and South, etc.

It was in response to the need to lower tensions that the world reacted to the Mongolian proposal made in May 1984 to call a conference of Asian and Pacific countries with participation of the permanent members of the UN Security Council to work out a mutual non-aggression convention and renunciation of force in relations between Asian and Pacific states.

There is, in essence, no shortage of peaceful proposals the implementation of which would bring about the reduction of tension in the world and the stabilization of the situation, including in Asia. Unfortunately, it has not been the case so far because the above mentioned approach failed to get a positive response from the opposite side. Evidently, there are certain reasons for the negative attitude to these proposals on the part of the United States and its close NATO partners. In this connection it seems appropriate to point out the accents which have recently become more visible in the U.S. military and strategic concept.

The United States has more clearly refined its opposition to the existing parity between the two major powers and between the two opposing alliances—NATO and the Warsaw Treaty states. It is against this background that the deployment of Pershing II and medium-range cruise missiles was started in Western Europe. In the USSR this was considered as the creation of a new first-strike stronghold close to the Soviet border.

On its part, the USSR tried to prevent these developments and suggested many times to bring Europe to an absolute zero as a result of eliminating all types of nuclear weapons and means of their delivery or to their substantial reduction. It should be emphasized that the USSR expressed its readiness to take an obligation to eliminate the removed missiles and not to transfer them into the Asian part of its territory, or in other words, not to target them against the countries that may present a potential danger to its security. This proposal may be viewed as a kind of "bridge" to reduction of nuclear weapons and means of their delivery in other regions apart from Europe. However, the opposite side remained deaf to these proposals.

Meanwhile, the U.S. action in Western Europe, no matter how dangerous it may be, was only an element of general U.S. military planning. It appears that—apart from improving the first-strike system based on the intercontinental means of delivery—the United States put stake in improving first-strike capability based on medium-range means. Such a concept directly implies active Asian involvement in U.S. plans. This system embraces relevant U.S. efforts in Japanese territory and the strengthening of its navy in the Pacific as well as the permanent presence of the American navy in the Indian Ocean and the Persian Gulf.

About 120 American bases and other military facilities were set up in Japanese territory, some of which are used by the forward-based U.S. forces. The Yokosuka and Sasebo naval bases are used by the U.S. Seventh Fleet as an anchorage of submarines and surface ships carrying nuclear weapons. The United States and Japan reached an agreement which allows for the stationing at Misawa air base—on Honshu island of two squadrons of F-16 new-type fighter-bombers capable of carrying nuclear weapons to the range of over 1,000 kilometers. The first squadron of twenty-four F-16s was stationed at Misawa in 1985.

While creating a first-strike stronghold in the area on the basis of a medium-range system, in addition to the above mentioned F-16 fighter-bombers, the United States began to deploy Tomahawk cruise missiles with a range of 2,500 kilometers on the Seventh Fleet ships. According to U.S. Navy Secretary John Lehman, these cruise missiles are already deployed on the *New Jersey* and four attack submarines. He did not deny that they carried nuclear warheads. The Pentagon also plans to modernize and arm with nuclear cruise missiles the *Long Beach* nuclear-powered cruiser which continuously uses the Yokosuka U.S. naval base in Japan. In effect, all this amounts to creating a new type of attack force as part of the U.S. Navy in the area meant to destroy targets deep in the Far Eastern and Siberian regions of the USSR.

The southern part of the Korean peninsula is continuously being transformed into a first-strike stronghold. U.S. Secretary of Defense Caspar Weinberger, in one of his statements, described the Seoul regime as an "ally of great strategic importance to the US and the entire free world." Around 700 to 1,000 nuclear charges of various kinds are believed stationed in the region. While presently their number is being reduced by the process of modernization, the overall nuclear situation remains unchanged. The United States plans to deploy Pershing II medium-range and cruise missiles in South Korea. The forward-based systems aimed at the USSR territory are deployed at U.S. air bases such as Osan, Kunsan, and Taegue. Within the framework of the modernization program of its armed forces in South Korea, the United States began to rearm its forces stationed there with F-16 fighter-bombers.

Development of various grounds of confrontation with the USSR has become a major thrust of U.S. policies in Asia. It entails greater emphasis placed on the formation and training of rapid deployment forces, the creation of facilities for the permanent presence of their advance detachment, and new forms of storing combat equipment for a possible use at the "D" hour. There is every reason to believe that the United States has begun to create a Pacific Theatre of War Operations (PTWO). Its zone stretches from Alaska to Australia, from the shores of Asia to California. Through the network of the military bases in the Indian Ocean, it meets the European Theatre of War Operations and thus forms a global ring of nuclear missiles around the USSR and the socialist countries. The PTWO is based on the ANZUS military alliance and the U.S. bilateral ties with Japan, South Korea, the Philippines, and Taiwan. Following the concept of the "island strategy," the United States has involved the archipelagos of its trust territories—the Pacific Islands (Micronesia) and Guam—in its military preparation. Improving the PTWO structure, the United States, by all appearances, pursues the policy of the stage-by-stage unification of the military organizations and alliances existing in the Pacific.

The facts indicate that the present U.S. administration has put a much stronger emphasis on the U.S. military and strategic ties with Japan than before. Recently, U.S. efforts to make South Korea equal in the military and strategic sense to Japan and to form a new anti-Soviet coalition shaped as a U.S.-Japan-South Korea triangle have become more and more pronounced. Given the tense situation existing in the Korean peninsula and the unresolved Korean conflict, these efforts present a serious destabilizing potential.

Japan has been joining the military maneuvers conducted by the United States, Australia, and New Zealand in the framework of ANZUS. Pressure is applied on the ASEAN member countries to make it a military-type organization. In the long perspective, it is planned to create a "Pacific Community" comprised of the United States, Canada, Japan, Australia, New Zealand, the ASEAN member states, and other Pacific states. Certain advocates of this idea visualize the prospective "Pacific Community" not only as an economic but also as a military and political alliance directed against the USSR.

The United States has intensified the use of local conflicts existing in Asia in enhancing confrontation with the USSR. As a clear departure from the policy of detente, the U.S. approach to local conflicts has been exposed more vividly in the following manner:

Increased U.S. military presence associated with the efforts to "control" the development of different conflict situations as well as with their unilateral settlement in the U.S. interests;

The efforts to introduce a NATO-type mechanism—along with the one existing in Europe and designed to be used in the region—capable of taking action in other parts of the world to "control" or "manage" the development of conflict situations;

Artificial linking together of the different conflict situations;

Monopolization by the United States of the process of political settlement of conflicts and creation of a better opportunity than before to
secure U.S. interests. Many of these have been already highlighted
in various reports by the U.S. Defense Department.

As for the USSR, on that problem, it also takes a stand opposite to the U.S. position. Soviet policy is aimed at the solution of
conflicts in Asia through their localization and renunciation of
their linkage to the global U.S.-Soviet confrontation and solving
them on a comprehensive basis in the interests of the peoples
involved in the conflict. The Soviet Union, in principle, is against
making the "management" of conflict situations a separate element dissociated from a comprehensive settlement. The USSR
negatively views any separate solutions of conflict situations with
the view to put pressure on this or that great power. This does
not, of course, imply that the USSR ignores any opportunity to
work out rules for the conduct of the greater powers regarding
local conflicts to prevent clashes between the two major powers
when the countries maintaining friendly relations with them are
directly involved in a conflict.

It should be clear from the above analysis that the entire international situation in Asia cannot be defined only from the
point of new trends or pronounced new accents in the U.S. strategic approach to the confrontation with the USSR. Other factors interact in Asia as well. They include the policies of Asian
countries, China and Japan, which simultaneously pose as
"centers of force" of global importance, and the Asian policy of
another "center of force," Western Europe, located outside the
region.

Recently the independent significance of Chinese policy in
Asia has grown even more. Sino-Soviet relations are being normalized. This fully corresponds to the interests of the two countries and the cause of Asian and Pacific security. The fact that
the United States hopes to extensively use China in the U.S.
confrontation against the USSR is another proof that Chinese
policy is in no case a derivative from the policy course of any
great power and that it is pursued on the basis of China's own
interests as they are seen and defined in Beijing. At the same

time, it should be clear that the United States did not discontinue its efforts to use the Sino-Soviet contradictions or give up its intention to make use of the Chinese policy in a system of measures taken against the USSR or its allies.

The conflict between China and Vietnam periodically takes the form of armed clashes. It is only the anti-Vietnamese line that prevents a full normalization in Kampuchea. Only unrealistically minded observers can deny the obvious fact that stability in Kampuchea cannot be achieved on an anti-Vietnamese basis or through a return to the state when, under the Pol Pot regime, the country was transformed into an anti-Vietnamese stronghold. The gradual improvement of Sino-Soviet relations since 1984 may at the same time positively influence the general improvement of the situation in Asia at large.

Approaching Chinese policy as an independent factor in Asia and the Pacific, one cannot employ a similar approach to Japan. Moreover, the inconsistency is increasing between the growth of Japanese economic, scientific, and technological potential—as Japan now ranks second in terms of economic development in the capitalist world—and the dependency in its foreign policy on the U.S. global and regional interests. This satisfies Washington for many reasons, including the consideration that such a dependency prevents to some extent an antagonistic development of the Japanese-American economic contradictions.

However, the active U.S. manipulation of Japan in its confrontation with the USSR both objectively and subjectively encourages Japan to militarize, while the tendency toward the growth of renewed Japanese militarism increases the imperial function of Japanese foreign policy. This tendency is manifested in the steady increase in military spending, expansion of military production, and accelerated growth of the Japanese armed forces.

According to the assessments of many observers, Japanese land forces are presently comparable to the British army. The Japanese air force ranks sixth in the Western world, while in submarines and naval tonnage Japan now occupies fifth and fourth places respectively. According to the sixth five-year program of the Japanese armed forces development in 1983–87, Japan plans to allocate $68 billion and to increase the annual military budget by 6.3 percent. During the next three years, Japan intends to purchase around 400 tanks, 14 destroyers, 6 submarines, 50 patrol aircraft, and 70 F-15 fighters. Accordingly, this clearly signifies a serious deviation from the present Japanese constitution by transforming Japan into a military power. This projected expenditure will certainly surpass the 1 percent GNP limit on military spending set in 1976. It is also evident that since Japan, apart from that, occupies a leading place in terms of scientific, technological, and industrial progress, the development of Japanese military strength may proceed at an even faster rate than previously envisaged.

Militarization of Japan is naturally bound to directly influence the situation in Asia, for it is quite impossible to limit the growth of the Japanese militarism within the limited framework of the confrontation with the USSR and other socialist countries. Indeed, a real military and strategic center is emerging in Asia. Given existing traditions, it may present a danger to the neighboring states and to other states as well.

Based on Japanese sources, the comparisons below are self-explanatory. In 1982 the Japanese self-defense forces possessed 400 tactical fighters, which substantially exceeded the strength of the U.S. Air Forces based in East Asia. Besides, Japan possessed 50 destroyer-type ships, which was twice the number of similar U.S. naval ships operated by the U.S. East and West Pacific Command. At the same time, the U.S. capability to control the rearmament of the Japanese army has been steadily decreasing. If the United States, feeling the danger of this process to its interests, would try to interrupt, it would be quite difficult to do so now and even more difficult in the future. Of the 155 F-15 fighters ordered by the Japanese self-defense forces in the early 1980's, 147 will be manufactured under license in Japan by Mitsubishi Heavy Industries. Presumably, militarizing Japan is part of the United States confronting the USSR.

No significant increase of Western European influence on Asian and Pacific developments has been recorded. It is possible to predict only the local activity of the Western European "center of force" in West Asia and the Near and Middle East. However, the policy of Western European states in this region plays, on the whole, a secondary role dependent on U.S. policy in this region.

It is quite obvious that modern Asia cannot be viewed as only an object of policy or an entity within the corners of a penta-gonal geometrical figure formed by the United States, USSR, China, Japan, and Western Europe, although, as has been stated before, the global situation in many ways determines events in Asia. The dynamics of international relations among the Asian countries presents the second dimension of changes in the Asian situation. These dynamics are determined by two conflicting trends—the centripetal on the subregional level and the centrif-ugal on the global basis.

Presently, the centripetal trend is most vividly manifested in the three subregions—in Southeast Asia, within the framework of the ASEAN; in the Persian Gulf, the Arab Gulf Cooperation Council, comprising Saudi Arabia, Kuwait, Qatar, Bahrein, Oman, and the United Arab Emirates; and in an embryonic state in the Pacific region. The rapprochement among the countries of these regions began mainly in the economic field. It would be pre-mature to speak about the processes of bilateral integration or even multilateral integration embracing a political or military-political field, although certain measures are being undertaken in these fields as well.

The policy of non-alignment is a factor which unites many Asian countries. From the start, it emerged as the reaction of the liberated countries of Asia, Africa, and Latin America to the global situation characterized by the opposition between the two military alliances—NATO and the Warsaw Treaty states. The policy of non-alignment has never been and is not equivalent to neutralism. It contains a positive element which works for strengthening peace and security of peoples.

Recently, the economic meaning of the non-alignment poli-cies has acquired an increased importance. This tendency is ac-companied not only by the struggle for the democratization of the international economic ties but by the growing tendency for strengthened economic unity among these states. Of course, we are quite far from overestimating this tendency, but "South-South" relations have been acquiring primary importance in the mid-1980's.

As regards the centrifugal trends in the international relations in Asia, they are mainly developing in the form of conflict situ-ations, such as the Iraq-Iran and the Middle East conflicts, the conflict around Afghanistan, Kampuchea, the conflict on the Korean peninsula, and the Indo-Pakistani conflict. There exist real prospects for solution of some of these conflicts provided the U.S. position changes correspondingly. Using the criterion based on the possibility of their settlement, these conflicts may be arranged into the following types.

The first involves the Middle East crisis, the settlement of which would evidently require joint USSR-U.S. efforts within the framework of an international conference convened under UN auspices and participated in by all the parties concerned and by the PLO—the sole legitimate representative of the Palestinian people. Given adequate preparation, the conference might become a real forum to solve the problem of the multilateral and comprehensive settlement of the Middle East in the interests of the peoples living in the area. Pursuing the policy of partial solutions, the United States ignores the opportunity to convene such a conference, although it is considered that the conference may open a unique opportunity to solve the whole range of problems related to the establishment of a just and lasting peace in the Middle East region in a "package deal."

The conflicts around Afghanistan and Kampuchea, on the Korean peninsula, and between India and Pakistan could be presumably referred to the second group. All of them may be settled on a solid basis provided the support given to the destructive forces working to destabilize the situation is discontinued. The USSR's position on the question of Afghanistan is well known. If the interference of outside forces into the affairs of Afghanistan is guaranteed to discontinue, the question of withdrawal of the Soviet military contingent could be solved. As is well known, the appropriate contact between the governments of Afghanistan and Pakistan was made in Geneva through the good offices of the UN secretary general. However, it did not bring about any positive result mainly because of U.S. pressure on Pakistan. Taking different forms, the supply of weapons and promises of economic aid included, this pressure was applied each time progress in the dialogue was about to be made.

Only one thing is required to solve the situation around Kampuchea—to stop outside interference in its internal affairs, to renounce the use of Thailand's territory for regrouping and training the forces hostile to the People's Republic of Kampuchea.

Recently, the Democratic People's Republic of Korea proposed a formula for a tripartite meeting between North Korea, South Korea, and the United States. Although the United States was taking interest in the idea and used to propose it itself, now it practically turned it down and preferred to build up American military strength in South Korea. Obviously, one cannot expect any progress in solving the Korean problem or any meaningful detente in the Korean peninsula under these circumstances. The only way out is to stop outside interference and to create the most favorable conditions for reaching an agreement between the two Koreas.

The acute character of the Indo-Pakistani conflict is intensified by the U.S. military supplies to the Zia ul-Haq regime. All this impedes the beginnings of the settlement which started with great difficulty several years ago. Receiving disproportionately large shipments of the most modern armaments from the United States, Pakistan has been making its position on the territorial problem more difficult and trying to gamble on the separatist tendencies of individual groups in some Indian states bordering with Pakistan.

The Iraq-Iran conflict, which cannot be solved due to the Iranian position, is a special case. However, there are certain indications that U.S. activities, to put it mildly, do not encourage the conditions for bringing the conflict to an end. Iran is being supplied with arms from the "free" arms market dominated by the American, West European, and Israeli arms suppliers. First, according to the views of American politicians, the war weakens the Arab countries' potential to resist the expansionist Israeli course. Second, the war intensifies the rightist tendencies in the involved two states. Third, it has created a pretext for the buildup of the U.S. military presence in the region.

Both the centripetal and centrifugal processes in Asia carry the mark of U.S. policy, which is trying to attach, in line with the above mentioned aspects, specific political and military character to the regional rapprochement among certain states, or as was mentioned earlier, "manage" development of conflicts and strengthen its position in the confrontation against the USSR and the countries of the socialist community. These are, in short, two conflicting concepts and approaches to the solution of the Asian problems of a regional and global nature.

Editors' note: These views by Academician Primakov were expressed prior to Gorbachev's Vladivostok initiatives in July 1986. How much Gorbachev's peace overtures would be implemented remains to be seen, however, particularly after the unsuccessful Gorbachev-Reagan meetings of October 1986 in Iceland.

3

The Japanese Concept of "Pacific Basin Cooperation" from the Soviet Perspective

HIROSHI KIMURA

In his inaugural speech (November 1978) Japanese Prime Minister Masayoshi Ohira advocated "the Pacific Basin Cooperation Concept" as one of his basic policy directions.[1] He repeated his idea in his Diet session speech on January 25, 1979, and elaborated it further: "I consider it my obligation to promote further friendly and cooperative relations with the U.S., Canada, Latin America, Australia, New Zealand, and other countries in the Pacific region."[2] In March 1979 Ohira organized a special policy-advisory group to study and work on "the Pacific Basin Cooperation Concept." His appointment of the chairman of this group, Mr. Saburo Okita, to be his foreign minister, demonstrates how much importance Mr. Ohira attached to this concept.

Ohira's successor, Prime Minister Zenko Suzuki, was more equivocal in his support for the Pacific Basin concept. On the one hand, it can be pointed out that in his general policy of following his predecessor rather faithfully, Suzuki was greatly interested in the continuation of the "Pacific Basin Cooperation Concept." He sent a delegation including Professor Tsuneo Iida, successor to Mr. Okita as chairman of the cooperation concept study group, and others to an international seminar on the Pacific Basin Cooperation in Canberra in September 1980, as promised by Mr. Ohira. On the other hand, Suzuki failed to include the term "Pacific Basin Cooperation Concept" in his Diet speech in August 1980.[3] In an interview with Asian correspondents prior to his trip to ASEAN countries, Suzuki stated that the "Pacific Basin Cooperation Concept" must be promoted by a voluntary rise of support for this idea.[4]

Regardless of Prime Minister Suzuki's more cautious support for the concept; and the subsequent ambitious policy of the administration of Yasuhiro Nakasone, the fact remains that the Soviets reacted very strongly to Mr. Ohira's "Pacific Ocean Basin Concept." Why? What were their points of criticism against this "concept"? Can any unique features be found in their way of criticizing Ohira's concept? Can any differences in degree and tone be found in their criticism? In order to answer these questions, this paper attempts, first, to introduce the three major points which have provoked strong criticism in Soviet official newspapers and periodicals; second, to detect the real meaning behind their words; and third, to provide various ways of interpreting apparently divergent views on the subject.

SOVIET GENERAL PERCEPTION OF U.S.-JAPANESE STRATEGY IN ASIA

The Soviets have been concerned over the Japanese idea of the "Pacific Ocean Community" for quite a long time. In his 290-page book, entitled *Japan in the World* (1973), Dimitri Petrov, Soviet expert on Japan, mentioned this phrase seventeen times![5] Petrov paid special attention to the "Asia-Pacific Design," which was advocated by Takeo Miki, Japanese foreign minister in the mid-1960's.[6]

Nonetheless, according to Petrov, this concept "was not put into effect successfully"[7] by any of the Japanese foreign ministers who succeeded Miki.[8] The reasons for it, as explained by Petrov, are the U.S.-Japanese economic rivalry, much closer relations of Australia and New Zealand with Anglo-Saxon states than with Japan, and apprehension in Asian countries that the "Pacific Ocean Community Concept" could be a tool of new colonialism.[9]

After the publication of Petrov's book (1973), significant changes in the political, economic, military-strategic, and hence psychological scene took place in the Asian-Pacific region. The debacle in Vietnam (spring 1975) forced the American administration to scale down the commitment-in-Asia-policy of Nixon's Guam Doctrine (and Ford's Pacific Doctrine, December 1975). While attempting to assure its commitment to the Asian-Pacific region, Washington redefined its own role and commitment in that region.

American strategy in the late 1970's under the Ford and Carter administrations was perceived by Soviet observers in the following way:[10] on the one hand, the United States remained fundamentally unchanged in its basic determination to remain, at least militarily, the major power in the Asian-Pacific theater, despite gestures of withdrawal. Consequently, the Soviet strategy in this area also remained unchanged in its basic orientation, regarding the United States as the principal enemy.[11]

On the other hand, the Soviets did not fail to observe some significant changes that took place in the late 1970's in U.S. strategy in the Asian-Pacific region. To begin with, they were observant enough to notice the shift in emphasis from the Nixon to the Carter administration in Asia: U.S. interests have been geographically moving "from continental Asia to Northeast Asia and the proper Pacific region."[12]

In other words, the so-called "selective commitment" policy of the U.S. administrations in Asian affairs was rightly taken note of by Soviet Asian watchers. Furthermore, the Soviets also became aware of the "division of labor" policy in the U.S. strategy in Asia. First, the United States gave an "extraordinarily," "decisively," or "exceptionally" great role in that region to Japan;[13] second, the United States tried hard to train both Australia and New Zealand to be "partners";[14] third, the United States considered promoting the People's Republic of China (PRC) to a position of "partner" as well as a "quasi-ally" country.[15]

What were the reasons for the second aspect, the change in American strategy in the Asia-Pacific area? Again, according to Soviet analysis, two basic reasons can be found: one on the American side, another on the Japanese side. Washington has become increasingly aware of the fact that Japan and other countries in the region have developed sufficiently to become its "partner." This recognition has led American decision makers to the idea that it would be desirable to leave Asia as Japan's sphere of interest. This idea is reinforced by the U.S. belief that it would be safe to do so as long as the United States holds military superiority over Japan, particularly in the field of nuclear weapons, which can serve as a sufficient means of controlling Japanese diplomatic and economic direction.[16] Tokyo has been increasingly aware of a changing power balance in the Asian-Pacific theater, the Soviet observers say. Recognizing the "decline of American power" in the region, the Tokyo government has come to think that Japan must fill the "power vacuum," taking the place of the United States. It has begun to think, in the Soviet understanding, that the chance has come to resume the traditional policy of expanding its influence in the area which it regards as its own back yard.[17]

The Soviets thus considered Ohira's "Pacific Basin Cooperation Concept" as one of the products of both changed and unchanged situations and policy orientations as described above by recent U.S. and Japanese administrations. Namely, Ohira's concept was formulated under Japan's sponsorship, but only with American approval and blessings.[18] This way of perceiving Ohira's concept as a combination of both changed and unchanged situations helps us to appreciate rather easily that among Soviet observers of Ohira's "Pacific Basin Concept" two views can be discerned, the one view emphasizing the new trend, the other the old and same element.

On the one hand, Vladimir Tsvetov, radio commentator of the Moscow Broadcasting Service, emphasized the newness of Ohira's "Pacific Basin Cooperation Concept." In an April 18, 1980, broadcast in Japanese, Tsvetov stated: "One would be urged to exercise vigilance over a *new* trend in Japan's foreign policy when one thinks of this pan-Pacific solidarity plan."[19] This emphasis on the "new trend" in Japanese foreign policy naturally connects the Pacific Community Concept closely with the name of Masayoshi Ohira. For instance, S. N. Nikonov, in his article entitled "On Plans of Creation of the New Regional Organization of Countries of the Basin of the Pacific Ocean," takes this position: "The initiator in promoting this idea, which has received the name of the 'Pacific Ocean Community' is considered to be Prime Minister M. Ohira."[20]

On the other hand, it is not surprising to note that some Soviet observers took Ohira's "concept" as nothing new. Rather, it was understood as a continuation of the policy that Japanese foreign policymakers have been tenuously pursuing. Yu. Bandura, Tokyo correspondent of *Izvestiia*, was a typical example of one taking this view. In an article for the May 1980 issue of the Soviet journal, *International Affairs*, Bandura wrote: "The idea of Japan-is-the-center is *not new* (*ne novoe*) for the Japanese ruling circle. From this evidence it becomes clear that the entrance of Japanese diplomacy into the international arena with the 'Pacific Basin Community Concept' is a *consequent* (*posledovatel'nye*) course of the long range policies of the ruling circle of this country" [emphasis mine].[21] Bandura does not connect the "Pacific Basin Concept" solely with the late Prime Minister Ohira, but rather traces back its roots to the 1960's by saying: "In Japan the idea of the 'Pacific Basin Community' is connected with the name of M. Ohira. . . . The fact, however, confirms that the 'Concept' which was put into effect by M. Ohira's government, has historically much deeper roots."[22]

Slightly different views are discernible elsewhere as well. These will be taken up shortly. The questions that arise at this point are: Do these differences simply represent differences in matter of degree or emphasis? Or do they indicate the existence of really plural viewpoints in the Soviet way of looking at things in the world and Asia? These questions will be discussed at the very end of this paper. In the meantime two or even three apparently different views and perceptions will be simply juxtaposed without further exploring what they really mean.

THREE MAJOR POINTS OF SOVIET CRITICISM

We will now examine the three major points that have generated the heavy criticism and hostile attitude toward Ohira's "Pacific Basin Cooperation Concept" from the Soviet side.

The Soviets, first of all, object to the capitalist orientation that they detect in the "Cooperation Concept." *The Interim Report on the Pacific Basin Cooperation Concept*, submitted to Prime Minister M. Ohira on November 14, 1979, says: "Our concept is, in the first place, directed to *open* cooperation. . . . Secondly, it aims at the formulation of a regional community based on *free* trade and capital transfer as the ideal to be achieved. In carrying out this task, it is especially incumbent on the advanced countries to take the lead in . . . making effective use of market-economy mechanisms, and also to keep in mind the maintenance and reinforcement of the free international economic system" [emphasis mine].[23] From the Soviet point of view it is nothing but a contradiction or "double-faced" (*dboistvennyi*) for the authors of the report to advocate both an "open and free" system at one and the same time. According to the Marxist-Leninist way of thinking, there are two kinds of "free systems or freedom," one being capitalistic and bourgeois and the other socialist. The fact that "free" means the first one is crystal clear from the interim report in that it continues to explain that "in the economic sphere promotion of *free* trade and capital transfer is the ideal to be achieved."[24] The Tokyo correspondent of *Izvestiia*, Yu. Bandura, for instance, interpreted "free economic system" as a capitalist system.[25] In January 1980 he wrote: "In the Report is emphasized the adjustment of interests, keeping in mind the maintenance and re-inforcement of the free international economic system, that is to say, capitalist system."[26] Therefore, argued the Soviets, the Japanese attitude on the nature of the "community" was based on a double standard: while they advocate a "free" system, they make it a "closed" one, restricting in practice the member countries only to capitalist, bourgeois countries. Yu. Bandura, for instance, in his article "The Pacific Ocean Community—Birth of Diplomatic Imperialism" in Soviet journal *International Affairs* (no. 5, 1980) said:

The attitude of Japan towards participation in the planned organization of capitalist countries of the Asia-Pacific region shows a double-standard: on the one hand, the planners repeatedly talk about the creation of an "open community"; but on the other hand, the explicit objective of this 'community' is the guarantee of "freedom of trade and capital transfer," an ideal which is pursued primarily by capitalist countries.[27]

S. N. Nikonov expressed concern about the possible development of the "community" into an anti-socialist organization in the future, but in a subjunctive mood: "If this organization is to be created as a closed group against the interests of socialist countries, which may allow South-East Asian and Pacific countries to integrate into the capitalist system of this 'Pacific Com- munity,' separating them from other developing countries, then its future is quite problematic."[28] While some Soviet observers regarded the "community" as an organization (de facto) closed to socialist countries (Bandura) or potentially anti-socialist (Ni- konov), others considered it simply as anti-Soviet. Vladimir Tsvetov, for instance, stated: "Judging from the recommenda- tion, this alliance is certain to take on a naked *anti-Soviet* char- acter."[29] Needless to say, there exist differences in implication between "anti-socialist" and "anti-Soviet." Whereas the former connotes the general capitalistic, bourgeois orientation, the lat- ter implies specifically Beijing's participation in the formation of the united front against the USSR.

What accounts for this subtle divergence of nuance in inter- pretation among Soviet commentators on one and the same sub- ject? Is it due to the difference in time of publication of the statements? Nikonov's and Bandura's articles were based on the Japanese interim report, but appeared respectively in February and May 1980, whereas Tsvetov's broadcast was on the air June 8, 1980, three weeks after the final report was submitted to Ohira. Divergent views may be ascribed to the different audiences that were addressed. While both Nikonov and Bandura wrote articles in Russian, Tsvetov's broadcast in the Japanese language was obviously addressed to the Japanese.

Regardless of their theoretical characterization of the "Pacific Basin Cooperation" as anti-socialist or anti-Soviet, what annoyed the Kremlin leaders seemed to be the possible practical effects of the formation of such a "community." One of the practical effects from the creation of a regional grouping in the Pacific area aimed at "strengthening relations of cooperation and inter- dependence" for which Moscow felt it should be prepared was the development of much closer economic ties and cooperation of the Japanese economy with Asian-Pacific countries rather than with other states, including the USSR. There is no need to be reminded here that the Soviet Union is expecting credit, tech- nology, and know-how from Japan in order to fulfill the plan of Siberia and the Far Eastern region of its country, a plan that was considered important to the Soviet economy in the decades ahead. Moscow had in fact been pushing Tokyo very hard to

conclude a long-term intergovernmental agreement on economic cooperation. Which direction is the Japanese economy
moving, to the north, i.e., the Soviet Union, or the south, i.e.,
the Asian-Pacific region? This was really a crucial question for
Moscow, keeping in mind the fact that the resources of Japan
are not, of course, unlimited.

It can also be suspected that in opposing Ohira's "Pacific Basin
Cooperation Concept," the Soviets were in practice concerned
about the creation of an Asian-Pacific version of the European
Economic Community (EEC). The late Prime Minister Ohira
himself made it clear that it was not feasible to create such an
organization as the EEC in the Asian-Pacific region, which was
said to include "a great number and variety of countries—very
and relatively advanced, developing, and resource-rich."[30] In an
address to the study group on Pacific Basin Cooperation on March
6, 1979, Ohira stated: "It is not realistic to have in our mind
such an organization as the E.E.C., when we think of solidarity
and cooperation among Pacific nations."[31] Despite these assurances, the Soviets were not convinced. Bandura, for example,
quotes the other statement of the Japanese prime minister, in-
dicating that what Mr. Ohira had in mind as a model for his
"Pacific Basin Cooperation Concept" was such economic relations as those between West Germany and the EEC. The Japanese prime minister is quoted by Bandura as having said in his
program speech in the Diet (January 25, 1979): "Japan draws
special attention to countries in the Pacific region. And this is
perfectly natural, exactly as the U.S.A. has relations with countries in Central and South America, as the F.R.G. has special
relations with the E.E.C., and as E.E.C. with Africa."[32]

The second major cause of Soviet distrust of the "Pacific
Community" came from their strong fear that the community
would not allow for the participation of socialist governments.
This fear was not dissipated by the repeated assertions of Mr.
Ohira that "there is no reason to decline the participation of any
nation that wishes to join the Community."[33] Ohira indeed made
it clear one time that he was "not opposed to the participation
of the Soviet Union nor the P.R.C."[34] The Soviet doubts were
well expressed by Mr. Bandura in *Izvestiia* when he criticized
the community's interim report submitted on November 30, 1979,

by the study group. He commented: "In the recommendation submitted to the Japanese government, no mention was made on the question as to which countries Japan would like to have as group members. Analysis of the Report, however, leads to a conclusion: The authors of the concept leave no room for the participation of socialist countries in the Pacific Ocean Cooperation."[35]

When it comes to the question of the possible candidate members of the community, there exists a variety of opinions among Soviet commentators. Bandura classifies candidate countries into four groups. The first group, which can be considered as "fixed candidates,"[36] members of "the Pacific Ocean Community" in the original Japanese planning, were Japan, the United States, Canada, Australia, New Zealand, and the ASEAN countries. In the second category, mentioned "occasionally"[37] as candidates, were some states in Latin America (Chile, Panama, Mexico). The third group consisted of such "special objects" as South Korea, Taiwan, and Hong Kong.[38] Such questions as how to deal with these countries in practice have not been solved even now. Finally, the PRC belongs to a fourth category. True, Bandura was aware that both Beijing itself and Australian Prime Minister Malcolm Fraser advocated the participation of the PRC in the community. But he did not seem to conceive that Japan would provide the PRC with membership in the organization, at least in the short run, as he wrote: "It is true that Tokyo feeds Beijing with the promise of taking China in the future into 'the Pacific Community.' "[39]

Commenting on Ohira's trip to Australia and New Zealand, Moscow's *Tass* in Russian on January 4, 1980, took a slightly different view on possible candidate membership of the "Pacific Community." It saw only two classifications, the first group being "Japan, Australia and New Zealand, and also ASEAN countries";[40] the second group, "China, South Korea, and also Hong Kong and Taiwan."[41] It provokes our interest to note that, while the United States and Canada are omitted here, the PRC is provided with the same status as South Korea, Hong Kong, and even Taiwan! It is strange indeed to see both the PRC and Taiwan joining one and the same organization. Some Soviet commentators took it for granted that the PRC, not Taiwan, would be a member of the community.[42] In his Japanese-language broadcast, clearly addressed to a Japanese audience, Tsvetov stated first: "The plan [of "Cooperation"] is to create in the Pacific basin a closed alliance incorporating Japan, the United States, Australia, New Zealand, the Republic of Korea, the Latin American countries and the ASEAN member nations."[43] Immediately after stating this, the Tokyo correspondent continues: "This alliance does not envisage the participation of socialist countries but *China's* participation is strongly recommended."[44]

There is no doubt that one of the reasons why the Soviets criticized Ohira's Pacific Basin Cooperation so bitterly lies in Soviet feeling that the USSR was not provided a rightful place in, and then is de facto excluded from, this proposed organization. It was seen as an impermissible disgrace, indeed, for that country which had recently conceived itself as a major leading Pacific power. It is hard to say exactly when, but from some time in the late 1970's, the USSR started to define itself as an Asian-Pacific power, not simply an Asia power.[45] And the fact that no mention at all was made of the Soviet Union in the interim report on the Pacific Basin Cooperation Concept caused most of the Soviet criticism. In the final report the USSR was, together with other countries, mentioned only once in a passage dealing with a not very significant subject, the study of a direct-broadcast relay satellite system. The sentence went as follows: "The United States, Canada, the Soviet Union, and Japan have been conducting experiments since 1974 on satellite broadcasting."[46] It is recalled that the Soviets were infuriated by the fact that U.S. President Ford de facto excluded the USSR in his "new Pacific Doctrine," which was made public after his trip to China in November 1975. Still remembering this disgrace even in 1978, two years after Ford had left the political scene, B. Zanegin, Americanologist of the IMEMO (Institute of World Economy and International Relations), stated: "In the Pacific Doctrine the Soviet Union, for instance, as a *Pacific power* was not mentioned."[47]

Thirdly, the Soviets have insisted that the establishment of a military alliance must be of primary interest to the cooperation. They think so in spite of repeated assurances from the Japanese side that the Cooperation's interests are of a cultural and economic nature. The late Prime Minister Ohira himself clearly stated, for instance, in the Lower House Budget Committee on February 5, 1980, that "we want to confine this idea of the Pacific Basin Cooperation only to economic and cultural spheres."[48] As a matter of fact, the final report submitted to Ohira did envisage such economic cooperation as in fields of "human resources and technology development" (Chapter II, 3), "trade expansion and adjustment of industrial structure" (Chapter II, 4), and "energy, marine, agriculture, forestry and fishery, and resources exploitation" (Chapter II, 5). It also envisaged such cultural cooperation as in "cultural, educational, academic and tourist exchanges" (Chapter II, 1). However, in contrast, nothing is spelled out on political or military relations. Nonetheless, the Soviets perceive that "it is hard to judge the real content of the Japanese model of world construction in the Asia-Pacific region only from the official materials of Tokyo,"[49] and thus it is necessary to detect "a plan hidden behind such flowery words as cooperation and mutual assistance."[50]

With regard to the real plan or purpose behind official words, there were again divergent opinions among Soviet observers. Some detected a political aim in Japan's version of the Pacific Community. Nikonov stressed that whereas in the 1960's it was academics and businessmen who were advocating the concept of the Pacific Ocean Community in Japan, now a special group appointed by the prime minister was involved. The shift in advocates indicates a shift in emphasis from economic to political considerations, according to Nikonov, who stated:

However, one main thing is quite clear: the major driving force of creating the new regional organization is not economic interests of development of countries in the region, but *political* purposes. And if formerly the concept of "Pacific Ocean Community" was discussed on the non-governmental level at the symposiums of scholars and representatives of the business community, then the concept has recently become the object of exchanges of opinion among politicians.[51]

Other Soviet commentators suspected worse and believed that the primary purpose of the Japanese design of the Pacific Community was military. Moscow's *Tass International* broadcast on

January 4, 1980, in Russian, was a typical example. Although citing the *Akahata* (Red Flag), the organ of the Japanese Communist party, it criticized: "Facts show that the 'Ohira Doctrine' is inseparably linked with plans to create a new military bloc in that region."[52] Nikonov also stressed the military purpose of Ohira's "Cooperation Concept" by saying that the statement of Japanese state officials had frequently drawn attention to the fact that "the proposed organization will have not merely a political but increasingly a *military* character" [emphasis mine].[53] Being concerned about the China connection as usual, Tsvetov suspected in Ohira's design the military motivation which had been, according to Tsvetov, pushed by Beijing. In a broadcast on the final report, Tsvetov said:

The Japanese government is not opposed to Beijing's proposal to form a *military* block to be comprised of *China*, the United States, Japan, and some developing countries in South Asia and in the Pacific basin. Thus, the so-called coordination of efforts to protect the free economic international system in the Pacific basin, as stated in the recommendation, actually means to unify the bilateral or multilateral *military* cooperation which either has already been established or is scheduled to be established in the days to come.[54]

Bandura took a sort of middle position on this issue, the characterization of Ohira's "Cooperation Concept," by stating that both economic and military-political aims could be distinguished in the concept. In an article entitled "Fact versus Words" in the February 24 issue of *Izvestiia*, Bandura complained: "Tokyo spares no effort to explain that the concept [of the Pacific Basin Cooperation] being pushed through by Japan pursues neither *political* nor *military* goals. . . . However, the facts indicate the opposite" (emphasis mine).[55] The Tokyo correspondent further wrote in an article in the May 1980 issue of *Far Eastern Affairs*: "The "Community" in reality has in mind to kill two birds with one stone: to organize in the Asia-Pacific region a *military-political* alliance with the U.S. at the head, which serves interests of the international reactionary forces, and to create a closed economic group, which will secure interests of Japanese imperialism" [emphasis mine].[56] Bandura, however, seemed to stress the military nature of the community. In another article entitled "Conspiracy in the Pacific Ocean," which appeared in the January 17 issue of *Izvestiia*, he wrote, "If the purpose of economic integration is put off beyond the present century, then a more evil purpose—military is coming to the fore already today."[57]

The participation for the first time of the Japanese Self-Defense Forces in Rimpac-80, Pacific Ocean naval exercises, together with ANZUS member countries, (the United States, Canada, Australia, and New Zealand), from February to March 1980, reinforced the Soviet suspicion that "there are military aspects in the Pacific Community design."[58] V. Gorovnin noted in the February 18, 1980, issue of the *APN News*: "The participants in these military maneuvers are those countries which will play a central role in the Pacific Basin Community design envisaged tenuously by Japan."[59] He concluded that "although Japan has defined this design to be of a purely economic and cultural nature, we see that the Pacific Ocean Cooperation has begun actual maneuvers in the military field."[60]

It is appropriate to be reminded here that the Soviet Union has its own design for almost the same geographical area as Japan's Pacific Basin Cooperation design—its Proposal of Collective Security in Asia. In his speech at the World Conference of Communist Parties in Moscow, on June 8, 1969, Leonid Brezhnev said, "We think the course of events is also placing on the agenda the task of creating a system of collective security in Asia."[61] Since this trial balloon, nearly twenty years have elapsed, and it is an undeniable fact now that, despite Soviet expectations, the "course of events" has not developed favorably enough for the creation of such an organization in the region. Only three neighboring countries formally endorsed the Soviet initiative: Outer Mongolia, Iran, and Afghanistan. In its proposal for "collective security" in Asia, Moscow had obviously been considering Tokyo as a crucial member. Thus the shock that Moscow had to encounter when it learned that Tokyo itself had its own idea for the same region was not small. It would not be incorrect to relate the Soviet Union's extraordinary sensitivity

demonstrated toward the Japanese version of Pacific Cooperation to its own unsuccessful efforts to create its own design in
Asia.

As its name clearly shows, the Kremlin's Asian collective security design is of a political-military nature. The Soviets themselves did not attempt to conceal this. In the address mentioned
above, General Secretary of the Communist Party of the Soviet
Union (CPSU) Brezhnev himself made it clear: "Asian collective security is the best substitute to the political-military grouping now existing."[62] One may suspect that the Soviets tended
to project their own way of thinking to other nations. The fact
is that the Soviets had no doubt that Ohira's Pacific Cooperation
design had political-military alliance in mind. Bandura, for instance, writes: "Behind these activities the intention to create
in the Pacific Ocean a huge military bloc of imperialist states is
quite clearly visible, as it is already receiving the name of JAN-
ZUS" (combination of the first letters of Japan-Australia-New
Zealand-United States).[63]

In summary, the reasons why the Soviets criticized Ohira's
"Pacific Basin Cooperation Concept" so bitterly can be assumed
to be the following, judging from their statements: (1) Moscow
did not like the concept's capitalist character. "The maintenance and promotion of the free international economic system"
envisaged in the recommendation is, in the Soviet perspective,
nothing but encouragement of the capitalist economy. Bandura
regarded the concept as "an attempt to knock together the capitalist bloc in the Asia-Pacific region."[64] In practice Moscow was
afraid that behind this concept, Japan was shifting its economic
emphasis from Siberia and the Far East to the south. (2) Moscow accused the concept of being anti-socialist or anti-Communist in character. The Pacific Basin Cooperation concept advocated by Mr. Ohira was, according to Oleg Skalkin, *Pravda*
correspondent at Sidney, "an attempt to knock together another
anti-communist military-political grouping."[65] Actually, Moscow
was more worried about the concept's anti-Soviet character. "Anti-
Soviet" in Soviet jargon connotes pro-Chinese; Moscow opposed
Ohira's concept, suspecting that it was encouraging the Chinese
to come into the organization. Tsvetov thus concluded that "this
alliance does not envisage the participation of socialist coun-

tries, but China's participation is strongly recommended."[66] (3) Moscow was greatly concerned about the cooperation's military character. This concern was reinforced by its unsuccessful attempt at putting into effect its own design of creating a military alliance in the region, i.e., an Asian collective security plan. Thus it envisioned the Ohira doctrine as a "modernized conception of the 'greater Asian coprosperity sphere,' which was promoted by the Japanese militarists during World War II."[67]

PLURAL VIEWS

Finally, a word about the existence, or non-existence, of multiple viewpoints in the Soviet system. As noted earlier, there seemed to be more than one Soviet view of Ohira's "Pacific Basin Cooperation Concept." There are some differences in opinion, for instance, between V. Tsvetov on the one hand, and S. H. Nikonov and Yu. Bandura on the other hand. The former appears to be more concerned with China's participation in the "Pacific Community." Subtle differences of nuance in perceptions on the community seemed to exist between Nikonov and Bandura. Thus a question arises as to how to understand this.

Of course, it is possible to dismiss the divergences described above as insignificant. One may argue that in general there cannot possibly exist multiple viewpoints in such a political system as the Soviet one under monolithic, one-party control. Even if there do exist multiple perceptions on the lower and intermediary levels, they will, and must, be in the end integrated into one on the central decision-making level at the very top. One-party dictatorship needs to arrive at one final interpretation.

It is my opinion, however, that the totally monolithic model has been increasingly inappropriate to explain what has been going on in the post-Stalin Soviet society. According to recent Western Sovietological research, the Soviet system is not and cannot be considered as monolithic now as it is supposed to be by official Soviet doctrine and in fact used to be to a large extent under Stalin.[68] Instead, as suggested by Western advocates of the "conflict model" approach to Soviet decision-making,[69] there does exist a considerable range of interests, perceptions, attitudes, and opinions in present Soviet society. And these divergences or conflicts are not necessarily solved unilaterally by the final voice of the one-man dictator but by bargaining among the reference groups and elite decision makers. Furthermore, it has been recently pointed out by some Western Sovietologists that in that bargaining process ad hoc alliances of convenience are formulated among different subgroups around concrete issues at a given moment.[70] In other words, different issues give rise to informal coalitions which cut across formal institutional lines.[71] This new alternative model of Soviet decision-making has been applied concretely to the analysis of Soviet foreign policy perceptions and decisions, such as Soviet self-images, Soviet images of the United States, Soviet intervention in Czechoslovakia, Soviet relations with the Middle East conflict, Soviet relations with world development, and Soviet foreign aid.[72]

In order to find some universal patterns of perceptions and behavior in the USSR, Western Soviet watchers have recently called for more "case studies" to be accumulated.[73] My paper is still a primitive and intermediate attempt to respond to that call from the Asian-Pacific part of the world, a region in which few studies have been done by the Western Sovietologists.

NOTES

1. Masayoshi Ohira, *Eien no ima* (Now is eternal) (Tokyo: Ohira jumusho, 1980), p. 304.

2. *Japan Times*, January 26, 1979.

3. *Asahi Shimbun* (evening edition), October 27, 1980.

4. *Sankei Shimbun*, December 5, 1980.

5. D. V. Petrov, *Iaponia v mirovoi politike* (Moscow: Mezhdunarodrye otnosheniia, 1973), pp. 40–41, 58–59, 133, 136, 159, 172, 176, 281–282.

6. Ibid., pp. 40, 58–59.

7. Ibid., pp. 58–59.

8. Ibid., pp. 40–41, 282.

9. Ibid.

10. *SSHAA i problemy tikhogo okeana: Mezhdunarodno-politicheskie aspekty* (Moscow: Mezhdunarodnye otoshniia, 1979); *Mezhdunarodnye otnosheniia v aziatsko-tikhookeanskom regione* (Moscow: Izdatel'stvo "Nauka," 1979); V. Mazurov, *SSHAA, Kitai, Iaponia: perestroika mezhgosudarstvennykh otnoshenii, 1969–1979* (Moscow:

Izdatel'stvo "Nauka," 1980); V. B. Vorontsov, *Kitai i SSHAA: 60-70-4 gody* (Moscow: Izdatel'stvo "Nauka," 1979); *Mezhdunarodnye ezhegodnik*: politika i ekonomika (Moscow: Politizdat, 1979).

11. *SSHAA i problemy tikhogo okeana*, p. 83.

12. Ibid., p. 302.

13. Ibid., p. 167.

14. Ibid., p. 37.

15. Ibid., pp. 31, 37.

16. *Mezhdunarodnye otnosheniia*, pp. 66–67.

17. Ibid., p. 67.

18. *SSHAA i problemy tikhogo okeana*, p. 303.

19. *Foreign Broadcasting Information Service: Daily Report (Soviet Union)*, April 30, 1981, p. 1. Hereafter cited as FBIS (SOV).

20. S. N. Nikonov, "O planakh sozdaniia noboi regional'noi organizatii stran tikhogo okeana," *Problemy Dal'nogo boscoka*, no. 2 (1980), p. 170.

21. Yu. Bandura, "Tikhookeanskoe soobshehestvo," *International Affairs*, May, 1980.

22. Ibid., p. 64.

23. *Kantaiheito rentai koso-chukan hokoku* (The interim report on the Pacific Basin cooperation concept) (unpublished), pp. 2, 4.

24. Ibid., p. 20.

25. *Izvestiia*, January 17, 1980.

26. Ibid.

27. Bandura, "Tikhookeanskoe soobshehestvo," p. 64.

28. Nikonov, "O planakh," p. 175.

29. *FBIS (SOV)*, June 9, 1980, p. c2.

30. Ohira, *Eien no ima*, p. 464.

31. Ibid.

32. Bandura, "Tikhookeanskoe soobschestvo," p. 67.

33. *Hokkaido Shimbun*, February 6, 1980.

34. *Nihon Keizai Shimbun*, January 22, 1980.

35. *Izvestiia*, January 17, 1980; exactly the same comment is repeated by him in his "Tikhookeanskoe soobshchestvo," p. 63.

36. Bandura, "Tikhookeanskoe soobshchestvo," p. 63.

37. Ibid.

38. Ibid.

39. Ibid., p. 70.

40. *FBIS (SOV)*, January 8, 1980, p. c2.

41. Ibid.

42. Both *Yomiuri Shimbun* and Nikonov take it for granted that ten countries—Japan, the United States, Canada, Australia, New Zealand,

and five ASEAN member countries—will be members from the start. According to the *Yomiuri Shimbun*, "the high official of the Japanese Ministry of Foreign Affairs stated that they take for granted the participation of *China* and South Korea." Nikonov, "O planakh," p. 173; *Yomiuri Shimbun*, January 22, 1980.

43. *FBIS (SOV)*, June 9, 1980, p. c2.

44. Ibid.

45. Osamu Miyoshi, professor of Kyoto Sangyo University and a regular participant in the closed joint Soviet-Japanese symposium, noted that in the meeting held in April 1976 in Kyoto, the Soviet delegation mentioned the USSR as a Pacific power. Osamu Miyoshi, *Soren-teikokushugi no sekai-senryaku* (Kyoto: PHP kenkyusho, 1980), pp. 267, 299; D. V. Petrov, ed., *Mezhdynarodnye otnosheniia v aziatsko-tikhookeanskom regione* (Moscow: Izdatel'stvo, Nauka, 1979), 280 pp.

46. Report on the Pacific Basin Cooperation Concept (unpublished), p. 73.

47. B. Zanegin, "Aziatskaia bezopasnost: dva podkhoda," *Asiia i Afrika sevodnia* (March 3, 1978), p. 3.

48. *Hokkaido Shimbun*, February 6, 1980.

49. Bandura, "Tikhookeanskoe soobshchestvo," p. 63.

50. *FBIS (SOV)*, January 9, 1980, p. c2.

51. Nikonov, "O planakh," p. 172.

52. *FBIS (SOV)*, January 8, 1980, p. c2.

53. Nikonov, "O planakh," p. 124.

54. *FBIS (SOV)*, June 9, 1980, p. c3; emphasis mine.

55. *Izvestiia*, February 24, 1980.

56. Bandura, "Tikhookeanskoe soobshchestvo," p. 69.

57. *Izvestiia*, January 1, 1980.

58. *Izvestiia*, February 24, 1980, p. 1.

59. *APN News*, February 18, 1980, p. 1.

60. Ibid.

61. Leonid Brezhnev, *Leninskim kursom* (Moscow: Gospolitizhat, 1970), vol. 2, p. 413.

62. Ibid.

63. *Izvestiia*, January 17, 1980.

64. *Izvestiia*, January 24, 1980.

65. *Pravda*, January 22, 1980.

66. *FBIS (SOV)*, June 9, 1980, p. c2.

67. *FBIS (SOV)*, January 22, 1980, p. c2.

68. Gen. John R. Deane, head of the U.S. Military Mission in Moscow and administrator of Lend-Lease at the Soviet end, once wrote: "Only one man in the Soviet Union can make 'on the spot' decisions

and he is Joe Stalin. The Molotovs, Vyshinskys, Gromykos, and Maliks are little more than messengers." John R. Deane, "Negotiating on Military Assistance, 1943–45," in *Negotiating with the Russians*, ed. Raymond Bennett and Joseph E. Johnson (Boston: World Peace Foundation, 1951), p. 27.

69. Carl Linden, *Khrushchev and the Soviet Leadership, 1957–1964* (Baltimore: Johns Hopkins University Press, 1966), pp. 6–7.

70. Jiri Valenta, *Soviet Intervention in Czechoslovakia, 1968: Anatomy of a Decision* (Baltimore: Johns Hopkins University Press, 1979), p. 17.

71. Christopher Johnson, *Soviet Bargaining Behavior: The Nuclear Test Ban Case* (New York: Columbia University Press, 1979), pp. 135–142.

72. Christopher Johnson, "Foreign Policy Ideas and Groupings in the Soviet Union," unpublished paper read at the panel of Political Science 14 of the Second World Congress for Soviet and East European Studies, Garmisch-Partenkirchen, September 30–October 4, 1980, pp. 5–28.

73. Ibid., p. 29. See also Hiroshi Kimura, "The Soviet Buildup: Its Impact on Japan and Its Aims," in *The Soviet Far East Military Buildup*, ed. Richard H. Solomon and Masataka Kosaka (Dover, Mass.: Auburn House Publishing Company, 1986), pp. 106–118; and Roy Kim, "Soviets Ponder Opening Port of Vladivostok," *Christian Science Monitor*, August 1, 1986.

4

The Pacific Economic Community: Unsettled Problems

VLADIMIR I. IVANOV

The international significance of the Twenty-Seventh Congress of the Soviet Union Communist Party in 1986 lay in the fact that it paid primary attention to international politics, to measures aimed at preserving and consolidating the trends of detente and at reducing military danger. Again, amidst the considerable aggravation of the deteriorating international situation and rising, growing tension between states, the congress advanced initiatives designed to improve the entire system of international relations, to solve important military-political issues and questions of bilateral relations, and to eliminate regional seats of tension. With regard to the Far East and western Pacific, the congress put forward important proposals whose implementation will undoubtedly contribute to a normalization of interstate relations in the region. The Soviet position as formulated in the Report of the Communist Party Central Committee to the Congress is defined thus: "There is a region where elaboration and use of confidence-building measures—naturally, with due consideration for its specific features—could not only defuse the situation locally, but also make a very useful contribution to strengthening the foundations of universal peace. That region is the Far East, where such powers as the Soviet Union, China and Japan border on each other. There are also US military bases there."

It is critically important to remember that all these processes are going on in a complex historical and political situation in

East Asia, and amidst growing instability in relations between the regional powers. This brings to the fore questions about the nature of the political atmosphere in which a system of economic ties can take shape and develop. In this context, the concept of the "Pacific Economic Community" acquires a certain international significance.

It is evident that the international environment in the Far East covers or includes not only political and strategic military questions, but problems of economic interaction of the countries of the Pacific. Furthermore, the intraregional structure of trade and economic cooperation undoubtedly includes the economic ties between two socio-political systems, which have been, and remain, a basis of detente and a factor of regional stability. At the same time, as the report to the Congress notes, the Soviet Union is "compelled to take account of the policy of the capitalist states. Not infrequently they try to use economic ties with us as a means of political pressure." In this connection attention should be turned to the trends in the economic development of the Pacific region, investment and commercial intercourse between the states bordering the Pacific, and also to the special economic and political activities undertaken by the so-called "advanced market economies" in the developing countries of the region.

The academics, businessmen, and government officials of the countries of the Pacific continue to discuss the Pacific Community idea. It boils down to searching for new methods and forms of economic interaction between the Pacific states, and approaches to the setting up of an intergovernmental consultative mechanism. Economists and political scientists of Japan, Australia, the United States, Canada, and other countries of the region have originated the concept of the "Pacific Economic Community." Fairly recently, the term "Pacific Community" has been used by government officials of the advanced industrial countries of the Pacific. A definite political atmosphere began to pervade academic discussions of regional economic problems. The most developed countries showed an explicit desire to use the concept of "Pacific Economic Community" for political purposes in order to adapt it as much as possible to the complicated international environment, which is characterized by changes in the correlation of forces between the socio-political systems, the markedly growing role of the developing countries in the world economy and international politics, and new developments in the whole structure of non-planned economies and regional economic relations.

The significance of the changes that have taken place during the past two or three decades in the economic pattern of the Pacific zone of the world economy goes beyond the boundaries of the region. The economic potentials of the principal Pacific countries have increased considerably; their economic growth rates now surpass the average level of the non-socialist part of the world. The western Pacific has turned into a most dynamic zone of the world economy through trade exchanges and new principal shifts in the system of the international division of labor. The operation, on a regional level, of the law of the uneven economic and political development of advanced countries and the growing economic and political differentiation of the developing economies have led to major changes in the whole structure of regional economy and political dimensions.

Postwar Japan has emerged as the center of economic gravity for the countries of the western Pacific and has become a most important factor of economic development in the region. Its rapid economic growth has resulted in a sharp rise in demand for minerals and energy, food, and agricultural raw materials for industry; and consequently, the entire system of regional economic ties has profoundly changed. The significance of the Pacific region for Japan has been growing along with the growth of the country's economic potential and industrial power. The countries of the western Pacific have become the most important field for the trade and investment expansion of Japanese corporations. Japan has become heavily dependent on raw materials and food supplies from Australia, the ASEAN countries, Canada, and New Zealand. Along with Japanese industrial growth, the Pacific Coast of the United States and Canada became in the 1960's the most dynamic region in North America in terms of concentration of population, urban areas, infrastructure, economic growth rates, and scope of industrial development. The countries of the western Pacific have become increasingly important for the foreign trade of the United States and Canada. By the end of the 1970's, Pacific trade had become more important for the United States than that with Europe. Small industrial countries of the western Pacific—Australia and New Zealand—have in their economic development passed through long periods of upsurge. The growing demand for mineral and agricultural resources has contributed to Australia, Canada, and New Zealand coming to the fore as major world exporters of raw materials.

The economies of the developing countries and territories of the Pacific region have undergone important changes, too. With the impact of foreign-policy factors as well as the domestic economic developments, regional political and economic integration has been accelerated and regional economic organizations of ASEAN and those of microstates of the South Pacific (the South Pacific Forum and the South Pacific Bureau of Economic Cooperation) have come into being. South Korea, Singapore, Taiwan, and Hong Kong have become sort of "industrialized islands" among the developing countries of Asia. Economic development strategy and industrialization of these and other developing western Pacific economies and the drawing of foreign investment and organization of export industries have led to substantial economic and trade expansion and closer interdependence between them and advanced capitalist states. The economic potential and participation in regional trade of South Korea, Taiwan, and Hong Kong have sharply grown. Their total share in international trade has reached 40 percent of that of Japan.

All these developments have contributed to the rapid expansion of economic links in Pacific Asia, a process that has been going on at a faster rate than the economic development of the countries of the region as a whole and the rate of increase of world trade. A trend has taken shape to concentrate economic interaction among the states of the Pacific zone within the framework of the Pacific region, and their economic development has begun to be centered around the inter-regional system of the international division of labor. By the end of the 1970's, 57 percent of the exports and 55 percent of the imports of the capitalist and developing countries of the Pacific region came from trade exchanges between them. For the majority of the developing economies or ASEAN members, South Korea, Taiwan, Hong Kong, and the microstates of the South Pacific whose external trade and investment relations are oriented mostly to the United States and Japan, Australia, and New Zealand, this share reached 70 to 90 percent.

Private capital flows and the activities of transnational corporations and banks have become an essential element of the system of inter-regional trade and economic contacts, and this has led to a consolidation of regional financial centers, such as Tokyo, Singapore, Hong Kong, and Sydney. Their role in the financial ties of the entire capitalist world has become much greater than before. Technological exchanges have intensified, and development assistance programs have expanded. The significance of transport and communication lines has increased. The rapid growth of export-oriented manufacturing and mining industries and the expansion of agricultural production and trade in food products within the region have increased economic interdependence. These changes and processes in the Pacific zone of the world economy have led to the emergence of the idea of a "Pacific Community."

By the end of the 1970's the concept of the "Pacific Economic Community," a term hitherto used in discussions in academic circles, had begun to enter the sphere of political decision-making. In 1979 and 1980 mention of and references to the "Pacific idea" appeared in statements made by Japanese Prime Minister Masayoshi Ohira, Australian Prime Minister Malcolm Fraser, and Assistant U.S. Secretary of State on Asian and Pacific Affairs Richard Holbrooke. On the initiative of the Australian and Japanese governments, the prospects of a regional economic organization were discussed at an international seminar held in Canberra in September 1980. The seminar was attended by scholars and representatives of the business communities and governments of the Pacific countries, including Australia, Japan, the United States, Canada, New Zealand, Indonesia, Malaysia, Singapore, Thailand, the Philippines, South Korea, several countries of the South Pacific, and a number of regional organizations. The government representatives, although they attended in their private capacity, lent a political character to the discussions. The Canberra seminar became, despite its "economic agenda," an international political event, the first at-

tempt to give a political interpretation of the basic aspect of the
"Pacific idea" as an alternative to divergent economic systems
and as a way of managing deep-rooted economic problems.

The main subject of discussion at the seminar was the inter-
nationalization trends in economic development, the emergence
of serious contradictions in the economic sphere, which began
to affect ever more deeply the interests of individual Pacific
countries, their governments, and business, politics, and other
groups of influence. The need to solve them and to avoid negative and destructive tendencies in interstate economic relations
has become an element of crucial importance in the "Pacific
Economic Community" concept. It is not accidental, therefore,
that the final documents of the seminar and speeches by its
participants highlighted the idea that it was necessary to take
coordinated steps in the economic sphere to preserve and develop the very structure of complex economic ties, and to reduce the gap between the long-term economic requirements and
the present national interests of individual countries.

The principal motive for the countries of the Pacific region to
discuss the "Pacific idea" was the growing narrowness of the
bounds of bilateral interstate relations, the existing international
economic organizations, and the national boundaries of economic management, as well as the growing interdependence of
regional processes and the domestic economic and socio-political situations.

The interaction of advanced capitalist states and the developing countries was a major point of heated discussion in planning for a "Pacific Economic Community." Unsettled problems
and potentially unstable relations between the two groups present a critical problem in the system of regional economic ties.
Despite some progress in economic development achieved by
individual developing countries of the Pacific region, the gap in
their levels of economic development and those of advanced industrial states continues to widen. The gross national product
of the five capitalist industrial countries of the region (the United
States, Canada, Japan, Australia, and New Zealand) and the nine
developing states (South Korea, Taiwan, Hong Kong, the Philippines, Thailand, Malaysia, Singapore, Indonesia, and Papua–
New Guinea) reached $3,000 billion in 1979, with the share of

the under-developed economies comprising only 6 percent while their population amounted to 46 percent.

The industrialization of a number of the Pacific developing countries (oriented to the intensive economic ties with advanced capitalist states) has not only caused serious changes in their economic structures, but has also increased the interdependence between them and the industrial states. Their importance as suppliers of agricultural and mineral raw materials to capitalist states has markedly increased; labor-, energy-, and material-intensive and ecologically impure industries were intensively transferred to their territories, and conditions were thus created which necessarily reorganized trade and investment flows in the favor of transnational corporations. All this inevitably connected the developing countries of the Pacific region and their industrial and natural resources, territories, and population with the regional structure of the international division of labor. It is not accidental that interest in the creation of the "Pacific Economic Community" has noticeably grown in Japan and the United States in recent years, precisely at a time when connections between the stagnation in this world of capitalist economy and the instability of the world market have become more evident.

The growth of unemployment in capitalist industrial countries, together with the rise of inflation, declining levels of consumption and demand, and measures to restrict imports, have seriously affected the vital interests of developing countries that export labor-intensive products. The curtailment of industrial production that followed in developing countries and the drop in exports and proceeds from them were accompanied by considerable rise in the import prices of equipment, food products, energy resources, and services which inevitably decreased the potentials of export and capital investment for advanced industrial states. It became evident that a profound and coordinated restructuring of national economies was needed, as well as expansion on that basis of the markets for export industries of the developing countries. Otherwise, the trend shaped during the 1960's and 1970's toward the growing economic integration of the developing countries of the Pacific zone in the world capitalist economy would weaken, and the links with which the industrial countries of the Pacific region tried to bind their junior partners to their own economic structures in order to use them as a reserve of the world capitalist economy would loosen. At the end of the 1970's the question of broadening development assistance programs to the developing countries, their growing indebtedness, higher costs of importing oil and industrial equipment, prospects of getting modern technology, stabilization of export incomes, and greater access to the markets of the developed countries of the Pacific, as well as the problems of food security and employment, become more acute.

Although the concept of the "Pacific Economic Community" connotes the existence of crucial regional problems, the future consultative organization is regarded by some developing countries as an instrument for strengthening economic domination, securing raw material supplies for advanced countries, and ensuring freedom of action for transnational corporations.

There is another important problem connected with the "Pacific Economic Community." Economic contradictions between industrial countries, competition for markets, for spheres of activities of transnational corporations, and for sources of raw materials on the one hand, and the increasing economic interdependence on the other, have led to the inability to solve many problems on a basis of bilateral relations. Containment, regulation, and neutralization of economic differences become in this context an important element of a stable economic environment. The economic rivalries among the industrial capitalist countries of the region are unfolding at three levels, as it were, in the bilateral relations between the United States and Japan; between these two leading centers of power of the non-socialist world and their "junior" partners (Canada, Australia, and New Zealand); and in the rivalry between all the advanced capitalist states (especially the United States and Japan) for economic and political presence in the developing countries of the western Pacific.

American-Japanese economic rivalry and a large imbalance of U.S.–Japan trade have an even greater impact on the stability of multilateral economic relations in the region. Beginning from the mid-1960's the U.S. share in Japan's foreign trade has diminished from 31 to 18 percent, whereas Japan's share in the U.S. foreign trade has risen from 8 to 10 percent. The expan-

sion of Japanese companies in the United States has been growing in scope; their investments in the American economy (in
the total volume of Japan's foreign investments) have increased
from 10.4 to 28 percent, amounting to $5.4 billion. Recently,
the extension of Japanese car-manufacturing companies to the
United States has become a matter of serious conflict in U.S.-
Japan trade relations. By 1986 the United States reached its worst
trade deficit of $51 billion with Japan—a potential source of se-
rious American-Japanese friction.

During the 1970–80 period, the share of Japanese motorcars
in total U.S. auto-imports had grown from 24.4 to 80.6 percent,
forcing U.S. producers to reorganize production and suffer great
losses. There are also other controversial problems, among which
are disagreements in the monetary sphere, shortages of energy
resources, and one-sided actions in trade relations, as well as
other manifestations of economic nationalism.

Economic rivalries are growing between the United States and
Canada, Australia and Japan, and Australia and New Zealand.
These rivalries are deep-rooted and often go beyond the bounds
of economic relations. The reason for this is the growing role of
mineral and raw material resources of the Pacific countries in
world trade, the capital investment flows, and the buildup of
intraregional structures of raw material consumption. On the
basis of the use of minerals and other raw material resources
the "regionalization" of trade relations is taking place and integration tendencies are being formed; their elements have appeared in the relations between the United States and Canada,
Japan, and Australia. Economic relations between these countries acquire a multilateral, interdependent character. For instance, Australia has become a leading exporter of mineral and
energy raw materials to Japan through the direct participation
of foreign, above all American, mining companies. American
transnational corporations are playing the role of a locomotive
in bilateral ties between Canada and Japan.

New circles of economic relations have emerged: the United
States–Australia-Japan; the United States–Canada-Japan. Their
functioning involves the operation of American mining corporations in Australia and Canada and the supplying of Japanese
industry with key raw materials from those countries. Finished

products of the Japanese steel and motorcar industry are being exported to the United States and also to Australia and Canada. At the same time Canada and Australia are important markets for American and Japanese industrial goods; the above mentioned countries also depend on the United States and Japan for the latest technology and science-intensive industries. The development of Australian and Canadian natural resources by transnational corporations, manipulation of the prices of raw materials, and the financial losses of the exporters of unprocessed raw materials and their growing technological dependence on U.S. and Japanese multinationals have become serious problems for the domestic economic policies of resource-producing countries, problems that impinge on their relations with the United States and Japan. Australia's and Canada's dependence on the economic situation in the United States and Japan is growing. Foreign capital increases its domination of the mining industries of Australia and Canada.

The formation of a zone of Japan's economic influence is becoming a crucial factor in the international and political ties of the Pacific region. With the economic growth of Japan and its turning into a relatively independent center of force in the world economy, Japanese-American rivalry for economic advantages in the developing countries of the western Pacific is mounting. American corporations have done much to bolster up their presence in the developing countries of Asia, especially in the ASEAN states, South Korea, and Taiwan. The aggregate share of Indonesia, Singapore, Malaysia, Hong Kong, Taiwan, and South Korea in the total of U.S.-Pacific trade reached 30 percent in 1978, or $23 billion.

American companies' private direct investment in these countries had increased many times during the 1970's. In 1978 Japan's trade turnover with the developing countries of the region exceeded $29.5 billion, which comprised 16.5 percent of its foreign trade, or 80 percent of Japan-U.S. trade. The share of Southeast Asian countries in Japan's foreign trade has remained stable since the early 1960's which is rather significant when viewed against the background of a thirtyfold increase in that country's foreign trade turnover, political instability in the region, a sharp rise in the prices of oil and oil products, and an

expansion and diversification of economic ties. Japan has become the most important trade partner of practically every country
in the region except Taiwan and Hong Kong, with which the
United States still retains its leadership in trade relations. In
this setting the "Pacific Economic Community" is regarded by
the supporters of the idea as a basis for a compromise between
U.S. and Japanese economic interests in the region.

It becomes evident that one of the reasons for setting up the
"Pacific Economic Community" is the inability of countries to
solve current economic problems by resorting to traditional
measures of protectionism or economic nationalism. Meanwhile, it should be admitted that all interested countries do recognize the complex situation in regional economic ties, the increasing interdependence of individual national economies, and
the inappropriateness of even a partial regimentation of economic activity.

The discussions of the prospects for "a Pacific Economic
Community" overlook another crucial question, namely, the
possible international consequences stemming from the organization of a regional intergovernmental institution and its influence on the political climate in the region. Any attempt to unite
a group of Pacific countries on the basis of economic relations
among them will inevitably have an impact on their political
ties, and in the prevailing international situation there is little
reason to believe that the projected organization would be neutral. This is shown, among other things, by its composition: an
overwhelming majority of participating countries are already
bound by mutual obligations in the political and military spheres
and are elements of a strategic relations structure.

This has influenced the evolution of the "Pacific Economic
Community" concept and the results of the Canberra seminar
proceedings. For instance, countries with a planned economy
were invited to take part only in the activities of the working
groups created under the auspices of the Committee of Pacific
Cooperation. There is a certain political inflexibility in the approach of the advanced capitalist countries of the Pacific region
to the crucial problems of international relations. This is connected not only with the cold war heritage, but also with the
growing new tendencies in the international politics of the Far

East, especially the attempts by the United States and Japan to augment their separate ties with the People's Republic of China. This suggests that they are using the "Pacific Community" in the interests of their alliance strategy in Asia and the Pacific.

Indeed, international relations in the region, especially in the western Pacific, during the entire postwar period have been marked by a high degree of tension, and the imperialists' desire to solve international problems from positions of power with the help of military-political alliances and other measures has split the region into confronting groupings. The United States has assumed the role of the initiator in setting up such military-political blocs and treaties as ANZUS, SEATO, ANZUK, and ASPAC, and it has also concluded bilateral agreements with Japan, South Korea, Thailand, the Philippines, and Taiwan, obtaining the right to deploy its military forces on their territories. The United States and other industrial Pacific states have for a long time utilized investment, trade, and aid ties to consolidate their military and political presence in Asia and to preserve or destabilize political regimes in some countries of the region. The United States and its allies continue to regard trade and economic contacts as a means of exerting pressure on the developing and socialist countries, and they use these contacts to obtain one-sided political advantages.

The plans to create a regional economic organization excluding the socialist countries can only be regarded as a way of ensuring growing participation in regional economic matters, and of bolstering economically a ramified network of already-existing military-political alliances directed against the USSR, Mongolia, Vietnam, North Korea, and, of late, Laos and Kampuchea. For example, the visit of Japanese Prime Minister M. Ohira to Australia and New Zealand in January 1980 and the official declarations and talks on the "Pacific Economic Community" were followed by military exercises of the naval forces of the United States, Canada, Australia, New Zealand, and Japan, code-named "Rimpac-80." Is it just a coincidence or a purposeful action? Are there real plans to use the idea of the "Pacific Community" for coordinating military activities and aggravating political tension?

The sphere of international economic connections in the Pacific region is not free from the influence of political and strategic considerations within the framework of the "East-West" dialogue. A cardinal criterion of the approach of the United States, Japan, and Australia to international economic relations in the Far East is now their feverishly active maneuvers to establish economic ties with the People's Republic of China. Today, when the fate of the "Chinese boom" is, to say the least, unpredictable, it can be seen especially clearly that attempts at a selective approach to the expansion of economic ties and the desire to influence the global alignment of forces with their help not only involve enormous financial losses, but also undermine international trust and block the establishment of genuine economic contacts with socialist states on a long-term basis.

It does not seem possible to solve the urgent problems of such a vast region as the Pacific, which has enormous resources and possibilities but is torn by most complicated contradictions, by creating a regional organization confined to the regional boundaries and including only some of the countries of the Pacific. In the conditions of the prevailing instability of international relations it is exceedingly dangerous to aggravate the situation in the Pacific and to try to use natural tendencies in economic life to increase political tension. A genuinely efficient regional cooperation can be established only through a really democratic and broad organization that will operate in stable conditions of peace and security throughout the Pacific area, and will itself become a factor of stabilization of international relations.

5

Soviet-American Economic Ties and the Pacific Community: Antecedents and Prospects

JOHN J. STEPHAN

The Soviet Union is a major Pacific power. A high level of economic development, rich natural resources, and internal market capacity make Soviet participation in economic relations of the Pacific region an objective necessity.

—Vladimir B. Yakubovsky (1976)[1]

A remarkable feature of recent dialogues about a Pacific Community is the virtual absence of any serious discussion of how the Soviet Union might fit into a multilateral structure of regional economic cooperation. There seems to be an unacknowledged but widespread assumption that whatever concrete form such a concept might eventually take, it would for the time being involve only market economies. Although not in principle barred from association, countries with planned economies are as a rule assigned peripheral roles.

This orientation toward the USSR in the Pacific is to some extent intentional. Decades of Soviet-American rivalry have conditioned our thinking about economic cooperation in a region where both Washington and Moscow have vital strategic interests. Consequently, the absence of any reference to the USSR in President Ford's 1975 "Pacific Doctrine" address was hardly accidental. Analogous omissions in statements on the Pacific (with the notable exception of perceived military threats) by spokesmen of succeeding administrations probably also contain an element of calculation.

Habit and ignorance also explain why the USSR figures so modestly in contemporary discussions about the Pacific Community. Americans tenaciously subscribe to the stereotype of "Russia" as a European state with a remote and desolate back yard called "Siberia." Russian history and culture are commonly viewed through a European prism. What happens east of the Urals tends to fall under the rubric of foreign affairs or penal servitude.

Our knowledge about the past and present relationship between the world's largest state and the world's largest ocean is rudimentary. Americans familiar with the names of Cook and Perry are unlikely to have heard of Dezhnev, Golovnin, or Krusenstern, whose contributions to Pacific exploration were hardly less noteworthy. Ignorance of history has gone hand in hand with ignorance of geography. There is only a hazy awareness of the Soviet Union's physical presence in the region. It even comes as a surprise to some that the USSR has a Pacific coastline. While the American public has been alerted to the expansion of the Soviet Pacific Fleet, far less attention has been drawn to trends in the Soviet Far East which are propelling the USSR toward new economic relationships with countries of the Pacific rim.

Possible modes of Soviet participation in a regional organization designed to promote economic cooperation can be gleaned from historical patterns of trade between Russia and the United States in the Pacific. Notwithstanding manifold changes in and around the basin during the last century, these patterns of Russian-American commerce have not lapsed into irrelevance. Indeed, they contain clues for fresh approaches to a superpower relationship in a region that in recent years has assumed critical importance in international relations.

HISTORICAL ANTECEDENTS

Russian-American trade in the Pacific originated in, and was sustained by, the demand for provisions in Russian settlements which at one time stretched along the basin's northern rim from the Korean frontier to California. One can even say that the search for food supplies constituted a leitmotif of Russian diplomatic initiatives in the Pacific for over two hundred years.

Since Cossacks reached the Sea of Okhotsk in the middle of the seventeenth century, the provisioning of settlements in Eastern Siberia and Russian America posed a serious impediment to colonization and development. Poor soil and harsh climatic conditions restricted agriculture. Immense distances and cumbersome transport facilities made overland shipments from European Russia slow and expensive.

Until the middle of the nineteenth century, the bulk of food for Russia's Pacific settlements had to be brought from Europe or from Siberia. Grain grown around Lake Baikal and livestock raised in Yakutsk supplied the Okhotsk region until 1800. Subsequently, overland transport was supplemented by sea shipments which until the opening of the Suez Canal in 1869 came via the Cape of Good Hope or Cape Horn. The cost of such methods of supply can be gauged from the fact that in 1800 provisions in Kamchatka fetched up to thirty-two times more than in Irkutsk.[2]

A number of attempts were made to solve the provisions problem, but none met with notable success. Penetration of the fertile Amur Valley was rebuffed by China in 1689. Trade missions sent to Japan in the eighteenth and early nineteenth centuries foundered upon the self-imposed isolation maintained by the Tokugawa shogunate. Not until the 1890's did Japan begin to play a significant role in supplying provisions to the Russian Far East.

Similar efforts were made to open trade relations with Spanish colonies in the Philippines, California, and Peru, but these also proved fruitless. An attempt to establish an agricultural colony north of San Francisco yielded disappointing results. An unofficial bid to secure a foothold in the Hawaiian Islands caused only political embarrassment in St. Petersburg.

Russian-American trade in the Pacific began shortly after 1800. It was conducted largely in Alaska and Upper California, areas in which the Russian-American Company enjoyed a monopoly of the fur trade. American merchants, largely from New England, brought provisions to Sitka and Bodega Bay and bartered them for pelts from employees of the Russian-American Company. The Americans then resold the pelts in Canton at a sizeable profit. The imperial government in St. Petersburg frowned upon this trade and chronically tried to curtail it; nevertheless, the demand for provisions in Russian America was such that Yankee entrepreneurs continued to find a ready market for their wares along the northeast Pacific littoral until the middle of the nineteenth century.

Although Russia and the United States signed a commercial treaty in 1832, trade between the two countries in the Pacific remained at modest, if growing, levels until the 1880's:[3]

	U.S. exports	*U.S. imports*
1866	$3,300	—
1868	$59,341	$15,849
1874	$134,583	—
1881	$207,061	$89,727

Modest levels of trade did not discourage American entrepreneurs from entertaining high hopes about commercial opportunities in the Russian Far East. In 1848 a New York businessman, Aaron Haight Palmer, presented President Polk with a plan to develop Sakhalin with American capital as an emporium for trade with Japan.[4] In 1856 Perry McDonough Collins, a California entrepreneur, persuaded President Pierce to appoint him "Commercial Agent of the United States for the Amoor River" and publicized the Amur Basin as a channel for American commercial enterprise throughout Northeast Asia.[5] Shortly after the Civil War, Collins raised three million dollars through Western Union to lay a telegraph line across Alaska, under the Bering Straits, and across Siberia to connect the United States and Europe.[6] Some dreamers envisioned connecting the Union Pacific Railroad with the Trans-Siberian by tunneling under the Bering Straits and opening Pullman service between Chicago and Paris via Irkutsk. None of these schemes came to fruition, but the spirit behind them has periodically resurfaced.

During the last half of the nineteenth century, Hawaii assumed increasing importance as a supply base for Russian merchant and naval ships operating between Asia and the Americas. Records of the Russian consulate in Honolulu indicate that several ships called annually, starting in 1859. In 1887 the subsequently illustrious navigator and naval strategist Stepan O. Makarov, then captain of the naval research vessel *Vityaz*, stopped in Honolulu.[7] During his visit, Makarov was approached by representatives of a local company regarding the establishment of trade between Hawaii and Russian Pacific ports. The results of these talks are not clear, but the expression of interest is in itself significant.

The acceleration of Siberia's development during the 1890's, promoted by construction of the Trans-Siberian Railroad and by peasant immigration, stimulated Russian-American trade in the Pacific. Imports from the United States through Vladivostok jumped from $566,512 in 1896 to $3,050,902 in 1900. Exports (largely furs) from Siberia to the United States did not keep pace with imports, leaving the United States with a favorable balance of trade in the Pacific from 1866 until the October Revolution.[8]

To equip peasant immigrants moving from the Ukraine and European Russia to Siberia, Russian firms purchased significant quantities of American agricultural machinery, which in terms of value came to predominate among commodities imported through Pacific ports after 1900. American harvesters were highly esteemed among cultivators along the Amur River. "Such is the demand," wrote the U.S. commercial agent in Vladivostok in 1903, "that private firms cannot fill orders."[9]

After the Russo-Japanese War, the range of American products entering Vladivostok grew to include automobiles, motorboats, sewing machines, and clothing.[10] American beer became so popular that in 1909 a brewery in Blagoveshchensk was bottling lager under the Schlitz label.[11]

Siberia's population growth boosted demand for fruits and vegetables which could not be locally grown. Around 1890 Russian merchants in the Far East became interested in the prospect of importing West Coast fruit.[12] By 1900 Oregon apples and California apricots, peaches, prunes, lemons, and raisins were being sold in Vladivostok, Nikolaevsk, and Khabarovsk. At first, shipping costs, delivery delays, and poor packing handicapped their competitiveness with European and Chinese produce, but after 1901 West Coast foodstuff exports mounted steadily until by 1913 they comprised over 20 percent of total U.S. exports to Siberia.[13]

World War I precipitated a surge of American shipments to Russia across the Pacific. With Baltic and Black Sea ports blocked by the Central Powers, Vladivostok emerged as Russia's principal maritime gateway. U.S. exports to the Russian Far East leapt from $5.7 million in 1914 to $160.7 million in 1916. Sixty-five percent of cargoes consisted of war materiel, but canned fruits, vegetables, meats, and milk comprised most of the remainder.[14] Despite American entry into the war as Russia's ally in April 1917, West Coast exports slipped during that year as a result of unstable political conditions following the February Revolution. The spread of civil war to Siberia caused a sharp decline of exports to the Far East in 1918.[15]

By disrupting internal transport and creating waves of refugees, the Russian Civil War eventually generated heavy demand for imported foodstuffs. American exports to Vladivostok rebounded from $8.4 million in 1918 to $52 million in 1919, with fruit, vegetables, meat, and milk retaining their prominence.

EXPORTS TO THE FAR EAST

The consolidation of Soviet power throughout the Far East brought a temporary halt to American food shipments to Vladivostok. Although Soviet-American Pacific trade grew from $813,000 in 1924 to $5,460,000 in 1930, foodstuffs did not regain their erstwhile position among American exports, which consisted largely of industrial products, particularly canning equipment. On the other hand, foodstuffs figured conspicuously among Soviet exports from the Far East to the American West Coast. In 1933, 27 percent of American crabmeat imports were coming from Soviet Pacific ports.[16] These structural shifts in trade derived from Soviet efforts to achieve self-sufficiency in food and to create a modern fishing industry in the Maritime Province, northern Sakhalin, and Kamchatka.

American food shipments to the Soviet Far East resumed during World War II as part of the Lend-Lease program. Most Lend-Lease tonnage came across the Pacific, transported on American-built ships under Soviet registry, manned by Soviet crews who brought the vessels through the Japanese-held Kuril Islands to Vladivostok. Supplies were also flown via Alaska and the Bering Straits to Yakutsk.

For a quarter of a century after 1945, Soviet-American trade in the Pacific was virtually non-existent. Since 1970 commerce has shown some signs of reviving, with foodstuffs again playing notable roles. Since 1972, when 200,000 tons of maize, barley, and oats were shipped to Nakhodka, grain has figured with erratic prominence in trans-Pacific trade, volume varying from year to year according to harvests and politics. Periodic cash sales of California citrus fruits recall patterns prevalent in 1900–1920. A joint fishing venture, the US-USSR Marine Resources Company, with offices in Seattle and Nakhodka, inaugurated operations in 1978. The firm's local representative in Nakhodka is the only American businessman stationed outside of Moscow.[17]

Despite a somewhat fitful growth during the past decade, Soviet-American commerce in the Pacific still amounts to only a fraction of Soviet-Japanese trade, which reached $4.6 billion in 1980. There appears to be a consensus that the potential for significantly greater Soviet-American trade in the Pacific exists. In looking for areas in which that potential can be realized, it is natural to ponder whether historical antecedents offer a useful guide to creating a stronger Soviet-American economic relationship in the Pacific and, by extension, to promoting Soviet participation in regional multilateral organizations such as those which might materialize under the Pacific Community concept.

PROSPECTS

In order to determine how realistic prospects are for deepening Soviet-American economic ties in the Pacific, it is important to identify and weigh obstacles which constrain the establishment of such ties. Some of the obstacles are structural: differences in socio-economic systems; institutional limitations (e.g., a Far East–based international trade organization does not include the United States within its purview); limited (if improving) capacities of Soviet Pacific ports; transportation bottlenecks between ports and inland areas; and inadequate awareness among

American businessmen of trade opportunities in the Soviet Far
East. The most stubborn obstacle, however, is mutual distrust.
Distrust was born from certain historical experiences, nurtured
by different societal values, hardened by postwar global rivalry,
and exacerbated by events during the late 1970's.

The Asian-Pacific component of Soviet distrust of the United
States springs from a conviction that Washington has chronically tried to use Japan and China against the USSR to further
its own global geopolitical strategy. Memories of American and
Japanese troops in the Far East during the Civil War are not
extinguished. Nor has the suspicion that the United States sur-
reptitiously encouraged Imperial Japan to move against Siberia
during the 1930's died. The current Japanese-American security relationship has in Moscow's eyes assumed ominous overtones as steady steps toward Japanese rearmament are accompanied by centripetal trends which have brought Tokyo,
Washington, and Peking together into a triangular alignment in
Northeast Asia. Meanwhile, unprecedented joint naval maneuvers of American, Japanese, Australian, New Zealand, and Canadian forces (Rimpac-80), prospective American arms sales to
China, and a statement by a Reagan administration official about
the strategic implications of a "Pacific Community" concept have
collectively convinced leading observers in the USSR that the
United States is attempting to forge a global anti-Soviet military
system involving NATO, ANZUS, China, Japan, Pakistan, and
the ASEAN nations. Conversely, American doubts about Soviet
motives, triggered by Bolshevik revolutionary rhetoric and nour-
ished by Stalin's domestic terror and territorial appetites, noticeably intensified during the late 1970's, to a great extent because
of events in Asia and the Pacific. The introduction of Soviet forces
into Afghanistan, Soviet support of Vietnam's occupation of
Kampuchea, and the growing reach of Siberia/Far East–based
sea and air power have all focused American concern on the
Asian-Pacific region. Mutual distrust has in turn given rise to
concrete barriers to developing Soviet-American economic relations in general and in the Pacific in particular. The 1972 Trade
Agreement has yet to come into force because of Soviet unwill-
ingness to accept American conditions for its implementation.
The Jackson-Vanik Amendment to the 1974 Trade Act linked

non-discriminatory tariff treatment of the USSR with Soviet emigration policies, and Congress subsequently imposed ceilings on Export-Import Bank loans to the USSR. In the wake of Afghanistan, the Carter administration took steps to restrict technology exports to the Soviet Union. Current Soviet attitudes on Pacific trade are an admixture of expectation and skepticism. On the one hand, there is an awareness of the Pacific Basin's growing importance as a locus of multilateral trade and investment. A recent Soviet source affirms that "economic processes occurring in recent years in the region of the Pacific Ocean have turned it into a new center of the economy of the capitalist world."[18]

There is a readiness to promote economic ties with market economies in the Pacific Basin, as has been demonstrated by large-scale commercial relations with Japan. In 1977 a Vladivostok official perceived an impressive potential for economic cooperation between the Soviet Far East and the American West Coast:

Vast possibilities for developing Soviet-U.S. trade and economic relations exist in the Soviet Far East. . . . Transoceanic trade between the Soviet Far East and the Pacific seaboard states (California, Washington, Oregon, Alaska) may become a very promising factor in Soviet-U.S. trade relations. An analysis of the commodity structure of the foreign trade of the U.S. Pacific seaboard shows it to correspond to the export possibilities and import needs of the Soviet Far East.[19]

On the other hand, recent American economic sanctions against the USSR, coupled with the award of most-favored-nation (MFN) status to China (while it was withheld from the USSR), have raised doubts about the feasibility of a long-term economic relationship if such a relationship is to be vulnerable to politically motivated disruptions.

Soviet commentary on the Pacific Community concept has reflected the same admixture of expectation and skepticism evident in attitudes toward trade with the United States. Published statements have criticized the concept as an instrument of American and Japanese aggrandizement, fraught with dangerous implications. On November 17, 1980, *Pravda* political columnist Vsevolod Ovchinnikov noted that recent international discussions about a Pacific Community (Ovchinnikov used the phrase "Pacific Ring") betrayed a political complexion, revealing that the idea was essentially an attempt to promote the interests of multinational corporations at the expense of developing countries.[20] Ovchinnikov discerned two types of motives. He suggested that Tokyo saw such a concept as a means to consolidate Japanese regional economic preeminence. The United States, he argued, intended to use the "Pacific Ring" idea as a mechanism to unite NATO, ANZUS, and the Japanese-American security arrangements into a single military alliance. Ovchinnikov concluded by warning that some architects of the "Pacific Ring" were planning to turn ASEAN nations into "accomplices of imperialist intrigues" and thus to prevent Southeast Asia from becoming a zone of "peace and neutrality."

Other published critiques of the Pacific Community idea vary in vocabulary (the appellation "Pacific Ring" did not endure) and emphasis, but they basically adhere to Ovchinnikov's negative characterization of the concept. Some writers affirm that Japan is using the idea to increase its political as well as economic presence in the region.[21] A number of commentators maintain that Peking, albeit not invited to take part in the Canberra seminar (September 1980), supports the Pacific Community idea insofar as it could serve as a means to isolate the USSR from the Pacific region.[22] One writer suggests that promoters of the Pacific Community have an eye on using cheap Chinese labor to serve the interests of "monopoly capital."[23] Nearly all observers affirm that discussion about such an organization is symptomatic of deepening Japanese-American contradictions in particular and of a crisis of the capitalist system in general.

Privately, some Soviet specialists offer more temperate analyses of the "Pacific idea." While they do not discount the presence of military overtones, there is a willingness to recognize that interest in a Pacific Community concept springs to a considerable extent from a broadly felt need to deal with problems raised by the growing magnitude and complexity of the area's economic relations, to rationalize the exploitation of its vast but limited natural resources, and to protect its natural environment. If the Pacific Community idea does indeed address these issues and does not turn out to be a political instrument aimed at "socialist" and developing countries, the USSR—according to these specialists—would not object to participation.

Even such tentative and qualified expressions of Soviet readiness to participate do not come easily, for the USSR has after a fashion its own version of a Pacific Community concept: the Asian Collective Security idea, proposed by Leonid Brezhnev in 1969 and periodically reiterated thereafter. The two ideas are dissimilar in geographical scope and political content, yet both propose a structure within which regional issues could be addressed in a multinational forum. The absence of a broad endorsement of the Asian Collective Security proposal, coupled with the Japanese-American imprint upon the Pacific Community concept, constrain Soviet acceptance of the latter, if only out of sensitivity to status and prestige.

The question of Soviet participation in a Pacific Community (in whatever form such an idea might take) raises political and organizational issues beyond the scope of this paper. However, there is reason to believe that a positive resolution of the question would be facilitated by a revival of Soviet-American trade in the Pacific, a trade patterned upon well-tested historical antecedents and addressed to current needs.

Today as before the October Revolution, development of the Russian Far East is inextricably linked with the availability of provisions. Soviet planners are well aware of this fact and have since the Third Five-Year Plan (1938–42) stipulated that the area was to achieve self-sufficiency in potatoes, vegetables, and grains. That objective has yet to be attained. At present, the only significant agriculture in the Soviet Far East is found in the Maritime Province and on Sakhalin. The Soviet Far East and Eastern Siberia together produce less than two-fifths of their food needs. The bulk of the remainder must be imported by rail from Western Siberia, Kazakhstan, and the Ukraine. The cost of shipping these foodstuffs by rail is heavy. For example, meat shipped from the Ukraine to Khabarovsk costs 33 percent more at the retail level.[24]

The Soviet Far East does import part of its food supply from abroad. During the 1950's China accounted for a large portion of the food imports. More recently, foreign food sources have

diversified: meat from Mongolia and Australia, rice and vegetables from North Korea, tea and fruits from Vietnam, and sugar
and pineapple from Cuba.[25]

Since 1965 fruit and fresh vegetables have been imported from
Japan in a special arrangement administered by a Nakhodka-
based trade organization called Dalintorg.[26] Dalintorg also con-
ducts, under strict guidelines, barter exchanges of food and other
products with North Korea and Australia. Despite these varied
sources, fresh fruit, vegetables, and meat are in short supply,
particularly during the winter months.

The limited variety of food products available to residents of
the Soviet Far East may be a contributory factor to the region's
high demographic mobility. Although workers continue to come
east, lured by incremental wage benefits and other induce-
ments, nearly an equal number leave the area. Two- or three-
year sojourns are not infrequent. A Soviet source asserts that
there exists a net westward migration in Siberia. Until recently,
the drain was most pronounced in the Amur region and on Sakhalin. High labor turnover has contributed to chronic labor
shortages which in turn inhibit the region's development, notwithstanding highly publicized construction projects such as the
Baikal-Amur Mainline (BAM), a railroad north of and parallel to
the eastern portion of the Trans-Siberian.

Significantly increased imports of high-quality foodstuffs, particularly meats and fresh fruits and vegetables, could exert a
salutary influence on the living conditions in the Soviet Far East
and thereby help reduce the exodus of skilled labor. Hawaii and
the West Coast offer attractive sources for these and many other
products. Hawaii, a major producer of pineapple and papaya, is
surprisingly close to the USSR's Pacific littoral. Petropavlovsk
(on Kamchatka) is closer to Honolulu than is any city in Asia.
Vladivostok is nearer to Honolulu than it is to the Ukraine. Soviet container ships, already active on Japan–West Coast routes,
could make deliveries of American foodstuffs directly to ports
along Siberia's Pacific littoral, obviating the cost and delay of
transshipment. A shift to Pacific sources of food supplies would
also relieve the overburdened rail network connecting the Far
East with the rest of the country.

Conversely, there are a number of potential exports from the

Soviet Far East which would find ready markets in the United States and could be used to pay for the foodstuffs sent to the USSR. In addition to such traditional items as marine products, there are ores, timber, oil, and natural gas whose accessibility is being improved by railroad construction and foreign investment. Nor should Far East exports be regarded solely in terms of raw materials. The region has acquired an increasingly variegated productive infrastructure and is already exporting a wide range of manufactured articles to European and Asian-Pacific nations. When Soviet exports receive MFN status, their price attractiveness to potential American buyers will no doubt also stimulate trade.

Participation of the Soviet Union in a regional trade organization would be an important step toward realizing an efficient division of labor among Pacific Basin countries. Such an organization could if necessary also bypass the MFN obstacle to Soviet-American bilateral trade by substituting a multilateral context. For example, Soviet exports could be sold in Japan, and Japanese corporations could remit payment to American firms, which would ship commodities of equivalent value to the Soviet Far East. Such a trilateral arrangement would prove mutually beneficial; moreover, it would encourage habits of cooperation applicable to other joint projects.

In the meantime, the United States might give serious consideration to the extension of Dalintorg's operations to include Hawaii, Alaska, and the West Coast. Such an extension should not raise serious diplomatic or bureaucratic problems insofar as Dalintorg only deals in barter arrangements which are not affected by MFN-related tariff barriers.[27]

American-Soviet relations have entered a difficult stage, but this is no time to postpone serious discussion of the USSR's participation in organizations which may emerge from current dialogues about a Pacific Community. Attempts to isolate the Soviet Union from the Pacific are at best likely only to reinforce suspicions and might in fact aggravate international tensions. Conversely, a willingness to reexamine the feasibility of Soviet-American economic cooperation in the Pacific may well reveal broad areas where the interests of both countries coincide. In this sense, a revival of their Pacific trade can make a real contribution toward building mutual trust, and by extension, toward securing a lasting peace. Such an idea, echoing Gorbachev's Vladivostok initiative, was stressed by Yuri Shcherbina, head of AMTORG Trading Corporation in New York, in his presentation in October 1986 in Washington, D.C.[28]

NOTES

1. Vladimir B. Yakubovsky, "Tendentsii skladyvaniia tikhookeanskogo khoziaistvennogo kompleksa i razvitie ekonomicheskikh sviazei SSSR so stranami regiona," in *Problemy izucheniia Avstralii i Okeanii*, ed. USSR, Akademiia nauk, Institut Vostokovedeniia (Moscow: Nauka, 1976), p. 72.

2. James R. Gibson, *Feeding the Russian Fur Trade* (Madison: University of Wisconsin Press, 1969), p. 220.

3. *Statistical Abstract of the United States, 1907* (Washington, D.C.: U.S. Government Printing Office, 1907), p. 357.

4. John J. Stephan, *Sakhalin: A History* (Oxford: Clarendon Press, 1971), p. 50.

5. Perry McDonough Collins, *A Voyage down the Amoor* (New York, 1860), p. 2.

6. Richard L. Neuberger, "The Telegraph Trail," *Harper's Magazine* (October 1946), pp. 363–370.

7. John M. Hackfeld to Captain Stepan O. Makarov, March 24, 1887, Russian Consular Papers, Honolulu, Record Group 261, Box Aj 2, Archives Division, Washington National Records Center, Suitland, Maryland.

8. *Statistical Abstract of the United States, 1907*, p. 377. Ibid., *1920*, p. 418.

9. Richard T. Greener, "American Interests and Opportunities in Siberia," United States, Department of Commerce, Bureau of Statistics, *Monthly Consular Reports*, no. 276 (September 1903), p. 35.

10. Department of State, Division of Commercial Affairs, Register of Consular Trade Reports, Vladivostok (1906–1923), National Records Center, Suitland, Maryland.

11. Lester Maynard, American consul in Vladivostok, to Secretary of State John Hay, October 22, 1909, State Department Archives, National Archives, M862, roll 1131, item 22363.

12. Platon Chikhachev, "Kaliforniya i Ussuriiskyi krai," *Vestnik Evropy*, vol. 25, no. 6 (June 1890), p. 550.

13. United States, Bureau of Foreign Commerce, *Commerce and*

Navigation of the United States, 1901–1914 (Washington, D.C.: U.S. Government Printing Office, 1915).

14. United States, Bureau of Foreign and Domestic Commerce, *Trade Information Bulletin*, no. 286 (1924), p. 19; *Statistical Abstract of the United States, 1920*, p. 418.

15. "Siberia as a Market for American Goods," United States, Bureau of Foreign and Domestic Commerce, *Commerce Reports*, no. 156 (July 5, 1919).

16. *Statistical Abstract of the United States, 1934*, pp. 428–429; *Handbook of the Soviet Union* (New York, 1934), p. 309.

17. Alex Beam, "A Trade Boom Tames the Soviet 'Wild West,' " *Business Week*, September 21, 1981.

18. I. B. Bulai and A. A. Kokoshin, "Tendentsii razvitiia tikhookeanskogo regiona i politika SSHA," *SSHA*, no. 4 (1978), p. 19.

19. Boris N. Slavinsky, "Siberia and the Soviet Far East within the Framework of International Trade and Economic Relations," *Asian Survey*, vol. 18, no. 4 (April 1977), pp. 324–325.

20. *Pravda*, November 17, 1980.

21. V. Golovnin, "Tikhookeanskie mirazhi tokiiskikh politikov," *Aziia i Afrika sevodnia*, no. 7 (1980), p. 8; Yu. Bandura, "Tikhookeanskoe soobshchestvo: porozhdenie diplomatii imperializma," *Mezhdunarodnaia zhizn*, no. 5 (1980), p. 68.

22. Golovnin, "Tikhookeanskie mirazhi," p. 9; I. Bulai, "Ekonomicheskoe soobshchestvo ili voennyi blok?" *Novoe vremia*, no. 28 (1981), p. 22.

23. G. Kim, "Osvobodivshiesia strany na rubezhe 70-kh i 80-kh godov," *Aziia i Afrika sevodnia*, no. 6 (1980), p. 5.

24. Paul Dibb, *Siberia and the Pacific* (New York: Praeger, 1972), pp. 32, 41, 144, 158–159. See also Allen S. Whiting, *Siberian Development and East Asia: Threat or Promise?* (Stanford: Stanford University Press, 1981); Theodore Shabad and Victor L. Mote, *Gateway to Siberian Resources (The BAA)* (New York: John Wiley & Sons, 1977).

25. A. N. Osorgin, N. L. Shlyk, V. G. Sakharov, and S. P. Bystritskii, *Vneshnetorgovye sviazi Dalnego Vostoka* (Khabarovsk: Khabarovskoe kn. izd-vo., 1973), p. 85; Dibb, *Siberia and the Pacific*, pp. 152, 156, 245–246.

26. Elisa B. Miller, "The Future of Soviet Participation in the Emerging Pacific Basin Economy: The Role of Border Trade," *Asian Survey*, vol. 22, no. 5 (May 1981), 565–578.

27. *Narodnoe khoziaistvo RSFSR v 1977 g.* (Moscow, 1978), p. 7.

28. The speech, sponsored by the American Committee on U.S.-Soviet Relations, was delivered October 23, 1986, to a business luncheon.

6

China, the Soviet Union, and the West: The Changing Ideological Terrain as a Factor in Pacific Community

FRANCE H. CONROY

No authentic vision of Pacific Community can fail to address the need for a stable relationship between China and the Soviet Union, the so-called, "East-East" factor, alongside the problem of East-West accommodation. Yet the Sino-Soviet relationship has been anything but stable in the last half-century, as shifting ideological winds have complicated the already difficult task of building brotherly relations between two proud societies with strikingly different cultures and the world's longest common border.

From the 1920's to the 1940's the Soviets maintained an awkward double relationship with the Chinese: party-to-party relations, which were rarely eye-to-eye between the ruling Soviet Communists and the upstart Chinese Communist Party (CCP), and a friendly relationship with the ruling Kuomintang that began naturally enough—as an enlightened Leninist policy, one might say—in the era of Sun Yat-sen, but became increasingly incongruous, an awkward kind of bet-hedging, as Sun's successor, Chiang Kai-shek, moved toward anti-communism and fascism. Then in the fifties, with Mao Zedong's revolution completed, the People's Republic of China and the Union of Soviet Socialist Republics became the best of friends, almost classic ideological older and younger brothers, whose seemingly unswerving solidarity frightened the West into a decade of policy

excesses. Even in the early 1960's when a Sino-Soviet split began to emerge, Western mainstream experts downplayed the
differences and emphasized a kind of eternal, metaphysical bond
among all Communists.[1] However, over the course of the sixties
close brothers changed almost to fratricidal enemies, with only
cooperation on the Vietnamese war effort as a remaining area of
commonality. That war's end in the mid-seventies left the chasm
deepening as the last inhibiting factor to mutual vilification was
removed. This led to a final bottoming out of the relationship as
the decade closed—even though all the while both countries were
still at least in their own self-perceptions guardians of Marxist-
Leninist ideology. Then in the eighties, a kind of thaw occurred,
the small beginnings of a new cordiality if not friendship, and a
cessation of mutual charges that the other was not Marxist or
socialist—ironically just as, year by year, the Chinese began increasingly to admit that they were moving away from Marxist-
Leninist orthodoxy.

This movement away from orthodoxy was heralded in the
United States as a pivotal turn toward the market system, a vin-
dication of Western values and a repudiation of Marx. Based on
these assumptions—and Beijing's dealings with the Pacific Economic Cooperation Conference mentioned in the Honorable Hugh
Scott's foreword—mainstream China experts began to speculate
that China would increasingly be drawn into the Western camp
and thus would be a candidate for a "Pacific Community" among
market nations.[2]

With predictions having taken such a complete reversal within
twenty-five years, caution suggests an attitude of some skepticism concerning the basic interpretive frameworks in use. When
supposedly permanent enemies turn into supposedly permanent
friends, one begins to wonder whether in each assessment the
"expert" is seeing all the contradictions within the perceived
unity.[3] Was the world Communist movement perhaps not cast
in such immutable essences in the fifties and early sixties as
Western experts thought? Was the Sino-American relationship
in the early 1980's perhaps not as confluent as the mainstream
was calling it? Were there certain contradictions in the Sino-
American relationship all along that would inevitably limit how
far China could be expected to go toward a Pacific Community

conceived up to now as a community of the exclusivist type but at the same time might challenge Pacific Community architects to consider redirecting the concept to a broader "cooperation," not so biased toward market economy and so exclusionary?

Multiple developments in 1986 and early 1987—including Mikhail Gorbachev's favorable comments about "Pacific cooperation" as opposed to "Pacific Community" and the shift by the PECC to use of the new term, joining of PECC by Beijing and Taipei in the November 1986 conference at Vancouver, and finally the Communist party shake-up in China in January pointing toward perhaps more political orthodoxy but continued economic liberalization—all bore witness to the importance of sensitivity to continuing contradictions between market and nonmarket economies in the Pacific. A continuation of the recent progress toward Pacific cooperation may depend considerably on continued adeptness at the handling of contradictions.

My purpose in this essay is essentially to uncover what contradictions and limits are still important between the PRC and the United States as well as the PRC and USSR after first establishing the extent of the changes in the ideological terrain of the 1980's from that of the 1950's. I have structured this essay in four propositions and a conclusion. The first two are somewhat convergent with the "mainstream expert" interpretation of Chinese and Sino-Soviet developments. The third, and especially the fourth, are more divergent—informed more by the interpretive framework of the Committee for Concerned Asian Scholars and other "radical" interpreters of the 1970's whose lessons seem to have been too quickly forgotten in the conservative glow of the Reagan 1980's.

PROPOSITION ONE

In the larger picture, the unity of world outlook shared by China and the Soviet Union in the 1950's was temporary, conditional, and secondary. Such a claim is controversial and even provocative. In essence, it says that history will judge the brief period of Chinese-Russian community between roughly 1949 and 1963 to have been an anomaly. If this is true, it does not bode well for the future of Sino-Soviet relations. Soviet and Chinese social scientists and policymakers who are in favor of restoring the fifties relationship might vigorously object to this judgment.

The proposition is based on a number of observations, historical, cultural, and philosophical. Overall the observations add up to the conclusion that the confluence of interests between the Soviet Union and China in the fifties were unprecedently and uniquely broad, and such a confluence probably will not be repeated.

First, there had been the recent worldwide defeat of fascism. The Soviets and Chinese shared in the joy of that defeat. In both countries, Communist forces had played the leading role in winning the struggle. Not long after this, there were the death knells of colonialism and neo-colonialism beginning to ring throughout the continents of Asia, Africa, and Latin America. China and the Soviet Union were again brought together in their jubilation over these developments. Lenin's theory was being vindicated. The peasant and proletarian backwaters of the earth were erupting to proclaim a new kind of freedom that Western liberal democracy had been unable to yield: freedom, however abstract and en masse, for the toilers of the lopsided world economic system.[4]

Then there was the intransigence of the West, particularly the United States of America, which seemed determined to move into the very shoes of the fascist enemy they had just defeated if this might only help stop the "Red" peasant/proletarian tide. In taking this option, the West actually helped perfect the conditions for unity between the metropolitan socialist countries, principally the Soviet Union, and the liberation movements in the third world, the most significant of which was the Chinese. Never before (and never again) could the Soviets declare so legitimately that they were the "natural allies" of the emerging third-world nations. Even the form of organization that Leninist Russia suggested for national liberation movements—the tight, secret, disciplined, full-time professional, armed Leninist party, gathering a larger mass movement around it—was uniquely suited to the moment when nationalist fury was gathering against a treacherous and no longer credible Western enemy. So was the Marxist-Leninist ideology, which preached collective strug-

CHINA, THE SOVIET UNION, AND THE WEST   103

gle, serving the people, and self-sacrifice at just the time when those ideals had the mix of conditions to catch fire.[5]

This was true even in cultures that had no tradition of societywide collective effort as life's raison d'être—which was certainly the case with the Chinese. Traditionally a decentralized people whose lives revolved around clan, village, or regional affairs, the Chinese only temporarily had what Marxists refer to as the "material conditions" for putting collective struggle first.[6] After these specific conditions began to change, the Chinese people's agreeableness to such slogans would gradually decline, for there is nothing in Chinese culture that is the same powerful unifying force as Mother Russia to the Russians. Collective soul, deep, joyous, sullen, capable of great suffering and terrible endurance, and at the same time of frenzied national orgasms of celebration: such qualities may be deeply embedded in Russian tradition, but hardly in Chinese.[7] China's empassioned national spectacle in Tien An Men Square in 1949 and its ultimately farcical rerun in 1966 were products of very special times. They were actually very un-Chinese phenomena.

The external factors that produced such temporary collectivism and centralism have already been enumerated; yet without several unique and probably unrepeatable internal factors as well, the world situation might have made little difference. First, the overriding shared fate of starvation and dislocation experienced by the Chinese peasantry in the twentieth century had wrenched a whole class beyond its customary familial and local horizons. Moreover, the national humiliation at the hands of foreigners inside China—first Westerners in their special "quarters" and then in the thirties the Japanese invaders—further motivated the Chinese toward an unprecedented unity. Then there was the nearness to a neighbor where collectivist ideology had its root, and where many Chinese leaders went to study. Add the genius of a Mao Zedong, who brilliantly converted the existing objective factors into subjective factors through nationwide consciousness raising, and a principle organ of this, the Long March, a journey calamitous in deaths and suffering, but fortuitous to New China in its spread of a collective spirit everywhere. Finally, in the 1950's China became the world's best laboratory for proving that collective and moral motivating factors in economics do work.[8] The Chinese people's collective verve was further buoyed by the Korean War and other Western reactions.[9] In sum, such is the way a historically family-, village-, and region-oriented people, wary of central authority, adverse to armies, who formed a cultural much more than a political unity, became for a few decades suitable clay for strikingly different ideological molding, embraced slogans like "Sacrifice for the motherland," "Put politics in command," "Long live the dictatorship of the proletariat," and "People's war is glorious," and accepted the leadership of a strong centralist party that demanded overriding loyalty, reaching its long arm into the most personal affairs of traditional village life.[10]

PROPOSITION TWO

In the eighties, what will prove in the long run to be the more "normal" situation undergirding any Sino-Soviet relationship resumed: that is, that the cultural and national differences between these two societies are lasting, deep-rooted, and primary, and tend toward markedly different world views.

One of the best ways to dramatize the changed conditions of the eighties is to go back to the type of statement the Communist world was making at the end of the fifties and note what is no longer the case. "It is perfectly obvious," the Communist Party of the Soviet Union (CPSU) wrote in 1963, that the "chief trends of the historical development of human society" are determined by "all the progressive forces struggling against imperialism for the reorganization of society along socialist lines. . . .The Soviet Union has already outpaced the leading capitalist countries of Europe in economic development and has taken second place in the world. The rising standards of living in the socialist countries are a great magnet for the working class of all the capitalist countries."[11]

These statements were part of the famous exchange of letters with the Chinese at the time of their momentous split. But the disagreement was not about these statements; the two parties agreed concerning socialism's optimistic position. What the Chinese disagreed with was whether any accommodation with the West could be tactically undertaken along the way. The Chinese said no: "The U.S. imperialists have thus placed themselves in opposition to the people of the whole world and have become encircled by them . . . to entrust the fate of the people and of mankind to collaboration with U.S. imperialism is to lead the people astray."[12]

Extraordinary conditions indeed were necessary to have brought the Chinese to the point of out-Russianing the Russians in their zeal for a socialist world future—and to a total writing off of the Americans who had, in fact, over many more decades than the Russians, found a special kind of compatibility with the Chinese. By the 1980's these conditions had drastically changed. The growth rates for socialist economies had long since stagnated. Experimenting with material incentives and limited forms of private enterprise had become common in Marxist-Leninist countries as confidence in Marx's charted path from socialism to communism waned.[13] Frozen, stultifying, unresponsive bureaucracies needed to be awakened by some thawing wind of human initiative, and the old capitalist model for that—some form of entrepreneurism—was the best model around. The new big story in East Asia, in fact, was the success of traditionally Confucian East Asian societies in making the entrepreneurial model work. Country after country—Japan, Hong Kong, South Korea, Taiwan, Singapore—was streaking out in front of the world in terms of growth rate, low unemployment, and low inflation. Some, such as Hong Kong, did it with unbridled, freewheeling competition and little rein on public morals or corruption. Others, like Singapore, tried to unleash the energy necessary to compete in world markets within the context of a traditional Confucian moral structure. What seemed to emerge from the experiences of all five East Asian capitalist principalities, however, was a sense that the extended family and clan loyalties of the Confucian tradition, including reverence for the dead and the unborn, when slightly transformed to fit the organizational needs of late twentieth century capitalism, became great attributes for economic success.[14] The East Asians were better at the free market competitive system than the Western originators themselves. In this environment, the long-latent Chinese propensity to go into business for the prosperity and glory of one's family, extended family, ancestors, descendants, village, and region became newly activated.

The quickness with which this new ideological situation descended in the mid-1980's is an indication of the extent to which it was already latent in the people's cultural and psychological makeup. An energy beyond anyone's prediction was released when the government began telling farmers, shopkeepers, and managers that they might start paying more attention to profits and less to the common good. Not that undue amounts of suppressed personal greed and love of high living were immediately unleashed: there were some cases, for example in the get-rich-quick schemes of certain Western-infatuated taxi drivers, who by 1985 had become the nouveau riche of Beijing and Canton.[15] But the cases of purely selfish greed were exceptional and quickly criticized by the public, as such behavior ran against the grain of not only Chinese Communist conservatism, which was now a bit out of fashion, but also the deeper traditional conservatism of the Confucian heritage. More prevalent and more interesting among the cases of new morality were the morally ambivalent ones: the cases of those who no longer tried to serve all the people, but only some, namely those people with whom they shared traditional ancestral, village, or regional bonds.

A case in point is what happened on Hainan Island in 1985.[16] Hainan is a place that prides itself on moral rectitude as much as anywhere in China; the island proudly displays, for example, its memorial to Hai Jui, the classic example of a good official who helped the poor, yet was wrongly exiled (in this case to Hainan) by corrupt superiors. Yet in 1985 Hainan officials were accused of what might be considered a shady misapplication of the Hai Jui legacy. Leading party and government officials were found to be importing tens of thousands of Toyotas at world market prices under its "open port" trade privileges and then reselling the cars at considerable profit to compatriots on the mainland who enjoyed no such "open port" setup. The profit was only partially, perhaps minimally, used to fatten individuals' pockets; beyond giving small bonuses to themselves, the officials' real use for the money was to help Hainan Island's dream of modernization. Loyalty to local people and the future of the island led officials to engage in a little clever entreprenuerism at the expense of the rest of China. It was, moreover, not clear that these actions differed more than perhaps in clumsiness and naivete from the new Chinese spirit that Beijing was preaching: "To get rich is glorious!"[17] China was more rapidly than anyone might have predicted reverting to a country where all that is expected of most people is that they pay careful attention to the business of their own families, districts, and provinces. Fewer people, i.e., those whom Confucius would have called "superior men," would be expected to act as guardians of all China. And those who do take charge of the larger picture would be expected to do so without a heavy hand, indeed as unobtrusively as possible, so as not to interfere with the important daily life of village, family, seasons, earth, and stars.[18]

Of course, in modern times all this will never return to where it was when China was literally a nation of villages, what Sun Yat-sen called "a sheet of sand."[19] The demands of defense, ecology, resource management, population, and communication ensure that China will always maintain some of the unity and collectivism bequeathed to it from its Marxist-Leninist period. The point is a more modest one: that China's traditional influences are in the opposite direction, and that therefore there will probably be fewer centralized features here than in other socialist (or even some capitalist) countries. Deng Xiaoping calls China's new system "Chinese socialism." The more important word here seems to be "Chinese." Whatever form of political economy the Chinese may adopt in the future, it is clear that it will, before long, be adapted to fit the lively, relaxed, traditional ways of Chinese local life. From the long-range point of view, the Communist revolution may be seen as an accident. It cleared out the grosser forms of foreign and class oppression in the end principally to give the Chinese people a fresh start at being Chinese. The best answer to Mao's question, "How can red political power exist in China?" may ultimately be, "Not very long."

So far we have been considering mostly economic factors in assessing China's drift away from the Leninist ideological framework prevalent in the Sino-Soviet unity period of the fifties. However, there is a dimension of political freedom and human rights to this as well.

I was surprised in my conversations with Chinese in Beijing,

Guangzhou, and Hainan in 1985 to find a vocal, unsolicited pride in the fact that a Soviet-type secret police apparatus had not been replicated in China. Of course there are some who might doubt the veracity of this. Fox Butterfield, for one, devoted the crowning book of his China career to "proving" just the opposite.[20] But the Chinese don't seem to buy Butterfield's "proof." They find it anecdotal and lightweight. The greater story for them is not the degree to which a spy network and gulag were replicated in China, but the degree to which they were not, at least not as a permanent feature of Chinese socialism, despite periods of lapse.

My conversation with one Hainan University professor was representative. After we had talked for hours about everything from Hainan's potential as a resort to American and Soviet politics, he suddenly remarked:

See how freely we are talking here? There is no fear of people watching us, or us spying on each other. Our Chinese system is really nothing like the Soviet system, is it? We are building something very different here. In many ways it has much more in common with your country.

I could not reasonably attribute the many remarks such as these that I heard to flattery of the American guest. The people who spoke to me like this knew me not to be an American flag-waver, but a strong social critic often more interested in the good in other systems than in my own. What I do attribute them to is the love of spirited verbal sparring and debate intrinsic to the Chinese traditional culture. I saw this in my visit to Beijing University as well: a rebirth of Chinese inquisitiveness into everything, colliding so directly with the thought-management system that has operated here in the past that I had to wonder why this outburst had not come sooner. The widespread student demonstration for "freedom and democracy" in winter 1986–87 accelerated this trend. In the end, I suppose the answer is that, for a time, inner and outer conditions in China were so extraordinary that a critical mass of people were willing to hold their tongues in the overriding interest of national unity and reconstruction. China could not have moved forward without its imported Communist, Leninist ways; but any communism in China's future will be no import; it will be Chinese first and Communist, or more likely socialist, second.

PROPOSITION THREE

Nevertheless (in spite of propositions one and two), a stable and friendly relationship between China and the Soviet Union is possible, on the basis not of similarity of ideology or world view, but acceptance of differences.

Up to now, the thrust of this essay might seem to be divisive, i.e., it might be viewed as a contribution toward driving a wedge between these two great societies, perhaps to the benefit of some third party or parties (although it is the author's view that such a wedge would in the long run benefit no one). However, divisiveness is not the real intent and hopefully will not be the product. A solid relationship cannot be built on a misunderstanding, a misperception, or mere wishful thinking. One of the most important reasons why it has taken so long even to begin to heal the Sino-Soviet wounds that opened in the 1960's is probably the inability of the Soviet Union to move beyond wishful thinking in its approach to healing. The perennial Soviet wish has been that some day the split would end when China rediscovered its proletarian internationalist obligation and rejoined the "socialist camp" with Moscow as its center. But no matter what ideological road China follows, this will probably never happen.

I had some firsthand experience of the grip with which this "Moscow-as-Vatican" view holds people's minds while attending an international young scholars' seminar in the Soviet Pacific port town of Nakhodka in 1981.[21] In informal conversations with delegates from socialist youth organizations of many Asian and Latin American countries, I came to realize that it was an anathema for these young socialists even to entertain the thought that Moscow could be wrong. This rigid mind-set was dressed up in a modern disguise: it was not because a Soviet leader was infallible (that would be primitive hero-worship) or because Soviet doctrine was infallible (that would be to downgrade Marxism-Leninism into a religion); it was because Moscow's policies were arrived at through the exercise of *science*. The structure of the Communist system was set up so that final decisions from CPSU leaders could only be scientific decisions, representing the summing up of knowledge from the four corners of the earth. Therefore any deviation from these policies by Marxists of other nations could only be a step back to pre-Marxism, pre-science—those unenlightened states of narrow nationalism, infantile leftism, or peasant mentality that so tragically hold back universal progress.

To see the Chinese Communists ever again fitting in with such a pageant of obeisance as I observed at Nakhodka would be unimaginable. In fact the one thread of continuity in China's foreign policy as it weaved left and right from the early 1960's to the mid 1980's was the conviction that a center to the world socialist movement was unacceptable. Each nation's Communist party was independent; each country also had the right to choose its own social system. Interestingly, if one puts these two together, one arrives at the right that China is so strikingly exercising in the mid-1980's: the right of a Communist party to choose its own social system—even if non-Communist. Furthermore, China insists that not only should powerful countries not interfere in the internal choices expressed by independent countries and parties, but that they should not discriminate against any country which chooses a different road by creating obstacles for this country in international economic bodies or other organizations. China's voice here is meant to speak as advocate not for itself alone, but for the whole third world. It is essentially an anti-imperialist position, descended from the anti-imperialism that opposed the domination of the world earlier in the century by the Western metropolitan powers. But now it is also being directed against the largest metropolitan Marxist power, in a twist that casts doubt on Marx's prediction that proletarian internationalism could lead to a withering away of the need for national boundaries within a socialist world community.[22]

With the Soviets maintaining a Kremlin-as-Vatican posture into the 1980's and the Chinese in no way fitting in, wherein lies the possibility of a better Sino-Soviet relationship? In part it is precisely because both parties are now conscious of the above characterization and are starting their negotiations from that consciousness that a modest relationship on stable ground is becoming again possible. Moreover, there are three additional favorable factors.

One is that the third-world–advocate posture that the Chinese have matured to in the mid–1980's is as much directed against the United States, and potentially Japan, as it is against the Soviet Union.[23] This gives the Soviets an entrée. In the late seventies when China seemed to be only selectively anti-imperialist—deploring Afghanistan but not El Salvador, for example— there was no chance for confluence. But with China edging in the direction of an Asian Yugoslavia or Sweden, in fact (defying Marxist logic) becoming more anti-imperialist as it becomes less socialist, the Soviets have more of a chance to retain their self-respect, yet respect China. The Americans, too, have to think of their relationship to China as built on "acceptance of differences." China is in nobody's alliance.[24]

Another factor is the Gorbachev ascendancy. The emergence of Mikhail Gorbachev was not just another change in Soviet leadership, it was probably the most significant change since Khrushchev succeeded Stalin. Gorbachev's fall 1985 assessment of where the Soviet socialist dream lay was the first really new assessment since Khrushchev. Gone are the grandiose designs: the nearness to world triumph for communism, the imminence of colonization of space, the promise of science to yield not only abundance for all but soon even immortality, the final triumph of the great experiment of Marx and Lenin to produce "the new man." It was these grandiose designs that made it so unthinkable that China would leave the fold; that Jews and others should want to leave; and that right-leaning internal reforms might be necessary. Gorbachev's assessments are more sober: the Soviet Union is not marching rapidly toward a Communist utopia, it is bogged down in a confused and mixed situation. Reform and dialogue are needed, yet party authority and vision must be retained. The Soviets would not entirely stop thinking of themselves as the Marxist-Leninist Vatican overnight, but the more overt and ponderous grandiose delusions seem to have subsided. And early in 1987 Gorbachev's call for "new thinking" on every subject, including increased artistic and economic freedoms, may indicate that the USSR is just now turning a corner toward reforms similar to those that China has embarked upon.

A final factor is the memory of the fifties. These two societies are not starting from scratch; there is a residue of good will. Despite the bitter acrimony that broke out in the early sixties and reached peaks in 1969 and again in 1979, the human-to-human contacts between Chinese and Russians in the 1950's were far from barren.[25] Peter Ustinov, the part-Russian playwright has humorously but aptly described Russians as a bit like reverse sugar-coated pills: they are pill on the outside and sugar on the inside. Many Chinese now in their fifties and sixties got to know Russians well enough in the 1950's to find that inner treasure. While the Russians may not be strong on the outward Chinese virtue of propriety, or social graciousness, at a deeper level Chinese and Russians share an appreciation for relaxed good times and an ability to "rough it." Both are more in contrast to the Japanese, for example, than to each other. Japan's intense drive for productivity and excellence, fueled as it is by nationalist undercurrents, contradicts the more relaxed pace of its two larger neighbors; if there is a cultural incompatibility to be watched for in the future in East Asian affairs, it might be the contradiction between Japan and the Soviet Union or Japan and China rather than China and the Soviet Union. In the long run, the bitter anti-hegemonist, anti-Russian talk that could be heard in China in 1979–80 was as much a temporary, conditional phenomenon as the earlier ideological coziness had been.[26]

PROPOSITION FOUR

Just as we find certain limits governing how far the Chinese and Soviets are likely to allow themselves to be drawn into new hostilities, there are also certain limits that stand in the way of fundamental Sino-American confluence. These could lead to a PRC exit from the Pacific Cooperation Movement should the United States begin to tilt the character of the movement toward a Western alliance. Such limiting factors, fundamental contradictions between the United States and China, seem to go undetected by the "mainstream experts."

There are four points to be made here. Each concerns a basic difference between a Chinese actuality and an assumption made in the mainstream framework.

1. Mainstream experts seem to assume that there is no "principal contradiction"—to go back to Mao's term[27]—to prevent China from sliding more and more into the American camp. However, for the Chinese there still is a principal contradiction in the international situation, and not only are the United States and China on opposite sides of it, the United States is the leader of the other side. This is the contradiction between rich and poor nations, or the "North-South" conflict. Chinese Vice Premier Qian Qichen recently reiterated China's primary concern with this conflict:

The emergence and growth of the third world is a major event in contemporary world history, and its influence on the whole international situation is growing. . . . Having shaken off the yoke of colonialism, [third-world] countries are now facing the task of safeguarding their national independence . . . while developing with other third-world nations.
China is a developing, socialist country, belonging to the third world. It is China's basic foreign policy to strengthen its unity and cooperation with other third-world nations.[28]

In the process of Pacific Cooperation negotiations, China can be expected to be consistently with the "have-nots" of North-South economic disputes, with the United States leading the "North" side. And if the South position is not respected, the movement will probably not amount to much, nor will China remain interested.

The importance of the above international contradiction to the Chinese is often overlooked by mainstream experts these days because in other ways China seems quite willing to unite with the United States and capitalism. This is because the Chinese see the principal contradiction within China as being between the present backward state of what they call "poor socialism" (sometimes "feudal socialism") and the goal of a modern socialist society with Chinese characteristics. And since China is finding that at its current level of development, market mechanisms and an "open door" policy are highly beneficial, there is ample opportunity these days for friendly relations with the United States as well as other market economies. However, it should be remembered that at the macro level China is still a planned economy, and its use of market mechanisms, profit motive, and private enterprise is a limited use guided by Marxist leadership.

2. A second divergence between a Chinese actuality and mainstream "expert" assumption is on whether the market system, as the "experts" seem to assume, is an eternal and self-evident good. Principles of planned economy (renamed "command" economy) are seen by the "experts" as unnatural and invariably forced on a population that would spontaneously resist them if it could. Donald Zagoria, for instance, writes confidently that China's "de-centralizing reforms will be very difficult to reverse now that the provincial authorities have tasted their fruits."[29] In his view, there seems to be no danger that the market system might someday give rise to contradictions that it cannot itself solve—the centerpoint of Marx's theory in his famous "Preface to a Contribution to the Critique of Political Economy"—thus leading to a situation in which the people themselves actually demand more socialist relations of production.

The adoption of American-style professional management; promotion of technocrats over "semi-educated peasant revolutionaries"; adoption of American-style hiring, firing and plant-closing policies; the dawn of a consumerist mentality; and even acceptance of the "trickle-down" theory: all these are, in the mainstream view, assumed to be self-evident goods for the Chinese. Phrases like "It looks encouraging" and "The picture is good" are used to describe these developments. On the other hand, problems with the market system—boom and bust cycles, unemployment, rural dislocation, hunger, growing inequalities, balance of payments disequilibriums, destruction of the environment, a morally decadent commodity culture—tend to appear only as "excuses" which might be seized upon by agitators with ulterior motives, in the analyses of such experts. For example, Jan Prybula, in "China's Economic Experiment: From Mao to Market," points out some of the above problems, but his conclusion is not that the market might be a mixed blessing to

China, but only that "mobilizations of resistance" might occur that upset that business environment.[30] There is a tendency in the mainstream framework to approach all problems from the perspective of the corporate investor or head of the market division.

The cap is perhaps Zagoria's laudatory description of Zhao Ziyang because he looks just like us: "the consummate technocrat," "a man . . . with enough worldliness to shed the gray Mao uniform for a Western coat and tie."[31] One wonders why we ever had to concern ourselves with Asians like Mao, Ho Chi Minh, and Gandhi; eventually there were bound to come along Asians more in our image.

3. A related assumption that the mainstream experts make is that one need not pay much attention to what the Chinese are saying about themselves. For example, if Chinese leaders keep saying, "We are still Marxists," and "We are still taking the socialist road," one can dismiss these statements as a kind of obligatory homage to official sacred cows. For we know all along that Deng Xiaoping really intends to go "all the way." We know that he already knows the answer to the "black cat, white cat" problem: that the white cat (the market cat) catches the mice.

A corollary to this assumption is that Marxism is a fixed, ossified dogma; that there is really very little room for criticism and reform within Marxism. It is interesting to contrast what Peng Zhen, chairman of the Standing Committee of the National People's Congress, says about Marxism with what the mainstream Western experts attribute to the Chinese as their "real" beliefs, "Reform," Peng explains,

is part of the self-perfecting process of the socialist system. . . . Marxism is essentially critical and revolutionary. Marx's materialist dialectics hold that a movement of opposites exists in everything. This movement will not stop even for a second . . . How can Marxism be described as conservative and against reforms? [It is] for continual reforms. It is the theories of the capitalist class and its apologists that are conservative and ossified. Bourgeois thoughts may look very fresh and jaunty today, but they serve only to defend capitalism's status quo . . . Even great early thinkers like David Ricardo and Adam Smith believed the capitalist system was "eternal and unchangable."[32]

Many Chinese Marxists feel that China is just now moving back on a course truly descended from the writings of Karl Marx. Marx was certainly no advocate of "poor socialism," they point out; he was a modernist. He also thought that capitalist relations would have to run through a rather full course of development before socialist and Communist relations could find fertile ground.

Yet when Han Xu, China's ambassador to the United States, writes in the Columbia *Journal of International Affairs*, "After weighing all sorts of options, we have come to the conclusion that in order to bring about maximum economic efficiency we must combine state planning with market mechanisms and open up to the outside world,"[33] the mainstream experts interpret this as a face-saving way of saying "Marx is out."

4. A fourth and final assumption contrary to the Chinese perception of reality that the mainstream experts make gets us back to a historical question, but one which still has great importance for China today. It is the assumption that the United States all along has had a non-imperialist Asian policy, including China policy, and in fact has had, in Robert Scalapino's 1965 phrase, "an extraordinary minimal objective for a superpower," involving only support for national independence and modernization.[34] As this view goes, the United States, although at first reluctant to recognize the nature of its responsibilities, came to find itself leading, in Kenneth Young's phrase, "the new world-oriented culture of technology and cosmopolitanism."[35] Young explains this as follows:

There is developing an ever more closely linked network of relationships around the world integrated by modern technology and communications, the common language of English, and the cosmopolitan customs of the younger generation in every urban center of the world—even in China. These are the new forces—a post-Marxian and post-capitalist twenty-first century, not nineteenth.[36]

Prominent Asian scholars John Fairbank and Edwin O. Reischauer also articulated this framework. Fairbank spoke of ourselves "caught in a role that has been partly thrust upon us."[37] Reischauer noted that the "impact of the West" on Asia might better be termed "impact of the age of machine production on Asia."[38] James Peck of the Committee for Concerned Asian Scholars summarized this notion, of which he was highly critical, as follows:

Underlying the various interpretations of China's confrontations with "the West" in American studies of China has been a basic seemingly obvious framework. Because of a unique constellation of pre-conditions, it is argued, the nation states in the West succeeded in unleashing an almost Faustian power, an exaltation of energy symbolized by the enormous "rationalization" of man's economic and social machinery . . . By the end of the 19th century, the dominance of the West in Asia was a symbol of more basic processes to which China had to respond: modernization and the evolving world culture.[39]

The disturbing thing about going back to descriptions of this 1950's and early 1960's mind-set is the continuity with the mainstream mind-set today. It is, in a nutshell, "We were right." There never was a need for the deep questioning of our Asian policy and national purposes of the late sixties and seventies. If we had waited just a little longer, it would have become clear to the Chinese that the technocratic, market solutions to their problems that we had been proposing all along were right. Indeed, as we were already saying in 1937, the year *Time* magazine chose Chiang Kai-shek and Madame Chiang as its "man and woman of the year." "The pattern for a new China is made in the U.S.A." Such views threaten to get us into the same troubles all over again in China and other parts of Asia. East Asian nations are striving to take their places as equal, modern nations on their own cultural and political terms. The United States can no longer look at itself as the purveyor of the world's modern universal culture. China's dynamic Marxism combined with its Confucian heritage has the potential of being a new kind of modernism, equally viable as the American. Twenty-first–century learning between East and West will be a two-way street.

In summary, the prevailing mainstream framework for approaching the question of China's future in general and possible candidacy for a Pacific Community in particular falls into some old traps. The conclusion that China will move toward the com-

munity concept seems based on the assumption that the Chinese
are finally, as one observer put it, "speaking the same language
as American businessmen."[40] This puts off the day when Americans might have to learn a new language. It forecasts a community that is no community; only oneself and a group of mir-
rors.

SOME CONCLUSIONS FOR PACIFIC COMMUNITY

We have determined that we can expect a future China that
is Chinese first, socialist second; that is an advocate for the
"South" in the North-South conflict; and finally, that is in part
a "market" economy—at any rate, the point here is that the PRC
is determined to become a modern socialist country, not the poor
socialist country she too long remained over the last three decades. Chinese leaders perceive this, and I believe quite accu-
rately, as not contradicting Marx's theory, but better adhering
to it and enriching it than the 1960's and 1970's. However, stormy
events in China in December and January 1986–87, showed
that the Chinese themselves are deeply divided about how
Marxism relates and how it should relate to both the economic
and political/ideological liberalizations their country has been
experiencing. Student demonstrations for "freedom and democracy" rocked major cities in December. Party General Secretary
Hu Yaobong was given a "comradely criticism" and removed
from his post in January as part of a general crackdown on "ideological laxness" and "bourgeois liberalism." But Deng Xiaoping
was careful to have Hu replaced, at least temporarily, by Premier Zhao Ziyang, the architect of China's economic liberalization. The message seemed to be that economic liberalization was
fine and conformed to Marxist theory as long as the Communist
party retained ideological and political leadership. Yet many
Chinese were clearly not satisfied with this: the January 23 *Wall
Street Journal* printed a letter from one thousand Chinese students in the United States and parts of an interview with Beijing University Professor Li Yining protesting the crackdown and
doubting if China can continue to liberalize politically and economically. "What China needs," Professor Li said, "is a big market and a small government." The question remains, can China

drop its Stalinist economic model if it retains its Leninist political model? But it should be remembered that few Chinese, even
the critics, agree with the *Journal* that China should abandon
Stalin, Lenin, and Marx in one load.[41]

While the Soviet future seems, by contrast, more slow to move
away from past economic-political models, the Kremlin is showing a more tolerant eye toward major economic and political reforms.[42] The relationship between China and Russia looks more
promising than in the last twenty-five years—more stable and
realistic—yet by no means as cozy as it once was. What then
are the implications of all this for the Pacific "Community" or
its revised "Cooperation" idea?

Since China is the more rapidly changing, pivotal country, we
can best draw out these implications by assuming China's perspective. How can we expect the Chinese to view this concept
if, indeed, it does gain momentum in coming years? The answer
leads us back into the initial discussion of the original Pacific
Community concept compared with its "Cooperation" redirec-
tion, as well as into the intricacies of the "three worlds theory."

First, Pacific Community has often been compared by its designers to the existing European Economic Community. Yet the
differences between EEC and PC, small to the original Pacific
Community architects, would loom much larger to the Chinese.
EEC is a union of developed countries, all second-world countries. These countries are grouped together geographically. Pacific "Community" would bring together countries of all three
"worlds": a superpower, the United States, with second-world
countries like Japan, Australia, New Zealand, and Canada, and
with third-world countries like the Philippines, Mexico, and
China. To the Chinese, this is a complicated problem. On what
basis are they to be united? How are the contradictions between
the interests of first- and third-world countries, or Japan and
third-world countries, going to be handled in this proposed unity?
One needs only to go back to the philosophy of Mao Zedong,
who, despite the excess of the Cultural Revolution, is still respected in the PRC on such theoretical matters, to see what a
problem this is: in terms of Mao's essay "On Contradiction," the
contradiction between the have and have-not nations of the world
is the *principal* contradiction in international affairs today. How

can an organization unite opposites of the principal contradiction?

Secondly, what would Pacific "Community" be for: uniting humanity for the progress of all, or uniting some as an alliance by which to compete better against certain others? No major alliance in modern world affairs has yet succeeded in being of that first, pure type. If Pacific "Community," as well, is of the second type, then against whom would this alliance be aimed? If China is moving toward neutrality in the Soviet-American contention, why would China join or look favorably upon a community which united one side against the other?

Thirdly, the original aim of Pacific "Community" seemed to be to unite market economies. But China is only "experimenting" with market mechanisms in an attempt to move toward a "modern socialism with Chinese characteristics" on a longer road to communism.

What China's very existence seems to dictate with regard to Pacific Cooperation in coming years is that no conventional type of alliance is possible. Having a China that is massive, part-East and part-West, neither Communist nor non-Communist, right in the middle of the Asian Pacific region might mean that East-West politics as usual is, in fact, dead. But after all, isn't that Beijing's purpose in taking its new stance: to force the rethinking of world affairs along North-South rather than East-West lines?

China's very existence means that the only type of Pacific Cooperation that has a real chance of succeeding is the more daring type: Pacific Cooperation which seeks to unite nations with all social systems, including perhaps not only China but the Soviet Union, both Koreas, and the Indochinese states. China could conceivably play a central role as the intermediary in creating such a community. This becomes much more apparent since both Beijing and Taipei joined the Pacific Economic Cooperation Conference at the fifth gathering held in Vancouver, Canada, in November 1986.

NOTES

1. The 1950's unity led American experts as late as 1962 to underplay the depth of the emerging Sino-Soviet conflict. Donald S. Zagoria, in *The Sino-Soviet Conflict, 1956–1961* (Princeton: Princeton University Press, 1962), wrote: "The framework that I suggest for analyzing the Sino-Soviet conflict is one in which it is clearly recognized that Communist China and Communist Russia have more in common with each other than with the Western world, which both view as a decaying social order doomed to the dustbin of history. This means that there are rational limits to the conflict between them. One obvious such limit is that the two communist powers cannot change partners in the world struggle" (p. 22).

2. Zagoria's later article, "China's Quiet Revolution," *Foreign Affairs* (Spring 1984), moves full circle from his 1962 prediction. The title phrase "quiet revolution" apparently supplies the rationale for such a complete turnabout; although the Chinese Communist party is still in command, he interprets what happened between 1978 and 1983 as a revolutionary change. He now predicts that the newest China "will also want to continue its open door policy and to develop substantial new trade and cultural ties with the West. Such a China will also want to be drawn increasingly into the new Pacific Community that is emerging in the Pacific region. All these developments will increase China's incentive for a long-term relationship with the West and diminish the incentives for fundamental rapprochement with the Soviet Union" (p. 903).

3. I refer the reader to Mao Zedong's essay "On Contradiction" in *Five Essays on Philosophy* (Beijing: Foreign Language Press, 1977), for Mao's use of such terms as "metaphysical," "unity," and "contradiction," which I have adopted.

4. Some of the best accounts of the struggles in the "peasant and proletarian backwaters" are Mark Selden's. See his *The Yenan Way in Revolutionary China* (Cambridge, Mass.: Harvard University Press, 1970), and his introduction to *The People's Republic of China: A Documentary History of the People's Republic of China* (New York: Monthly Review Press, 1979).

5. On the relevance of the Leninist party to Chinese conditions, see "The Role of the Chinese Communist Party" and "Some Questions Concerning Methods of Leadership," in *Selected Readings from the Works of Mao Zedong* (Beijing: Foreign Language Press, 1971); and compare them with "Lenin's Teaching about the Party" by the Communist International, 1931, as well as Lenin's "What Is to be Done."

6. On the traditional localism of the Chinese, see Joseph Levenson, *Modern China: An Interpretive Anthology* (London: Macmillan, 1971), especially chs. 5 and 20.

7. A good popular description of the Russian character can be found in Peter Ustinov, *My Russia* (Boston: Little, Brown, 1963).

8. On the successes of the fifties, see Mark Selden, "The Socialist Transformation, the First Five-Year Plan and the Soviet Model, 1953–1957" in *The People's Republic of China: A Documentary History of Revolutionary China*, pp. 40–75. Also helpful is a volume by Selden and Victor Lippitt entitled *The Transition to Socialism in China* (Armonk, N.Y.: M. E. Sharpe, 1982).

9. A good firsthand account of the psychological effects of the Korean War in forging Chinese unity is in Allyn and Adele Rickett's *Prisoners of Liberation* (reprint, San Francisco: China Books, 1981).

10. On how the slogans caught hold, see my "China: Dream and Reality," in the journal *Peace and Change*, vol. 7, no. 3 (Spring 1981), pp. 75–84. For more contemporary accounts, Maria Antonietta Macciocchi, *Daily Life in Revolutionary China* (New York: Monthly Review Press, 1972) is excellent on the Cultural Revolution period; and Joshua S. Horn, *Away with all Pests* (New York: Monthly Review Press, 1969) captures the slogans and spirit of the fifties.

11. "The Letter of the Central Committee of the CPSU to the Central Committee of the CPC," March 30, 1963, in *A Proposal Concerning the General Line of the International Communist Movement* (Beijing: Foreign Language Press, 1963), p. 71.

12. *Reply to the Letter of the Central Committee of the CPSU to the Central Committee of the CPC* (Beijing: Foreign Language Press, 1963), p. 12.

13. See Lin Zili, "Socialism: Theory and Practice," in *Beijing Review*, August 24, 1981.

14. See Roy Hofheinz and Kent Calder, *The Eastasia Edge* (New York: Basic Books, 1982).

15. For more details, see my "China Ferment," in the *Courier-Post*, Cherry Hill, N.J., September 22, 1985, Forum Section, p. 1.

16. On the Hainan scandal, see Jim Mann, "China Discloses Profiteering Scandal," *Los Angeles Times*, August 1, 1985, p. 16; and "Peking Pops Hainan's Capitalist Balloon," in the *Wall Street Journal*, October 1, 1985, p. 37.

17. There is a book by this name worth noting by Orville Schell, *To Get Rich Is Glorious: China in the 80s* (New York: Pantheon, 1984).

18. See *The Analects of Confucius (Lun Yu)*, book two, "On Government," and the Confucian classic *Great Learning (Da Xue)*.

19. On the "sheet of sand" tendency, see Jonathan Schell's article, "Watch Out for the Foreign Guests," *Mother Jones*, December 1980. On the collectivist inheritance, see "Public Ownership of Land," *Beijing Review*, November 16, 1981.

20. Fox Butterfield, *China: Alive in the Bitter Sea* (New York: New York Times Press, 1982).

21. "Problems of Cooperation in the Pacific Ocean Basin Region," an international seminar sponsored by the Academy of Sciences and the Committee of Youth Organizations of the U.S.S.R., August 19–24, 1981, Nakhodka.

22. On China's position vis-à-vis the third world, see "Deng Ties World Peace to Growth in Third World," *China Daily*, March 4, 1985; and "China Belongs to the Third World Forever," *Beijing Review*, November 28, 1981.

23. See, for example, "Stop the Bullying," *China Daily*, March 2, 1985, directed against U.S. Nicaragua policy; and "United States: Arrogant Anti-China Elements," *Beijing Review*, December 14, 1981.

24. See Bernard Gwertzman, "U.S. Fears a Shift by China on Soviet," *New York Times*, March 16, 1985.

25. See I. Alexandrov, "On Soviet-Chinese Relations," *International Affairs* (Moscow, July 1982): pp. 16–19; and the *Beijing Review*, September 13, 1982, p. 30.

26. I was in Beijing to meet with officials of the Central Committee Propaganda Department as part of a delegation of young American journalists in March 1979, at the height of the bitter rhetoric. One of the Chinese propagandists' favorite in-print phrases to describe the Soviet system was "fascism of the Hitler type"; yet face to face they admitted that they had little theoretical or empirical basis for this claim, and asked us what we thought.

27. "There are many contradictions in the development of a complex thing, and one of them is necessarily the principal contradiction." Mao Zedong, "On Contradiction," in *Five Essays on Philosophy*, p. 51.

28. "Qian Qichen Reviews China's Foreign Policy," *Beijing Review*, January 6, 1986, p. 15.

29. Zagoria, "China's Quiet Revolution," p. 886.

30. Jan Prybula, "China's Economic Experiment: From Mao to Market," *Problems of Communism* (January–February 1986), pp. 21–38.

31. Zagoria, "China's Quiet Revolution," p. 904.

32. Peng Zhen, "Reform Conforms to Marxist Principles," *Beijing Review*, April 3, 1986, p. 14.

33. Han Xu, "Economic Reform and Sino-U.S. Relations," *Journal of International Affairs* (Columbia University, Winter 1986), p. 27.

34. Robert Scalapino, testimony, *Sino-Soviet Conflict*, Hearings before the Subcommittee on the Far East and the Pacific of the Committee of Foreign Affairs, House (Washington, D.C.: U.S. Government Printing Office, 1965), p. 241, cited in Mark Selden and Edward Friedman, *America's Asia* (New York: Vintage, 1971), p. 64.

35. Kenneth Young, *Diplomacy and Power in Washington-Peking Dealings, 1953–1967* (Chicago: University of Chicago Press, 1967), p. 28, cited in Selden and Friedman, *America's Asia*, p. 48.

36. Kenneth Young, "Asia's Disequilibrium and America's Strategies," in *The United States and Communist China*, ed. W. W. Lockwood (Princeton: Princeton University Press, 1965), p. 45, cited in Selden and Friedman, *America's Asia*, p. 48.

37. John Fairbank, "The Great Wall," *New York Review of Books*, March 28, 1968, p. 28, cited in Selden and Friedman, *America's Asia*, p. 46.

38. Edwin Reischauer, *Wanted: An Asian Policy* (New York: Knopf, 1955), p. 70, cited in Selden and Friedman, *America's Asia*, p. 42.

39. James Peck, "The Roots of Rhetoric: The Professional Ideology of America's China Watchers," cited in Selden and Friedman, *America's Asia*, p. 41.

40. "China after Mao: Open for Business?" *Fortune* (February 18, 1985), p. 29.

41. On the debate in January 1987 concerning the future of China's economic and political liberalizations after the ouster of General Secretary Hu Yaobang, see the *Wall Street Journal*'s editorial "China's Hope," January 23, 1987, and the *Christian Science Monitor*, January 20, 1987.

42. On Gorbachev's openness to reform, see the three-part series by Heidi and Alvin Toffler, "A Conversation with Mikhail Gorbachev," *Christian Science Monitor*, January 5–7, 1987.

7

United States Policies Toward Pacific Cooperation

MARK BORTHWICK

INTRODUCTION

This chapter reviews U.S. official responses to the idea of Pacific economic cooperation and examines the role government so far has played in the Pacific cooperation dialogue. It describes the process by which an international dialogue about Pacific cooperation has grown and matured and suggests future directions this process may take.

While organized international discussions on this subject have not involved governments in formal capacities, governmental representatives have participated informally in privately sponsored conferences and seminars. These meetings have pointedly avoided the type of official representation and position taking that would suggest the beginnings of direct intergovernmental discussions on the subject. The reason for this caution is that the Pacific Basin, its vast economic potential notwithstanding, remains an extremely heterogeneous region in which any new framework for cooperation must bridge a variety of economic, political, and cultural gaps. Moreover, unless regional consultations are carefully defined as having general global benefits, they can give rise to anxieties among countries that perceive themselves as excluded and even conspired against.

The political and economic developments that have encouraged consideration of Pacific economic cooperation are by now well documented.[1] Only in recent years, however, have these trends begun to be more clearly and generally recognized in the United States, particularly since the major economic downturn in the early 1980's (the "Great Recession") which forced Americans to confront the international economic challenges and opportunities that face them in Asia and elsewhere. Japan's economic surge, the similarly dynamic growth of the newly industrialized countries, and the opening of China have been important elements in this development. The political emergence and economic growth of ASEAN has been important also but of lower overall visibility. In sum, Americans are finding Asia's economic impact increasingly difficult to ignore. Part of the national debate over our economic future is implicitly one of how to cooperate and compete in the western Pacific. As will be discussed below, this has encouraged a delayed but growing U.S. governmental interest in Pacific cooperation which is based on global as well as regional interests.

BACKGROUND

The earliest proposal for Pacific regional economic cooperation was largely ignored by the United States. In 1965, Kiyoshi Kojima suggested that a Pacific Free Trade Area (PAFTA) should be formed, consisting of the United States, Japan, Canada, Australia, and New Zealand, but the proposal was deemed unsuited to America's global economic and trade policy aims. After flirting with the idea briefly, the Japanese government too recognized that its global policies should take precedence. Since then, proposals for a preferential trading system in the Pacific Basin, along the lines of an EEC, have gained little support.

Even more limited forms of cooperation on an intergovernmental level were initially criticized by the developing countries of the region as merely a means of promoting the economic and political dominance of the developed nations. As will be seen, however, the compelling facts of strong regional interdependence and the absence of any concerned Japanese-U.S. initiative for a "Pacific Community" apparently have calmed some of these fears and have left the way open for substantive discussions of common economic interests.

Following the Kojima PAFTA proposal, serious discussion of regionwide cooperation remained limited to academia for a while. U.S. perceptions of its role and interests in the Pacific Basin were being shaped by other events. In the early to middle 1970's, the trauma of the Vietnam War left few Americans with an optimistic vision of the U.S. regional involvement in the Pacific. The withdrawal had created the secondary effect of encouraging the western Pacific nations to develop stronger regional or subregional perspectives of their own. The Association of Southeast Asian Nations (ASEAN), for example, emerged as a political force to be reckoned with largely in response to the vacuum left by the U.S. departure from mainland Southeast Asia. Japan began cautiously to revive its interest in support for Pacific regional cooperation and to attempt to improve its relationship with Southeast Asia, while Australia and New Zealand as well began to adapt to their growing economic interdependence with the Pacific nations.

Meanwhile, private regional forums such as the PAFTAD conferences of leading economists continued to refine and develop the rationale and proposals for Pacific economic cooperation. Yet if it were to receive a serious hearing in the United States, the "Pacific Community" idea would require a forum outside the bureaucratic channels of the administration and in an arena that would gain governmental and regional attention. Clearly, this was a prescription for congressional involvement.

CONGRESSIONAL INTEREST

In April 1978 Senator John Glenn, then chairman of the Subcommittee on East Asian and Pacific Affairs in the Senate Foreign Relations Committee, requested that the Congressional Research Service (CRS) provide an evaluation of proposals for a Pacific area economic association. CRS enlisted the help of then Yale University economist Hugh Patrick and the Australian National University's Peter Drysdale to provide the analysis. Their report, published in July 1979, suggested that the United States should join in discussions concerning the possible formation of a regional cooperative institution.[2]

Arguing that the United States could not afford to overlook its

strong national interests in connection with any new Pacific regional arrangements, the authors suggested that an Organization for Pacific Trade and Development (OPTAD), comprising
Pacific free market economies, could become a forum for discussion and cooperation and a stimulus to new investment. The
Patrick/Drysdale report to the Glenn subcommittee essentially
fleshed out the argument for OPTAD from the U.S. standpoint
in terms of U.S. interests in the Pacific. These interests were
summarized as (1) the preservation of U.S. leadership in liber-
alizing international trade, (2) improved adaptability to shifts in
relative economic power and intent within the Pacific region,
(3) better prospects for resolving problems of international economic competition, (4) the furtherance of U.S. relations with
the Communist states of Asia, and (5) and expanded network
for the U.S.-Japan relationship which would embrace the entire
Asian-Pacific region.

The authors argued for an increased appreciation by U.S. policymakers of the economic importance of the Pacific area and
for a general broadening of the U.S. perspective with respect to
Asia. Implicit in the latter view is the assumption that U.S. policy in Asia is dominated by the bilateral relationship with Japan,
a relationship which the authors conceded would remain fundamental to the security and prosperity of the Pacific region for
the foreseeable future.

As a counterpoint, the committee report included an adden-
dum by CRS Senior Specialist in International Economics Alfred
Reifman, who took a "skeptical view" of the OPTAD proposal.
In brief, Reifman argued that existing institutions are adequate
for Pacific consultations, that lines of communication are already available for the purposes OPTAD would achieve, that its
regional emphasis could undercut U.S. emphasis on a global
approach to trade liberalization, and that such a regional organization would be viewed as divisive by the Group of 77. In his
preface to the committee print, Senator Glenn noted that he found
the Patrick/Drysdale thesis "both thought-provoking and generally persuasive," whereas the arguments by Reifman were, for
him, not convincing.

The central arguments contained in the Patrick/Drysdale report had been made in earlier pieces by its authors and others,

but publication of the document by the Senate Foreign Relations Committee gave the Pacific Community thesis a wider U.S. audience. As an additional if less plausible element, it warned that the potential costs of a failure by the U.S. to play an active role included a possible coalescence of Japanese, Australian, and ASEAN interests which would undermine U.S. influence and leadership in the region.

Another committee demonstrating an interest in the Pacific Community during the 96th Congress was the House-Senate Joint Economic Committee (JEC). Chaired by Senator Lloyd Bentsen, the JEC gave attention to America's trade relationship with the Pacific region. In January 1980 Bentsen led a study mission of committee members to Asia and conducted unofficial hearings in Manila, Hong Kong, Taipei, and Seoul. While the report issued by the committee did not deal specifically with the Pacific Community concept, the concerns it expressed over the decline of the U.S. market share in East Asia underscored a growing congressional awareness of America's considerable stake in Pacific trade.[3] In June 1981 the committee issued a compendium of papers titled "Pacific Regional Interdependencies" written by U.S. and Asian scholars from a variety of national and interdisciplinary perspectives. The compendium did not include a statement on Pacific economic policy by a U.S. government official, however.

The most recent effort by the JEC (and the Congress) to deal constructively with East Asian economic issues is contained in a paper released by the JEC prior to a special symposium conducted by the CRS.[4] Authored by several CRS researchers, the paper and a forthcoming committee print attempt to provide insights into the policy options available to the United States as it confronts an increasingly competitive East Asian region.

One member of the Joint Economic Committee, Senator William Roth, has taken a special interest not only in Pacific trade issues but specifically in the idea of a Pacific Community institution. In mid-1979 Roth argued in support of an intergovernmental organization, albeit one less structured than the Patrick/Drysdale proposal for OPTAD. Since then, Roth has shifted his emphasis to non-governmental initiatives as a beginning stage for an evolutionary process of institution building. He had advocated the following guidelines for considering the future of a Pacific Basin institution:[5]

1. Institutions ought to be created organically, in response to agreed needs.
2. At least in their initial stages, institutions should be consultative rather than appellate or activist.
3. Membership and leadership should be treated flexibly, with partici- pation possibly through different functional groups.
4. Any Pacific institution should take care to relate to global organiza- tions that already exist.
5. Progress should be made through a trial-and-error process rather than by implementation of a grand design.

In the House of Representatives, the congressional inquiry was led by the chairman of the Subcommittee on Asian and Pacific Affairs, Lester Wolff. After an initial interest in a pro- posed "Asian and Pacific Parliamentary Assembly," Wolff turned to the "Pacific Community" proposals such as the PAFTAD idea. In the summer of 1979 the subcommittee held a series of hear- ings on the Pacific Community idea with the stated objective of encouraging movement "from academic debate to concrete ac- tion." The hearings were of an exploratory nature, however, without preconceived notions as to the appropriate structure and basis of a Pacific institution. Testimony was heard from a num- ber of U.S. experts in Asian affairs, resulting in a report that considered both academic and committee views about the idea at the time. The general tone of the hearings was strongly pos- itive toward the idea of closer cooperation but did not result in recommendations by the committee for specific U.S. govern- mental initiatives.[6]

The changes brought about by the November 1980 elections affected the members of the House and Senate who were active in exploring the idea of Pacific regional cooperation. Congress- man Wolff was defeated in his bid for reelection and Glenn lost the chairmanship of the Senate Subcommittee on East Asian and Pacific Affairs when the Democratic party lost the Senate majority. However, Senator Daniel Inouye, another supporter, recently criticized the slow U.S. response:

We need to develop long-term policies for our relations with Pacific Basin countries, particularly by creating an institutional mechanism to stimulate cooperation in the economic, foreign-assistance and political spheres.

We must be more responsive to opportunities to construct multilateral institutions that emphasize regional harmony . . . The time has come to end our rhetorical obeisance to Pacific cooperation and formulate the policies that will translate the proposal into reality.[7]

ADMINISTRATION RESPONSES

Following World War II, the United States' basic objectives in Asia were shaped primarily by security considerations. The central concern was to prevent anti-U.S. offensive operations from being launched from the Asian mainland. This eventually was formulated by Secretary of State Dean Acheson in his "defensive perimeter" speech before the National Press Club, January 12, 1950.

At that time the linkage between the security and prosperity of the Asian nations and that of the United States was clearly recognized and so stated by the National Security Council in its 1949 outline "The Position of the United States with Respect to Asia." Notably, however, the NSC specifically ruled out any initiative by the United States to form regional associations with the non-Communist states of the Pacific. Much of what is contained in the document continues to apply to the current U.S. stance toward Pacific Basin Cooperation:

1. Any association formed must be the result of a genuine desire on the part of the participating nations to cooperate for mutual benefit in solving the political, economic, social and cultural problems of the area.

2. The United States must not take such an active part in the early stages of the formation of such an association that it will be subject to the charge of using the Asiatic nations to further United States ambitions.

3. The association, if it is to be a constructive force, must operate on the basis of mutual aid and self-help in all fields so that a true partnership may exist based on equal rights and equal obligations.

4. United States participation in any stage of the development of such an association should be with the view of accomplishing our basic objectives in Asia and of assuring that any association formed will be in accord with Chapter VII of the Charter of the United Nations dealing with regional arrangements.[8]

The NSC also cited the need to "obtain the adherence of Asiatic countries to the principles of multilateral, non-discriminatory trade as embodied in the General Agreement on Tariffs and Trade, as a means of reducing trade barriers and expanding the international and intra-regional trade of the region."[9]

The long-standing interest of the United States in Pacific regional associations therefore is not in question, but economic and political relationships were hardly conducive to the development of the idea until the mid- to late 1970s, when burgeoning Pacific trade, the end of the Vietnam War, and a rapprochement with China lent added force to suggestions for new institutional arrangements.

These multilateral consultations and in general the concept of a Pacific Community had developed sufficiently within the State Department by 1979 to support a September mission to Asia for the purpose of exploring ASEAN and other Asian attitudes toward these and related issues. Thus in September 1979 the East Asia Division's deputy assistant secretary for economic affairs, Erland Heginbotham (later to become director of the Foreign Commercial Service in the Department of Commerce), and Donald Zagoria, Columbia University, visited several Southeast Asian capitals to assess, among other things, interest in a consortium of private, Asian-Pacific institutions and to explore Asian views concerning regular, informal, non-governmental discussions about economic issues. The Heginbotham mission did not represent an official U.S. initiative toward pan-Pacific institution building. Rather, it assessed and discussed which people and institutions might wish to participate in an informal network for regular communications about the Pacific Community concept.

For a short time, there was some discussion of forming an academic network among Pacific Basin countries along the lines suggested by the Heginbotham inquiry. The proposal faded, however, when Prime Minister Ohira of Japan, having decided to make the Pacific Community concept a centerpiece of his regional policy, pressed for a more ambitious scheme. Along with Prime Minister Malcolm Fraser of Australia, he advocated a systematic and cooperative exploration of the Pacific Community idea. It was suggested that a series of private, business-academic-government "seminars" be held with participation by the ASEAN nations, Australia, Canada, New Zealand, Japan, Korea, the United States, and representatives of the South Pacific Forum.

Participants at the Canberra seminar—a detailed account of which can be found in James Morley's chapter—were not designated as official representatives of their governments, but Assistant Secretary of State Richard Holbrooke signaled continued American interest in the Pacific Community concept by accepting an invitation to attend. Neither Holbrooke nor the other two American participants, Lawrence Krause (Brookings) and Richard Wheeler (senior vice president, Citibank) made formal presentations. In a briefing paper prior to the seminar, however, Krause outlined the options available for improving pan-Pacific consultations and noted the need to develop an American constituency to support the Pacific Community process.[10]

Holbrooke later described the Canberra seminar as an extremely useful meeting. He took the view that continued U.S. participation in any such discussions was essential. On the other hand, the State Department sought to avoid any appearance of taking the lead regionally in exploring the Pacific Community concept. To do so, it was felt, would create the inaccurate impression that the United States eventually would seek to dominate a formal Pacific Basin arrangement.

For the remaining period of the Carter administration, the U.S. position was to treat the ASEAN response to the Pacific Community as a determining factor in shaping the U.S. response. As a result, American comments on the idea were constrained in deference to ASEAN while, paradoxically, ASEAN leaders awaited a clearer enunciation of American proposals.

This situation continued well into the Reagan administration as a new leadership became even more preoccupied with developments outside the Pacific region. Thus U.S. governmental participation in a follow-up meeting to the Canberra seminar held in Bangkok in 1982 was downgraded to the level of a single deputy assistant secretary whose open skepticism at the meeting left a growing impression of U.S. indifference to proposals for closer regional associations.

In further acknowledgment of this sensitivity, the Bangkok meeting was called a "Pacific Economic Cooperation Conference," the second in the series proposed by Fraser and Ohira, without reference to a Pacific Community. The new Standing Committee and task forces were charged with preparing for a third conference to be hosted by the Indonesian think tank, the Centre for Strategic and International Studies (CSIS).

Meanwhile, with the entry of George Shultz as secretary of state, U.S. governmental interest in Pacific cooperation began to widen. Shultz's natural interest in Asia was perhaps indirectly supported by other California-oriented officials, not the least of whom was President Reagan himself. An international economist and former business leader, Shultz has found little difficulty in understanding economic cooperation as a means of reducing the growing trade frictions that had accompanied expansion of Pacific commerce. In informal remarks, moreover, his enthusiasm for the export-oriented growth of the region has indicated a hope that the Pacific can be an anchor for resisting protectionist pressures in the global trading system.

Former U.S. Trade Representative William Brock echoed this sentiment in his enthusiasm for a constructive trading relationship with the western Pacific countries. The administration clearly was impressed by the relative level of support it received from Pacific rim countries as opposed to Europe in the November 1982 ministerial-level meeting of the General Agreement on Tariffs and Trade (GATT). But because Pacific Basin cooperation is often proposed in terms of being a primary bulwark for the GATT, Brock's position on some aspects of Pacific cooperation may lie slightly askew those of Shultz. In Singapore, February 1983, in a speech that went relatively unnoticed in the United States, Brock proposed the "phased elimination of all barriers to trade between the United States and ASEAN." Whether this proposal would be implemented consistent with the MFN principles of the GATT has not been made clear. The idea has been well received by the ASEAN business community, but there are no signs yet that ASEAN and the United States plan to conduct formal discussions on the subject.

In the White House, the importance attached to the Pacific region was expressed most directly in May 1983 by the NSC director of international economic affairs, Norman Bailey. Referring to the Pacific Basin as a "huge, poorly defended and fabulously rich prize," his remarks before a European audience reflected a concern more with ensuring the region's security than with its economic potential, although his remarks were too brief to cover all aspects of U.S. interests in the area.

The formative stages of a broader U.S. perspective toward the Pacific region were evident in Secretary Shultz's May 5, 1983, speech before the World Affairs Council of San Francisco.[11] While Shultz stressed the necessity of maintaining a common vigilance with other non-Communist countries against the threat posed by the Soviet Union and its allies, the economic dynamism of the Pacific was recognized as having placed the region in a position of increased global importance in U.S. eyes.

Citing Douglas MacArthur, Shultz reiterated an American belief in a global outlook, one that perceives Asia's interests, those of the United States, and those of Europe as inextricably linked. Yet a crack in this consistent theme of postwar American policy has opened slightly under an increasingly strained relationship with Europe. On issues ranging from the gas pipeline contract with the Soviet Union to Euromissiles to protectionism and subsidized exports, Europe and the United States have tested the endurance of the Atlantic Alliance as never before. Perhaps in sheer exasperation, Under Secretary of State for Political Affairs Lawrence Eagleburger, one of Shultz's most senior and experienced foreign policy professionals, forecast a "shift in the center of gravity of U.S. foreign policy interests from the transatlantic relationship toward the Pacific Basin and particularly Japan."[12] Brock seemed to reinforce this sentiment when, on the same day, he suggested to the Joint Economic Committee that America's "more intractible" trade problems now were with Europe rather than with Japan.[13] The relationship with Japan is indeed, in President Reagan's words, America's "key partnership in the Pacific,"[14] apparently taking precedence across all fronts with other Pacific nations including China. As the Pacific coopera-

tion idea gains credibility in the United States, a fresh infusion
of interest could develop in Japan where the idea was originally
nurtured but has lain somewhat dormant.

From a European perspective, however, a "Japan-U.S. axis"
is developing which threatens to leave the EEC members in a
permanently second-class economic position. European reaction
to the Eagleburger remarks was sharply critical, and the United
States sought to allay possible EEC fears about America's increasing Pacific interests by stressing the goal of strengthened
ties between the Pacific and other regions.

If any further evidence is needed that there exists a new level
of U.S. interests in the Pacific, it is provided by President Reagan's remarks during his trips to Japan and Korea in 1983 and
to China in 1984. These remarks were meant to convey that the
administration saw the trips in more than merely bilateral terms,
as a part of an approach to the region as a whole, according to
former Assistant Secretary of State Paul Wolfowitz.[15] Yet the
declarations that the U.S. is a "Pacific nation" and that "the
entire Pacific Basin is the world's future" have so far expressed
feelings of enthusiasm and optimism, not an underlying strategy. They appear meant to solidify the principle of shared interests among friends and allies in the region, but not to lay the
groundwork for a new initiative.

In this respect, the U.S. government has looked to a partnership with the privately sponsored process begun in Canberra in
1980. Following the Second Pacific Economic Cooperation Conference (PECC) in Bangkok in 1982, the Third PECC was held
in Bali, Indonesia, in November 1983 with a record attendance
from participating and observing countries and the largest representation of U.S. governmental representatives yet to be sent
to a PECC. Both Shultz and Wolfowitz sent messages of support
to the meeting, although the United States still did not play a
leading role in the preparations and task forces.

Then in 1984 Shultz gave Ambassador-at-Large Richard Fairbanks a new portfolio for examining broad U.S.–Pacific Basin
interests. Fairbanks traveled extensively in the region, soliciting
the views of the private sector and governmental figures concerning possible dimensions of future Pacific economic cooperation and the ways in which the United States could be suppor-

tive. The extensive consultations by Ambassador Fairbanks led to his recommendation to Shultz that the United States take a more active part in organizations and networks such as the Pacific Economic Cooperation Conference. Consequently, Shultz privately encouraged a number of business leaders, members of Congress, administration officials, and academics to join in a broadly bipartisan U.S. National Committee for Pacific Economic Cooperation. Formed as an independent, non-profit organization, the committee was inaugurated in September 1984 by President Reagan, Vice President Bush, and Secretary Shultz in a White House ceremony. With offices in Washington, D.C., and in the Asia Foundation in San Francisco, it functions as a private policy forum for both national and international discussions about U.S.–Pacific Basin relations and serves as the primary link for the United States to the PECC.

It should be stressed that the underlying assumption of the U.S. government is that the ongoing discussions between the committee and regional bodies such as the PECC will relate to how to improve the working of international free market principles by countries that to some significant degree are using capitalist principles. The recent suggestion by the Soviet Union that it should be part of the regional discussions on Pacific economic cooperation, as evidenced by Mikhail Gorbachev's speech in Vladivostok on July 28, 1986,[16] has elicited no formal U.S. response as of this writing, but such expressions of interest, by themselves, are not likely to be viewed as a significant basis for participation by the USSR without substantial political improvement.

CONCLUSION

By now it is clear that Pacific regional economic cooperation is not, as many had predicted, an academic topic of diminishing interest and importance to governments in the area. Among these signs can be counted the efforts by President Reagan and Secretary Shultz to pointedly develop the idea of a community of interests in the Pacific and to underscore the global importance of the Pacific Basin. Nor can it be doubted that their support of the establishment of a National Committee for Pacific Economic

Cooperation has had an additional stimulative impact on similar committees in other countries and has added momentum to regional economic discussions.

On the other hand, leaders in both political parties recognize the limits of government intervention in the process, particularly in this early and exploratory stage. While they are aware of the economic underpinnings of political stability in East Asia, they also are under increasing pressure to take defensive policy stances toward the region in the face of an overwhelming trade deficit.

Given these limitations, and the desire of the United States to encourage the development of closer consultations among the Pacific nations, it is likely that the future U.S. governmental role will be somewhat limited and determined largely by developments in three areas. First, the new round of global trade negotiations, the so-called "Uruguay Round," will test the common interests of the Pacific nations and their abilities to work together with reference to global trade issues. From the outset of initiatives to launch a new trade round, it has been clear that an incipient "Pacific bloc" within the GATT could become an effective spur toward trade liberalization.

Second, the ability of the United States to reduce its trade deficit with the Pacific region will influence the climate for closer regional cooperation in matters of trade and investment. To the extent that this will be accomplished by export-oriented rather than protectionist solutions, the prospects for cooperation will improve from a U.S. standpoint.

Third, the willingness of three or more ASEAN nations to accept the desirability and viablity of a Pacific Basin framework for trade and other economic policy discussions will at least prevent stagnation in the process, however much or little it will add to its momentum. This appears to be the current situation with three ASEAN nations, Indonesia, Thailand, and Singapore, showing an increased commitment to regular regional discussions. Also, the United States can be expected to continue to support consultations within the "6 + 5" group of Pacific foreign ministers, but ASEAN appears too indecisive as a body to move that group into a more activist mode of cooperation. Within the "private" PECC framework, governments are active participants whose views exert a considerable influence in the deliberations of that regional body. The U.S. government has indicated that the PECC will be, for the foreseeable future, the preeminent voice for the United States in the search for Pacific Basin cooperation. In so doing, it has shown that governments can usefully follow as well as lead the private sector in creative applications of public diplomacy.

Yet the United States seems likely to remain more a follower than a leader in actual discussions of regional cooperation. While the Pacific Basin movement is generally seen as a positive development which is supportive of American policies in the region, the United States remains sensitive to the misunderstandings that could arise both within and outside the region as to its advocacy of closer Pacific Basin ties.

Meanwhile, other Pacific governments are taking more aggressive stances. South Korea's President Chun advocated a Pacific summit meeting of regional leaders, Australian Prime Minister Hawke has pushed for and achieved a meeting of western Pacific trade officials as a follow-up to the Third PECC, and Indonesian Foreign Minister Mochtar Kusmaatmadja has suggested that the ASEAN Ministerial Dialogues with the five developed Pacific countries should become a forum for discussing Pacific regional economic cooperation. If this trend continues, the concern for the United States will be, as critics such as Senator Inouye have suggested, not whether its overbearing presence is detrimental to regional dialogues, but whether it is keeping pace with events.

NOTES

1. *Asian Survey*, vol. 23, no. 12 (1983), *"Perspectives on the Pacific Community Concept"*, pp. 1245–1304; Sir John Crawford and Greg Seow, eds., *Pacific Economic Co-Operation: Suggestions for Action* (Heinemann Educational Books (Asia) Ltd., 1981), 246 pp.; United Nations Economic and Social Commission for Asia and the Pacific (ESCAP), *ASEAN and Pacific Economic Co-Operation* (Bangkok: ESCAP, 1983), 365 pp.; Paul F. Hooper, ed., *Building a Pacific Community: The Addresses and Papers of the Pacific Community Lecture Series* (Honolulu: The East-West Center, 1982), 176 pp.; Japan Center for International Exchange, *The Pacific Community Concept: A Select Annotated*

Bibliography (Tokyo, 1982), 68 pp.; U.S. Congress, Joint Economic Committee, *Pacific Region Interdependencies: A Compendium of Papers*, June 15, 1981, 97th Cong., First sess. (Washington, D.C.: U.S. Government Printing Office), 148 pp.; Hadi Soesastro and Han Sungju, eds., *Pacific Economic Cooperation: The Next Phase* (Jakarta: Centre for Strategic and International Studies, 1983), 302 pp.

2. Congressional Research Service, Library of Congress, *An Asian-Pacific Regional Economic Organization: An Exploratory Concept Paper*, prepared for the Committee on Foreign Relations, United States Senate (Washington, D.C.: U.S. Government Printing Office, 1979).

3. U.S. Congress, Joint Economic Committee, *Study Mission to East Asia* (Washington, D.C.: U.S. Government Printing Office, 1980).

4. *Economic Changes in the Asian Pacific Rim: Policy Prospectus*, Economic Division, Foreign Affairs and National Defense Division, and Office of Senior Specialists of the Congressional Research Service, August, 1986, mimeo.

5. "Pacific Trade Symposium Addresses Multilateral Issues," *Pacific Community Newsletter*, vol. 1, no. 3 (1981), p. 4.

6. U.S. Congress, House of Representatives, Subcommittee on Asian and Pacific Affairs, *The Pacific Community Idea* (Washington, D.C.: U.S. Government Printing Office, 1979).

7. Daniel K. Inouye, "The U.S. Role in the Pacific Basin," *Leaders* (April–June 1984), pp. 4–12.

8. National Security Council, "The Position of the United States with Respect to Asia," NSC 48/2, December 30, 1949, in *Containment: Documents on American Policy and Strategy, 1945–1950*, ed. Thomas H. Etzold and John Lewis Gaddis (New York: Columbia University Press, 1978), p. 270.

9. Ibid., p. 272.

10. For further discussion of the Ohira plan, see James Morley's essay, Chapter 1 of this book.

11. George Shultz, "The U.S. and East Asia: A Partnership for the Future," *Policy*, no. 459 (Washington, D.C.: U.S. Department of State, 1983), 4 pp.

12. "Europeans' Self-Centered Concerns to Alter U.S. Policy, Eagleburger Says," *Washington Post*, February 1, 1984, p. A6; "Eagleburger Warns of Growing Strains in NATO Alliance," *Washington Post*, March 8, 1984, p. A31.

13. "Brock Sees Trade Deficits Continuing Several Years," *Washington Post*, February 1, 1984, p. D1.

14. Address by the president to the National Diet, November 11, 1983, and Reagan's other speeches during the visit to Japan.

15. *Pacific Community Newsletter*, vol. 4, no. 1 (p. 1).

16. For the complete text of the speech, see *Pravda*, July 29, 1986. William Safire had two essays on the speech in the *New York Times*: the first on September 8, 1986, the second on October 20, 1986.

8

Security Dimensions of Pacific Basin Cooperation

NORMAN D. PALMER

The concept of Pacific Basin Cooperation has been given added importance and significance because of the growing role of the Pacific Basin Cooperation (PBC) concept in international affairs, the increasing number and variety of transactions and interactions within the region and between the region and the rest of the world, and the growing awareness of the region as an area of extraordinary activity and change. Many observers believe that the Pacific era has already begun, and that in the twenty-first century the Pacific Basin will be the center of world progress.[1]

The one major aspect of Pacific Basin Cooperation that is often neglected is that of security. Emphasis is usually on economic aspects, which do encompass the most obvious and most extensive kinds of associations and activities in the Pacific Basin. Considerable attention is also given to certain political, technological, and cultural aspects.

Most promoters of PBC agree on several main approaches: that the concept is an important and a potentially unifying one: that much needs to be done to promote greater consultation and cooperation among the countries of the Pacific region; that in developing PBC it is desirable, indeed essential, to begin slowly, and to concentrate on areas, such as economic and trade matters, in which the interactions are already extensive and the possibilities of cooperation for mutual benefit seem to be particularly great; and that security aspects of the movement should be somewhat deemphasized in the early stage of the development of the community approach, because they are too controversial and because agreement on the nature of security threats and needs is lacking.

TWO NEBULOUS CONCEPTS: SECURITY AND PBC

As would be expected in the vast Pacific region, where the nearly forty littoral states are so separated by geographic, cultural, political, economic, and psychological differences, there is little consensus regarding security approaches and needs. There are wide divergencies regarding the source and nature of the threats to security and national survival, and vast differences in power and capabilities. Some of the Pacific countries, especially the small, weak states, seem to be more concerned with internal than with regional or global threats.[2] Others, including most of the more highly developed states, seem to be more concerned with external threats. Some, notably the United States and some of its Pacific allies, seems to be primarily concerned with security against the Soviet threat; but there are fundamental perceptual differences between the United States and almost all of its Pacific allies regarding the Soviet Union.

Some of the smaller nations of East and Southeast Asia seem to regard China, and even the United States and Japan, as real or potential threats, and to have more ambivalent views regarding the Soviet Union. The many nations of Central and South America that border on the Pacific may be more concerned with possible threats from the United States, "the colossus of the North," than with threats from the Soviet Union, even though most of them are associated with the United States in a major multilateral security arrangement—the Rio Pact of 1947. The Soviet Union, of course, denies that it threatens any country, in the Pacific or elsewhere, and claims that the real security danger to the nations of the Pacific and to all nations comes from the United States and other nations associated with the United States, perhaps now including the PRC, in alliances and alignments that the Soviet Union insists are basically anti-Soviet in nature and intent.

Many of the countries of the Pacific Basin, notably Japan and the ASEAN states, are inclined to deemphasize the military aspects of security and to emphasize the less military aspects. They favor what the Japanese have popularized as the "comprehensive national security" approach. This approach was recommended by the Comprehensive National Security Group, established in 1979 as an advisory group to Prime Minister Ohira. Its nature was indicated in the group's report, submitted in July 1980:

In the abstract, national security can be defined as the protection of the people's life from various kinds of external threats. . . . National security policy is comprehensive by nature. . . . [It] must be composed of efforts on different levels. These efforts come under three levels of (1) self-reliant efforts, (2) efforts to turn the overall international environment into a favorable one, and (3) efforts to create a favorable environment within a limited scope. . . . Security policy requires a comprehensive range of measures. . . . The dynamism of international relations is governed by an all-encompassing mix of both military and non-military means.[3]

The distinguished authors of this much-discussed report did not neglect the military dimensions of security or the importance of paying special attention to Japan's relations with the three other major Pacific powers, but they tended to place special emphasis on "a comprehensive range of measures" to promote security and on "non-military." They laid down for Japan five "security tasks": (1) promoting Japanese-U.S. relations; (2) strengthening defense capability; (3) improving the management of relations with China and the Soviet Union; (4) achieving energy security; and (5) achieving food security. They reported that "Japan's national security efforts thus far . . . have been deplorable indeed." Japan, they concluded, "has survived so far by leaving external crisis management to the United States and internal crisis management to the society at large."[4] They insisted that this evasion of national responsibility was particularly dangerous because of the changing nature of Japan's security environment. "The U.S. military power is no longer able to provide its allies and friends with nearly full security,"[5] and the responsible leaders of the nation could no longer leave "in-

ternal crisis management to the society at large." Japan's security, in short, must henceforth be sought within the framework
of "comprehensive national security," in which the Japanese
government must take central responsibility, and in which greater
"self-reliant efforts" must be supplemented by national participation in external crisis management in collaboration with Japan's friends and allies, particularly but not exclusively the United
States.

This "comprehensive national security" approach was widely
praised in many other Pacific Basin states. It was, in fact, a
Japanese version of an approach that was gaining worldwide
popularity, especially among states that were particularly defi-
cient in military power and capabilities. It was carried to ex-
tremes in the well-known report of the Palme Commission (the
Independent Commission on Disarmament and Security Issues)
entitled *Common Security*.[6]

Certainly the broader and more comprehensive dimensions of
security are being more generally recognized and accepted by
most security analysts and by most responsible political leaders.
It was endorsed in these words by a major organization dedi-
cated to promoting security in the Atlantic rather than the Pacific Community, in a report significantly entitled *The Growing
Dimensions of Security*: "In the nuclear age, in an increasingly
crowded and interdependent world, security is not a matter merely
of military strength. Security also involves a combination of many
other factors, including domestic as well as foreign ones: political, economic, social and psychological. It is the combination of
these factors which Communist doctrine calls the 'correlation of
forces.' " The report also called attention to the "growing dimensions of security" in a geographic sense: "Nor can security be
limited to any specific geographic area. Its ramifications are
global."[7] This underscores the importance of the point that various dimensions of security must be considered, including internal and external dimensions, and that the external dimensions
must encompass problems and considerations of security on both
regional and global levels.

Within such a broad and comprehensive framework almost all
of the many interactions and contacts among Pacific Basin states
have significant security dimensions. This applies particularly

to economic and trade relations, which are the relations that are usually emphasized in discussions of the emerging PBC. But these non-military aspects of growing intracommunity relationships are seldom discussed from a security perspective. In fact, as has been noted, almost all of the official pronouncements on this subject, and almost all of the writing and public discussion about PBC,[8] have tended to avoid the security dimensions altogether, or, if security problems are mentioned, they are usually cited as matters that should not be included in any early stages of the development of the PBC concept. They are, in essence, "swept under the rug," although almost everyone recognizes that while they are temporarily out of sight, they are almost never out of mind.

If security, one of the central concerns of people and politics throughout history, is still a concept with many meanings, ranging all the way from the concept of "comprehensive" security (which itself is used in many different ways) to detailed and technical matters of strategy and tactics, weapons systems, and military capabilities (on which, again, there is little consensus), it is hardly surprising that an emerging concept such as that of PBC is a very nebulous one, meaning different things to different states and people. This does not mean that the concept is not real or not important. Many nebulous concepts that have been of central importance in determining national policies and ideologies have defied precise definition and have been interpreted in manifold ways.

But, as the director of the Pacific Basin Project at the Center for Strategic and International Studies at Georgetown University has pointed out, PBC "is an idea without a program, a goal without an agenda."[9] The idea or the concept of PBC is now generally recognized and accepted; but it may not only be "an idea without a program," but also an idea without a community, an idea without a region. Some years ago, a British scholar described South Asia as "a region without regionalism." The PBC concept may be dealing with regionalism without a region.

If the Pacific Basin is classified as a region, it would surely be one of the most amorphous regions in the world. It encompasses several of the generally recognized world regions and subregions, such as East Asia, Southeast Asia, North America,

Central America, the Pacific Coast members of the Latin American region, and even some "regions" in the Pacific Ocean, such as Micronesia and Polynesia, in which a number of small oceanic or island states have emerged. If the Pacific Basin is a region, it is characterized by an extensive pattern of subregionalization, with several of the subregional components functioning much more actively and more effectively as regions than the "subregion" of which they are a part. It would probably be better to preserve the prevailing tendency to continue to recognize these regional components as regions—not as subregions—and to consider the Pacific Basin "region" in a looser sense, rather than as a new world regime.

The major actors in the Pacific Basin—the independent nation-states—may also be classfied in terms other than those of regionalism or subregionalism. For example, the superpowers in the Pacific Basin, as in the entire world, are clearly the United States and the Soviet Union; the major actors in the region, in terms of power and influence, are the superpowers plus Japan and the PRC; the most developed states of the region are the United States and Japan (the world's two economic giants), Canada, Australia, and New Zealand. The countries with the most formidable military power, in addition to the superpowers, are China, Japan, North Korea, South Korea, Taiwan, and Vietnam. Most of the states of the region are developing countries, ranging all the way from small new oceanic polities to rapidly developing countries such as "the four little tigers" or "the four little dragons" of Asia—South Korea, Taiwan, Hong Kong, and Singapore.

Clearly much more spade work must be done before any major all-Pacific organizations of a comprehensive and influential kind can emerge with widespread acceptance. In the meantime a great variety of patterns of cooperation, well short of major institutionalization, may be considered. This was well explained in a report, *The Emerging Pacific Community Concept*, by the Pacific Basin Congressional Study Group that was set up by the Center for Strategic and International Studies at Georgetown University:

The concept of a Community need not, of course, signify a formal organization of Byzantine complexity. There are various gradations of the

Pacific Basin Community, ranging from casual discussion groups, to groups that meet on a regularly scheduled basis, to a highly structured organization. Less formal groups, such as the task forces that grew out of the 1982 Bangkok meeting, have their role to play at present.[10]

In any case, various associational patterns, subregional, regional, and international, may develop, as a part of the many forces and trends that will give greater reality and significance to Pacific Basin Cooperation. This point is emphasized by Peter A. Poole:

The Pacific community will require forums in which the advanced and developing states can meet together—as well as separate organizations, such as ASEAN, in which countries which have most in common can meet. The advanced countries may develop a formal or informal organization of their own, or they may decide that the existing array of rich men's clubs provides an adequate framework for consultation. In either case, they will continue to belong to international (nonregional) organizations such as the World Bank and OECD, while the developing Asian states will remain in the Group of 77 and other nonregional organizations. The entire Pacific community can benefit from these multiple and overlapping memberships.[11]

These comments suggest that at least some of the proponents of the PBC idea think in both regional and global terms. They are interested in promoting increasing cooperation within the Pacific Basin and increasing acceptance of the concept of the Pacific Basin in the entire area, whether regarded as a region in the formal sense or not. They are also interested in promoting increasing cooperation between the PBC and the rest of the world. They regard these objectives as complementary, not conflicting, and indeed as inescapable imperatives. In the words of the famous Japanese report, *Pacific Basin Cooperation Concept*, "We are fully aware that a regional community without a perspective for a global community, a regionalism that excludes globalism, has no possibility of developments and prosperity."[12]

SECURITY ARRANGEMENTS AND ALIGNMENTS IN THE PACIFIC BASIN

In this context the interlinkages between the two nebulous but important concepts of security and PBC become more apparent. Security is a major dimension of both regionalism and globalism. This observation applies particularly, of course, to regional or larger organizations, such as NATO, the Rio Pact, and some other multilateral security arrangements, which were created primarily as instruments for promoting mutual security. But security-oriented organizations are the exceptions rather than the rule in virtually all the world's regions. This is obviously the case in the Pacific Basin, where regional cooperation is still in an early stage of development and a PBC approach is even more underdeveloped, and where there is still little agreement among the diverse members of the "community" on basic approaches and policies in the security field.

The reluctance of most states of the Pacific Basin to form security-oriented organizations seems to be in sharp contrast to the already quite extensive pattern of security alliances and the even more extensive pattern of security alignments in the Pacific Basin region. In this pattern of alliances and alignments the United States obviously has played a central role. Many of the Pacific Basin nations, on both sides of the vast ocean, are associated with the United States in formal security arrangements of a multilateral or bilateral nature—all of the Pacific littoral states of Central and South America in the Rio Pact, Canada in NATO, New Zealand and Australia in ANZUS, and Japan, South Korea, and the Philippines in bilateral security pacts with the United States.

Until the "opening of China," beginning in the early 1970's, the United States and the Republic of China in Taiwan had a formal security arrangement. The United States was publicly committed to the defense of Taiwan, and apparently still is under the Taiwan Relations Act of 1979. It is still providing military equipment and weapons to Taiwan. At the insistence of the PRC it has withdrawn its recognition of the Taiwanese regime, and it no longer maintains troops or bases in Taiwan. It has also agreed to cease to provide Taiwan with military assistance; but the final date was not specified, and in the meantime it is continuing this assistance on a limited scale.

If special security relationships or limited forms of security collaboration and support are included in this inventory of security arrangements and alignments in the Pacific Basin, several other relationships with security dimensions could be cited. Perhaps the most interesting, and potentially the most important, is that between the United States and the PRC. Since the advent of the Reagan administration, the United States has offered to supply some types of military equipment and arms to China on a highly selective basis, and it has already provided certain advanced technology and equipment that could easily be utilized for military purposes.

A more limited security arrangement among non-Communist states of the western Pacific, to which the United States is not a party, is the Five Power Defense Pact, in which Australia, New Zealand, and the United Kingdom have entered into certain defense commitments with Malaysia and Singapore to help these two Southeast Asian countries to improve their capabilities for dealing with both external and internal threats. This is an interesting example of a limited intra–Commonwealth of Nations security relationship, and it is obviously a legacy of the period before Malaysia (then Malaya) and Singapore became independent of British rule.

Not all of the security arrangements in the Pacific Basin have been confined to non-Communist states. Until the Sino-Soviet split in the late 1950's and early 1960's, the treaty of 1950 between the Soviet Union and the People's Republic of China, and other agreements in the following years, created a kind of security alliance between these two countries. The Soviet Union has long been committed to the defense of Mongolia and Vietnam.

Some security associations in the region that are now defunct, most notably the Southeast Asia Treaty Organization (SEATO), might also be mentioned. SEATO was a security arrangement in which five Pacific Basin states—Australia, New Zealand, the Philippines, Thailand, and the United States—were associated with one other Asian state, Pakistan, and two European powers, Britain and France. Since the demise of SEATO the United States has continued to be formally allied with Britain and France in NATO, and with Pakistan and the Philippines in bilateral security arrangements. It has also an agreement with Thailand to maintain many of the ties, mostly of a security nature, that had existed between the two states in the SEATO era.

This kind of continuing security commitment has taken on added significance in the light of developments in the Indochina area, the activities and pressures of major powers in Southeast Asia, and the added pressures on Thailand because of the conflicting roles of China and the Soviet Union in Vietnam and Kampuchea, the influx of refugees from Vietnam, Laos, and Kampuchea, and the continuing subversive activities of Communist infiltrators inside Thailand.

At least two other associations in the Western Pacific—ASPAC, now defunct, and ASEAN, the only major regional arrangement that has emerged in Southeast Asia—have important security dimensions, although they deliberately refrained from placing security issues as such on their formal agenda. ASPAC—the Asian and Pacific Council—was organized in 1966, mainly on the initiative of South Korea, by representatives of nine Western Pacific states—Australia, Japan, Malaysia, the Repubic of China, New Zealand, the Philippines, South Korea, South Vietnam, and Thailand. It announced its intention to give primary attention to the promotion of economic cooperation among its members, and to be a non-military, non-ideological, and non–anti-Communist organization; but it was clear from the beginning that it had strong security overtones, and that its real intentions, at least on the part of its main sponsor, South Korea, were quite different from its professed objectives. For this reason, and because few of the member states other than South Korea had much enthusiasm for the organization, described by an American journalist as "an association of nations with perhaps the greatest racial, religious, political, economic, cultural, and historical differences in the world,"[13] ASPAC had a brief and rather unproductive life.

The ASEAN experience has been quite different. It started in a very modest and tentative way, but it gathered momentum and has become one of the most exciting regional organizations anywhere in the world. Like ASPAC, it eschewed direct consideration of security matters; but security considerations were clearly in the minds of its founders, and they have been frequently discussed by high-level member-state officials. Since the American withdrawal from Vietnam, and what they regard as threatening moves from the Communist Vietnamese regime, including invasion of Kampuchea, the security pact with the Soviet Union, and the sponsoring of subversive activities in Thailand, ASEAN members have been increasingly concerned with problems of security.[14]

SECURITY CONSIDERATIONS IN PBC FORUMS

The ASPAC and ASEAN experiences, and those of many other organizations in or focusing on the Pacific Basin that are not primarily concerned with security problems, show quite unmistakably that common security problems and concerns can, and will, be discussed at various forums. Consideration of items on formal agendas are often not the most important business that takes place when high-level officials of cooperating countries come together in regional or other gatherings. The fact that so many matters of common concern among nations, definitely including economic and political issues, have important security dimensions reveals the virtual impossibility of avoiding security and security-related matters whenever top-level officials of several states convene, whatever the special focus of the formal discussions. Moreover, if the concept of comprehensive security is accepted, as it is by many of the states of the Pacific Basin region, it becomes quite clear that the emerging Pacific Community, whatever form it will take and whatever the intentions and formal statements of purpose of its promoters may be, will provide forums for a discussion of security as of other matters of common concern. The question therefore becomes not whether security matters should be a part of the agenda for consideration by the Pacific Community, whatever form it may take, but how such matters should be considered.

Since most of those who are interested in Pacific Basin Cooperation are agreed that the movement should begin in a modest way and should limit its areas of concentration and cooperation to a few subjects of a non-security nature that are clearly of concern to all possible participants—which would be mostly economic matters—how could and should security concerns be considered by members of the emerging community? They cannot be neglected completely, for they are of central concern to most or all possible participants, especially if the concept of comprehensive security is accepted. The security dimensions of most of the items on any Pacific Community agenda will be apparent to all, although these dimensions may not be given formal consideration. Most of the types of Pacific Basin cooperation that are mentioned by supporters of PBC suggest that first steps are likely to be a broadening of existing practices and patterns of cooperation. As Peter A. Poole has observed, "the present practice of round-robin discussions and overlapping caucuses of several groups of states may be the best that can be devised at present."[15]

Many commentators have recommended concentration on informal discussion groups, conferences, and seminars with either official or unofficial participation, or both, and various kinds of exploratory meetings. The CSIS Pacific Basin Congressional Study Group took special note of the task forces established at the conference on the Pacific Community idea in Bangkok in 1982. The group suggested that attention should be focused "on participation in informal functional groups, not on membership in an official organization." One member of the group advanced the view that even if PBC began to assume some institutional form, it would still be desirable to approach problems of security in indirect rather than in direct ways. "Let security be discussed in the corridors," he advised, "and when and if it becomes a common enough interest, a security aspect will naturally evolve into organized discussions."[16] While stating that the "long range goal" of PBC should be "an international organization formed by the governments concerned," the Japanese Pacific Basin Cooperation Study Group proposed, as a more feasible short-range program, the establishment of "a committee to manage a series of international conferences, and working groups on a government or private level to be entrusted with particular projects."[17]

Even if the Pacific Cooperation Movement begins to assume some organizational forms, this will probably be limited for some time to ad hoc meetings and groupings on both official and unofficial levels. If at some future stage a more institutionalized structure emerges, it will probably not be a single all-regional organization but a series of functional and other types of organizations, perhaps with some loose form of coordination arrangements. Even more probable are patterns such as the Western economic summit—in which Japan participates—which brings together the heads of government of the world's major economic powers at least annually, and which provides an opportunity for these top leaders to exchange views and even to agree on measures of cooperation on a wider variety of matters, often including security concerns, and the annual meetings of the foreign ministers, and less frequent meetings of the heads of government, of the ASEAN countries, where again discussions take place "in the corridors" on a variety of issues of common concern, often including security problems. In the newly emerging South Asian Association for Regional Cooperation (SAARC), the deputy foreign ministers and the foreign ministers of all the South Asian states played a central role in bringing the new organization into being. In their annual meetings, now well established, the foreign ministers have been reported to discuss a variety of subjects of common interest, well beyond the formal agenda, including even external security concerns and, at least on a bilateral basis, security and other problems that have created tensions in intraregional relations.[18]

The example of ASEAN, which may be described as the most important regional arrangement that now exists in the entire Pacific Basin, is one that proponents of a Pacific Community should study, and perhaps borrow from and emulate. This would be particularly useful for those who believe that the emerging PBC cannot and should not neglect security considerations, and who are looking for some formula by which security matters can be considered within the Pacific Community framework but at the same time can be kept off the formal agenda and the formal programs of institutional development. Peter Poole believes that "ASEAN offers the best available model of the kind of informal arrangement for consultation that seems to be needed by the Pacific basin region as a whole. . . . The ASEAN ministers can and do discuss with one another, usually in a private, informal setting, issues of concern to the group, and they have ready access to the leaders of other [Pacific Basin countries]."[19]

THE ROLE OF ADVANCED COUNTRIES IN PBC

Poole also sees patterns of growing cooperation among the more powerful nations of the Pacific Basin, and between these nations and ASEAN. The five advanced countries, he observes, "are not far from having such a framework of their own. The existing patterns of U.S.-Canadian, U.S.-Japanese, and Japanese-Australian consultation could quite easily be expanded into a five-power caucus. . . . The advanced countries and the ASEAN five are rapidly improving their habits of consultation."[20] The "post-ministerial" consultations which the ASEAN foreign ministers now hold regularly each year, after their formal ASEAN meeting, with their major trading partners may provide examples for PBC,[21] and this in time might lead to a broader network of interlocking interdependencies that would give greater vitality to PBC.

Some pitfalls exist in Poole's proposals for the expansion of the existing patterns of consultation and cooperation among the five advanced countries of the Pacific Basin, and between them and ASEAN. ASEAN states and almost all other countries of the Pacific region, aside from the five advanced countries, would view any signs of growing collaboration among these advanced countries with considerable misgivings. Some would even feel that such growing collaboration would add to the threats and tensions in the region. This view would obviously be shared by the Communist states of the region, most notably the Soviet Union, and to a lesser extent by the PRC as well. There would also be widespread doubts that advanced-nation collaboration would be a good way to promote the Pacific Community idea. Some of the ambivalence and hesitation regarding the Pacific Community concept that are entertained by many Pacific states, including the ASEAN nations and China, as well as the Soviet Union, are occasioned by fears of increasing the already-great asymmetries in the Pacific area and of making the area one of confrontation among the great powers, notably the United States and the Soviet Union, and of involving other Pacific Basin states in great-power rivalries and conflicts. Hence concern about the security dimensions of PBC would be enhanced, to the detriment of the larger goals and purposes of the movement. Genuine "cooperation" could hardly be based on such shaky foundations.

This raises the whole question of the proper role of the more advanced countries, and particularly of the two most advanced, the United States and Japan, in PBC. Much of the initiative for the movement has originated in Japan and the United States, on the part of both official and unofficial leaders and organizations. Without active support in the Pacific Basin's two greatest economic powers, the whole Pacific Basin Cooperation idea will be stillborn. But it is also true that if these powers promote the idea too vigorously, and if other Pacific countries do not show greater enthusiasm and support for the idea, no real cooperation will emerge. Many commentators, including some in Japan and the United States, have warned against too-active promotion of the movement in these countries, and have stressed the importance of a low-key approach and the need for more widespread support. "The United States and Japan," advised the members of the CSIS Pacific Basin Congressional Study Group, "should take pains to avoid taking a leading role. If either appears overbearing it will arouse suspicions and may inhibit acceptance of the idea." This advice would seem to be most relevant with respect to the United States, as the members of the study group pointed out: "The Pacific Basin initiative is, after all, largely an Asian initiative, and it might be well to rely on the diplomatic imagination of our Asian neighbors to create the framework in which the forum might occur."[22]

MEMBERSHIP AND SECURITY

If the emerging Pacific Basin Cooperation is given organizational form, much will depend on the membership.[23] This is particularly the case with regard to the cooperation's security dimensions. If the membership is confined to the five advanced countries of the Pacific Basin, or even if it has a larger membership, but still mainly consists of U.S. allies, security matters will be given considerable prominence; but this kind of organizational framework will in many ways place the whole future of the movement in jeopardy. "Cooperation" in this form will be regarded as a thin facade for a U.S.-dominated Pacific NATO. It will be viewed with doubts and suspicions by other non-Communist Pacific states, and it will give some basis for Soviet charges that "a new military bloc in the Pacific Ocean," anti-Soviet in essence, instead of real PBC, is emerging.[24] If most of the non-Communist nations of the Pacific actively participate from the outset in the institutionalization and development of PBC, the Soviet Union will doubtless make the same charges, but they are less likely to have an impact outside of the Communist world. Many of the non-Communist members, while sharing the U.S. concern about the Soviet military buildup in the Asian-Pacific area and overall Soviet intentions, will be critical of U.S. policies toward the Soviet Union on the ground that these policies are overly confrontational and military. These states will want no part of an organization or organizations that might involve them in great-power conflicts.

If the PRC or the Soviet Union were associated with the formative stages of a PBC, the nature of the cooperation, and especially its security dimensions, would obviously be quite different. Communist membership seems quite unlikely, but some of the main proponents of the cooperation idea, such as President Chun Doo Hwan of South Korea, have advocated open rather than closed membership in any PBC, and in 1980 Prime Minister Ohira of Japan, one of the chief proponents of the cooperation idea, said that he was not opposed to Chinese and Soviet participation.

Most of the PBC's supporters, however, are agreed that the cooperation would have little coherence if the Communist states were included. Hence they are opposed to any Communist participation, at least until and unless the cooperation is well established. Communist membership from the outset would probably doom any prospects for the emergence of a real PBC, and it would certainly limit and change the character of any considerations of a security nature. On the other hand, one can also argue that a Pacific Cooperation system without two of the largest and most important states along the Pacific rim would be a travesty, a truncated pattern of relationships that would create further divisions in the vital Pacific Basin.

Various patterns of limited cooperation between Communist and non-Communist states have developed in many parts of the world, including the Pacific region, but nowhere has such limited cooperation led to joint membership in effective regional communities. The Pacific Basin, where regional cooperation of any kind has been quite limited, at least until recent years, would not seem to be a promising theater for the emergence of the first Communist/non-Communist "PBC."

Even if Communist (and perhaps other) Pacific states are not centrally involved in the emerging PBC, it is vital that any cooperation that may emerge be open with respect to outside contacts, if not in membership. The Pacific Basin, for all its vast area and the extensive trade and other relationships within it, has extensive involvement with other countries and other parts of the world, and much of the rest of the world is involved in the Pacific Basin in a multitude of ways. European involvement is particularly extensive and important, "nor is Europe's increasing involvement . . . limited to trade and investment." As Peter A. Poole has stated, "the creation of a Pacific Community is far more likely to succeed if Western Europe's variegated interests in the region are encouraged rather than ignored."[25] Some of these interests are related to security; but on the whole, in considering the relationship of Pacific states in any PBC, either with each other or with the outside world, the "cobweb" model of international relations—the model of interlocking interdependencies—would seem to be more relevant than the "billiard ball" model—the model of clashing interrelations among a few great powers.[26]

ON THE PBC'S SECURITY AGENDA

Assuming that a Pacific Cooperation system emerges in some identifiable form, in which most of the non-Communist states of the Pacific—but no Communist states—are involved, what will be its security dimensions, and what security issues or security-related items, if any, will be on its agenda? In all probability security issues, as such, will be kept off the formal agenda, at least for a considerable time. But many of the agenda items will certainly be security-related, as indeed almost all matters of mutual concern are. This is especially true if the Japanese approach to "comprehensive national security" is extended to embrace comprehensive regional security, or comprehensive or common security in the international system. Certainly issues of trade, investment, technology transfer, resources, energy, and other matters that are often referred to as issues with which emerging Pacific Cooperation should be primarily concerned have definite security dimensions and implications. Some of the developing forums of the emerging PBC, including unofficial forums and meetings of top political leaders, will undoubtedly be avenues for exchange of views and plans of security matters. They will be discussed mainly "in the corridors" rather than in official sessions. They will be more openly discussed in unofficial gatherings—seminars, conferences, and the like, under private sponsorship—and they will be treated much more extensively than has been the case so far in publications by private scholars and institutes concerned with PBC themes.

Some items certain to figure prominently in any agenda and in some specialized cooperation forums are so centrally related to security that they can hardly be discussed adequately without due recognition of their security dimensions. An outstanding illustration, as far as Pacific states are concerned, is the question of the protection of vital sea lanes, a question that inevitably arises whenever representatives of Pacific states discuss the economic bases of their survival and growth. These states are dependent on distant sources for essential resources, energy, and so on (the importance of the long and vital sea lanes from the Persian Gulf to Japan and South Korea would come immediately to mind). Some American students of PBC affairs, official and unofficial, have suggested that this question might even provide a central theme for cooperation itself. In remarks to the members of the CSIS Pacific Basin Congressional Study Group, Congressman Paul Findley said: "The question of the safety of the sea, with or without military connotations, is certainly a logical part of the investigations" of PBC, and a 1983 staff report of this study group carried Congressman Findley's observation at least one step further: "The Pacific Basin countries may be reluctant to discuss regional security issues, but they will discuss preserving their vital commercial links to each other. The security of sea lanes could provide one organizing concept for" PBC.[27]

In an address before the Los Angeles World Affairs Council in October 1984, U.S. Secretary of State George Shultz said: "Today, a new sense of Pacific Cooperation is emerging with the potential for greater collaboration among many nations with an extraordinary diversity of cultures, race, and political systems. . . . There is an expanding practice of consultation, a developing sense of common interest, and an exciting vision of the future. We may well be at the threshold of a new era in international relations in the Pacific Basin."[28] The new era, like past eras, will doubtless witness many trends that will run counter to the direction which Mr. Shultz envisions; but if it also witnesses a growing "sense of PBC" and "an expanding practice of consultation," this may set in motion trends that may in time become even stronger than the continuing divisions and tensions. This would still be a far cry from a real PBC, but it could provide the momentum that is needed for translating the growing "sense of Pacific Cooperation" into something much more concrete and enduring. It could be an impressive demonstration of the transnational dimensions of national and regional as well as international life. In this broader conceptual framework the concept of "security" and especially of "comprehensive security" should take on a new meaning and significance.

A similar vision for a new Pacific era was observed by Soviet General Secretary Mikhail Gorbachev in his Vladivostok speech on July 28, 1986. Challenging the entire Pacific region, but particularly the major powers—China, Japan, and the United States—Gorbachev called for an active dialogue to reduce tensions and to increase mutually beneficial economic intercourse in the region.[29]

NOTES

1. An American specialist in Pacific affairs has called attention to several major and scientific innovations that mainly originated in the Pacific region: "Perhaps the most exciting aspect of the emergence of the Pacific Basin as an influential area is its creative contributions to innovations and new trends with dramatic implications for future culture and civilization. The microprocessing revolution, robotics, Theory Z and industrial democracy, ecotopia, cultural democracy and *dependencia* are significant new concepts and theories all having their origins in the Pacific Basin." Gerald W. Frey, "The Pacific Challenge: A Transnational Future," *Asia Pacific Community* (Summer 1983), p. 37.

2. This was a central finding of Rear Admiral (Ret.) L. R. Vasey, now executive director of the Pacific Forum in Hawaii, and Professor

Bernard K. Gordon of the University of New Hampshire during a study tour of eight East Asian and Pacific countries in mid-1981. A report of their study tour is presented under the title "Security in East Asia-Pacific," in *Threats to Security in East Asia-Pacific National and Regional Perspectives*, ed. Charles E. Morrison (Lexington, Mass.: Lexington Books, 1983), ch. 4.

3. Comprehensive National Security Study Group, *Report on Comprehensive National Security* (Tokyo, 1980), p. 19.

4. Ibid., p. 35.

5. Ibid., p. 7.

6. *Common Security*, Report of the Independent Commission on Disarmament and Security Issues (Olof Palme, Chairman) (London: Pan Books, 1982).

7. *The Growing Dimensions of Security*, a report by the Atlantic Council's Working Group on Security (Washington, D.C.: Atlantic Council of the United States, November 1977), p. 1.

8. A partial exception is Robert L. Downen and Bruce J. Dickson, eds., *The Emerging Pacific Community: A Regional Perspective* (Boulder, Colo.: Westview Press, 1984).

9. Bruce J. Dickson, ed., *The Emerging Pacific Community Concept: An American Perspective*, a Staff Report on the CSIS Pacific Basin Congressional Study Group (Washington, D.C.: Center for Strategic and International Studies, Georgetown University, 1983), p. 1.

10. Ibid., p. 12.

11. Peter A. Poole, "The Emerging Pacific Basin Community," *Asian Affairs* (September/October 1980), p. 51.

12. Pacific Basin Cooperation Study Group, *Report on the Pacific Basin Cooperation Concept* (Tokyo, 1980). Like the Comprehensive National Security Study Group, the Pacific Basin Cooperation Study Group was formed as an advisory group to then Prime Minister Ohira.

13. *Philadelphia Inquirer*, June 23, 1982.

14. See Donald K. Crone, *The ASEAN States: Coping with Dependence* (New York: Praeger, 1983).

15. Poole, "Emerging Pacific Basin Community," p. 53.

16. Dickson, *Emerging Pacific Community Concept*, pp. 17, 21.

17. *Report on the Pacific Basin Cooperation Concept*, p. 77.

18. See S. D. Muni and Anuradha Muni, *Regional Cooperation in South Asia* (New Delhi: National Publishing House, 1984).

19. Poole, "Emerging Pacific Basin Community," p. 53.

20. Ibid.

21. See "ASEAN Ministerial Conference with the Dialogue Partners in Jakarta," *Indonesia News and Views* (July 20, 1984), pp. 2–3.

22. Dickson, *Emerging Pacific Community Concept*, pp. 21, 47.

23. See Stephen Uhalley, Jr., "The Membership Dilemma and What to Do About it: The Non-Market Economy Nations and the Pacific Community," in Downen and Dickson, *Emerging Pacific Community*, pp. 22–31.

24. See, for example, Y. Stolyarov and A. Shmyryvov, "The Pacific Community: Economic Integration or a Military-Political Bloc?" *Far Eastern Affairs*, no. 3 (Moscow, 1983); and I. Bulai, "The Shady Aims of the Pacific Community," *International Affairs* (Moscow, January 1983).

25. Poole, "Emerging Pacific Basin Community," p. 52.

26. For an explanation of these two models, see J. Burton, A. J. R. Groom, C. Mittchel, and A. deReuck, *The Study of World Society: A London Perspective* (Pittsburgh: International Studies Association, 1973); and John W. Burton, *Global Conflict: The Domestic Sources of International Crisis* (Brighton: Wheatsheaf Books, 1984), pp. 4, 67.

27. Dickson, *Emerging Pacific Community Concept*, p. 20.

28. "A Forward Look at Foreign Policy," address by U.S. Secretary of State George Shultz before the Los Angeles World Affairs Council, October 19, 1984, Washington, D.C.: Bureau of Public Affairs, U.S. Department of State, *Current Policy*, no. 625, October 19, 1984.

29. The complete text of the speech is found in *Pravda*, July 29, 1986. A detailed analysis is provided in the Conclusion to this book.

9

Pacific Basin Cooperation: Problems and Prospects

ROY KIM

INTRODUCTION

The Pacific era has dawned. Today the region in and around the Pacific Basin—the largest of the world's oceans—holds most of the human and natural resources and is the most dynamic and prosperous area of the world. The region also has had its share of past conflicts, including World War II and wars in Korea and Vietnam. In fact, the region has long been militarized; yet given the nature of the economic dynamics, the region as a whole has the real potential for tremendous mutual economic benefits.

It is generally recognized in the study of international trade that the world's major trade center shifted from the Mediterranean to the Atlantic, and since the early 1980's it has been changing again from the Atlantic to the Pacific. We are witnessing the historic advent of the Pacific era, as the volume of trade in and across the Pacific has been larger than that in and across the Atlantic. If current trends continue, British historian Arnold Toynbee's prophecy that the twenty-first century will be the Pacific Century may indeed be fulfilled. Fully recognizing this dynamic change, particularly in the United States, the *Economist* of London observed in May 1984 that California's 26 million people produced more than $460 billion in goods and services in 1984, about what Britain's 54 million people produced. This

would give California, were it an independent country, the world's
sixth or seventh largest GNP and, apart from a few small oil-
producing countries, the world's highest per capita GNP. The
11 million people of Los Angeles alone had a larger gross product than India's 750 million. More to the point, each Los Ange-
leno produced more than ten times as much as each Mexican.[1]
Growing, dynamic cities—Los Angeles, San Diego, the San
Francisco Bay area, Seattle, and Portland—seriously challenge
the East Coast cities—New York, Boston, Philadelphia, and Baltimore—as commercial centers. California in 1984 accounted for
about 12 percent of total U.S. production. The purpose of this
brief essay is to analyze some of the sources of conflict and potential opportunities for mutual benefits in the Pacific.

What, then, are the problems and prospects for realizing
Toynbee's dream? As is well known, the original designers of
the Pacific Basin scheme—Kiyoshi Kojima, Peter Drysdale, and
Hugh Patrick—assumed that if the economies of the western
Pacific and North America could be brought together, they would
all benefit on the principle of an international division of labor.
The initially suggested model was that of the Organization for
Economic Cooperation and Development (OECD), which was
established in Western Europe to act as a clearinghouse for the
major capitalist countries involved in world trade. The originally
recommended Pacific Basin Cooperation membership consisted
of five developed countries (Australia, Canada, Japan, New Zealand, and the United States), five ASEAN countries (Indonesia,
Malaysia, the Philippines, Singapore, Thailand), South Korea,
Hong Kong, and Taiwan. They also suggested that the several
independent states of the Pacific islands (Papua, New Guinea,
Fiji, and Tonga) should join as a group.

There were several anomalies in the original design. First, if
an association was to bear the label "Pacific," what of those Latin
American countries bordering on the Pacific Ocean? The originators did not, apparently, regard them as essential, largely because of their low volume of trade. Would they eventually join
the envisioned PBC at some point, or would they be completely
left out simply because of their underdevelopment? A more difficult problem concerned adherence to the free market frame-

work. This raised membership problems particularly for social-ist-modeled economies in the region—China, North Korea, and Vietnam, but most of all the Soviet Union. While Beijing desires trade with Washington and Tokyo on a wider scale, its trade policy has been and will be, in all probability, guided by its own "unique socialist" criteria. The USSR is, of course, another case in point. Two-thirds of its territory lies in Asia, and the Soviet Far East has a 5,000-mile coastline stretching from the North Korean frontier to the Bering Straits. Moreover, the world's largest ocean is growing in tandem with the development of various natural resources in the Soviet Far East, notably the construction of the Baikal-Amur Railroad, and expanding trade with Japan through Japan's monopolized annual trade fairs in the Soviet Far East. The port of Vostochny near Nakhodka was exclusively designed and constructed by the Japanese to expand their trade with the region. The question then was, Should these Pacific but socialist states be left out simply because of their different economic systems?

These two anomalies aside, there were a number of serious security, economic, and political problems. Most of them are old problems, including the still remaining division of China and Korea, Vietnam's tensions with China and Kampuchea, the restless Philippines, continuing tensions along the Sino-Soviet border, and finally but not least, much-strained American-Soviet relations which, undoubtedly, will affect the prospects of PBC.

Since the end of World War II we have witnessed in the Pacific region shifting alignments in the ongoing competition between Moscow and Washington. In the Atlantic, the pattern of alliances between NATO and Warsaw Pact countries has remained relatively stable for more than thirty years. Yet in the Pacific region, the postwar years have produced major periodic alterations. The Sino-Soviet alliance of the 1950's gave way to geopolitical feuding in the 1960's and a limited military confrontation in the 1970's. The fundamental forces animating these changes have been the state of Sino-Soviet relations and Soviet-American competition. But now Japan, China, the Soviet Union, and the United States are faced with choices about how far they should proceed in building coalitions to contain the influence of adversaries and their allies. In other words, their decision whether a stable balance of relationships could be achieved or a protracted conflict would drive them toward confrontation will undoubtedly affect the vision of PBC.

Essentially, there are four overlapping triangles in the Pacific. They are (1) Beijing-Tokyo-Washington, (2) Beijing-Moscow-Washington, (3) Beijing-Moscow-Tokyo, and (4) Moscow-Tokyo-Washington. The Soviet linkage with the other three powers appears, on the whole, the weakest. For reason of limited space, these four evolving triangles cannot be fully analyzed. It suffices to say, that the Beijing-Tokyo-Washington seems the most agreeable and the Beijing-Moscow-Washington the most conflictive. Undoubtedly, the Japan-U.S. linkage is the most important bilateral relationship in the Pacific whereas the much-strained U.S.-Soviet relationship is the most troublesome. Let us, with these in mind, closely examine the Japan-U.S. relationship—a key determinant in the prospects of PBC.

Four-Power Relationship

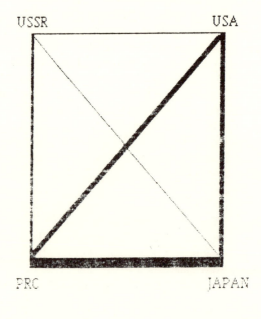

JAPAN-U.S. RELATIONS

The bilateral U.S.-Japanese relationship is the indispensable link to PBC. It offers many mutual economic and political benefits, and it holds the potential for international cooperation to foster a more stable world environment. Having the world's largest economies, the United States and Japan are emerging as the two most significant players in the field of high-technology development—a field that is likely to define fast-paced economic development and prosperity in the years ahead. As we enter the twenty-first century, they are likely to be either the world's major economic competitors or economic partners. Needless to say, if the present tensions over economic competition lead to protectionist measures, not only Japan and the United States will suffer but these tensions will, without any doubt, adversely affect the world economy as a whole, including the Pacific region. Essentially, there are two key issues causing U.S.-Japanese economic tensions: (1) the rising U.S. trade deficit with Japan, and (2) U.S. insistence that Japan increase its defense spending and military capabilities. How these two difficult problems are handled between Tokyo and Washington will inevitably affect the prospects for PBC more than anything else.

Perhaps with this in mind, President Ronald Reagan urged Japan, during his November 1983 visit, to join the United States in a global "Partnership for Good," claiming that "Japanese-American friendship is forever." Reagan's speech was the first address by an American president to the Japanese parliament. Indeed, much time has passed since President Franklin D. Roosevelt's "day of infamy" speech to the U.S. Congress after Japan's attack on Pearl Harbor in 1941. U.S. Ambassador to Japan Mike Mansfield claimed:

The Japanese-American bond is the most important bilateral relationship in the world, bar none. The Japanese have no doubts about America's importance to them in many spheres—economic, diplomacy and security, to name a few—but I sometimes think that we Americans do not fully appreciate Japan's importance to the United States.[2]

While the bond is, indeed, indispensable to PBC, it is highly uncertain what degree of American-Japanese cooperation will emerge in the process of establishing such an entity.

This uncertainty has been largely caused by a fundamental change in U.S.-Japanese relations. For instance, the postwar Japanese *amae* (dependent) mentality toward the United States does not apply any longer. Referring to Japan's exclusive dependent reliance on the United States, it used to be said, "When Washington gets a cold, Tokyo gets pneumonia." Yet the present reality is that if the Japanese economy gets a cold, the U.S. economy is likely to get one as well.

JAPANESE-U.S. ECONOMIC RELATIONS

Historically, postwar U.S.-Japanese economic relations have gone through three major stages: (1) American military-economic hegemony over a subdued Japan until the reversion of Okinawa in 1972; (2) relative politico-economic cooperation, up to the 1979 Afghan crisis, rather reluctantly on the part of Japan; and (3) since then, an open competition, if not conflict, in trade, investment, and manufacturing on a global scale.

What causes conflict in U.S.-Japanese trade? After examining five key cases (steel, automobiles, agricultural products, telecommunications equipment, and macro-economic policy coordination), I. M. Destler and Hideo Sato suggest four major reasons.[3] To begin with, the enormous expansion of bilateral trade and its shifts in composition intensified the conflict. Over the last twenty years there has been a fivefold real increase in U.S. exports to Japan and a sevenfold real increase in imports. This increase far outstripped the growth of overall U.S. production.

The trade balance has also shifted dramatically from a steady surplus in the U.S. favor through 1964 to a growing deficit thereafter, reaching an all-time high, $20 billion, by 1983, $50 billion by 1985, and $51 billion out of the global trade gap of $173 billion in 1986. There has been a remarkable change, of course, in the composition of Japan's exports. Today Japan's major exports to the United States largely consist of high-technology goods, instead of textiles as in the 1960's, whereas agricultural products and raw materials still dominate U.S. exports to Japan.

In other words, what the Japanese supply is abundantly available—albeit with differences in price and quality—from competing U.S. firms. From a purely economic point of view, a bilateral merchandise trade deficit should not be a great concern as long as a nation's worldwide current account is in rough balance. This argument, however, can hardly ignore the political reality of the highly volatile U.S. trade deficit and the huge federal budget deficit—both of which have been somehow claimed to have been caused, ironically, by free trade, a subject of much controversy itself. Free trade, in many ways, very much like beauty, is in the eye of the beholder. Naturally, there is a glaring gap, if not contradiction, between rhetoric and reality in free trade. President Reagan, in his 1983 *Economic Report to the Congress*, stated:

Intervention in international trade by the U.S. Government even though costly to the U.S. economy in the short run, may, however, be justified if it serves the strategic purpose of increasing the cost of interventionist policies by foreign governments. Thus, there is a potential role for carefully targeted measures, explicitly temporarily aimed at convincing other countries to reduce their trade distortions.[4]

Yet such temporary measures—to protect a domestic industry only until it can get back on its feet—turn out to be very difficult to remove once installed. For protection encourages the industry to delay making much-needed adjustments rather than to speed them up. In his 1984 *Economic Report to the Congress*, President Reagan returned to his favorite free trade rhetoric by declaring:

I remain committed to the principle of free trade as the best way to bring the benefits of competition to American consumers and businesses. It would be totally inappropriate to respond by erecting trade barriers or by using taxpayers' dollars to subsidize exports. Instead, we must work with other nations of the world to reduce the export subsidies and import barriers that currently hurt U.S. farmers, businesses, and workers.[5]

Many previous U.S. presidents also deviated from a free trade policy. Gerald Ford raised barriers against specialty steel imports. Jimmy Carter sheltered the domestic footwear industry. Contrary to the rhetoric, import protection has greatly expanded since the Reagan administration took office. An estimated 35 percent of manufactured goods—autos, textiles, carbon steel, specialty steel, motorcycles—are now reportedly protected.[6] Moreover, U.S. logs from federal lands are legally prohibited to be exported to Japan, largely for the benefit of special interests in the United States. In brief, U.S.-Japanese trade is hardly free trade; and, in all probability, it is likely to be even less so with increasing friction.

A second cause of the U.S.-Japanese trade conflict is the erosion of the postwar international system. During the height of the cold war, the United States, as long as its economy was strong and healthy, was excessively generous to Japan and other Western industrial allies. While leading a global anti-Communist crusade, the United States not only provided a relatively open market for Japanese products but in fact allowed Japan to engage in severe import and foreign-exchange restrictions on goods, services, and capital.[7] Meanwhile the relative decline of the U.S. macro-economic position during the detente era was accompanied by Japan's sustained economic growth, its increasing penetration of the U.S. market, and its control over economies quite often in defiance of Washington. Even if the United States succeeded in energizing military strength vis-à-vis the Soviet Union, whether the United States could possibly regain economic hegemony over Japan remains highly doubtful.

A third contributor to the U.S.-Japanese trade conflict is differences in national trade machinery and policies. As is well known, the U.S. government has traditionally functioned as an arbiter—under anti-trust laws—in order to maintain healthy competition nationally and internationally under free trade. Japan, in contrast, has given the top priority to enhancing its world trade expansion. The top U.S. trade decision-making machinery—the Office of the Special Trade Representative in the president's executive office—is not likely to match Japan's comprehensive Ministry of International Trade and Industry (MITI). Not only has the U.S. Trade Representative Office failed to formulate a comprehensive long-term trade policy but it has even failed to mediate bureaucratic conflict among competing executive branches—Agriculture, Commerce, Defense, State, and Treasury—over critical trade issues (for example, the grain embargo, pipelines, and technology transfer). The late Theodore White, as the dean of U.S. election scholars, in his *America in Search of Itself*, asked:

Is a new American Department of International Trade and Industry (a DITI) necessary? Is American anti-trust legislation still useful? It is now almost a century since the passage of the Sherman Anti-Trust Act, which succeeded in its purpose in its time and for generations thereafter. But is it now time to review the traditional faith in free-for-all industrial competition? Is our concept of industrial management obsolete? Above all, how can government coordinate the vital dynamics of free private enterprise with federal guidance? . . . So the question: what remains valid and useful to Americans of their recent history of free trade, and what must be changed to protect the jobs of American working people in the endangered sectors?[8]

A final cause of the U.S.-Japanese trade conflict is perceptual differences. As noted above, there is still some residue of the customary U.S. perception of Japan as its weak Asian protégé and of Japan's own dependent mentality toward the United States. These perceptions are, of course, both grossly inconsistent with present economic realities. For some Americans, it is simply inconceivable that they could lose in free competition to their Asian client, and they automatically suspect Japan of resorting to unfair competition. Much irritated by this U.S. attitude, the Japanese feel that they are blamed for their hard work and efficiency, for living out what Professor Michio Morishima calls the Japanese Confucian work ethic.[9]

Consideration of these four basic causes of U.S.-Japanese trade friction does not, at present, indicate much prospect for improvement. Naturally, these problems inevitably and adversely affect the prospects for PBC, for they tend to have a propensity for intensification and proliferation horizontally as well as vertically.

In coping with these bilateral problems, the Japanese lately seem to be adopting two basic trade policy modifications: (1) voluntary export restrictions, and (2) merging with troubled U.S.

industries. How these two Japanese trade modifications will, directly or indirectly, affect the future of the Pacific Community is difficult even to conjecture at the present time. For the moment, however, they seem to be lowering somewhat the heightened U.S.-Japanese emotional temperature.

Greatly alarmed by the prospects for protectionist measures in the U.S. Congress and under considerable U.S. government pressure, Japanese automakers themselves imposed, for a sixth year, export quotas. In 1984, beginning April 1, for instance, Japan had an export limit of 1.85 million passenger cars, although this was a 170,000-unit increase in the quota from 1983.[10] Japan had reportedly unsucessfully sought to have a limit of 1.9 million cars, while the United States had tried to place the limit at 1.8 million cars.[11] Should auto quotas be continued? If so, for whom, for what purposes, and for how long? Not only auto but general trade protectionism became entangled with the 1984 U.S. presidential election politics. Democratic front-runner Walter Mondale came down on the side of the U.S. labor unions in support of continuing auto quotas, whereas the Reagan administration's former trade representative William Brock proposed not to extend the existing import quotas on Japanese cars when they would expire in 1985.

Because of much-improved productivity and income for labor, Brock did not favor extending the auto quotas. Extending the existing auto quotas would temporarily benefit organized labor—particularly the United Auto Workers—and top auto management at the expense of American consumers as a whole. The U.S. International Trade Commission, on a 3–2 vote in July 1984, recommended five years of import quotas and additional tariffs to help the ailing U.S. steel industry.[12] Expectedly, Japanese steelmakers sharply criticized the decision.[13]

A second Japanese trade policy has been direct investment in the United States. Initially urged by labor and business leaders alike to alleviate increasing U.S. trade deficits with Japan, Japanese investment has been trickling to American shores for more than a decade. The United States has become Japan's prime foreign investment target and accounted for 24.7 percent of total outstanding Japanese investment by 1982. For Japan the United States is the most important market abroad, so vital that

Japan could not live without it. Yet in order to keep the U.S. market stable, Japan is changing from a policy of simple exporting to overseas production in the United States. From Japan's point of view, this is happening not a moment too soon: there are numerous reciprocity bills and a local content bill—clearly protectionist measures—before the U.S. Congress. Besides obvious fear of rising U.S. protectionism, the United States—with abundant natural resources, relatively low costs, a high level of technology, and a large market—is most attractive for Japan's investment.[14]

How has Washington reacted? In 1983 President Reagan issued a policy statement welcoming foreign, including Japanese, direct investment in the United States, as long as it is based purely on economic reasons. Exclusively economic considerations as such, though, rarely exist. In April 1984, in fact, William J. Casey, director of the CIA, denounced Japan's big stake in American computer industries as "Trojan horses." He warned that excessive dependence on Japanese technology could undermine American pace-setting skills in the field.[15] Indeed, the long-term economic, strategic, and political impact of the increasing Japanese share of ownership in the American economy is very difficult to predict—whether it would fuel a nationalistic protectionist drive within the United States or facilitate a much closer economic international division of labor between the United States and Japan, thereby positively contributing toward establishing PBC. The present $10.5 billion stake in American business makes Japan the fourth-largest foreign investor, just behind Canada in the value of its total holdings. The Japanese are far ahead of the $8 billion that the United States has invested in Japanese business.[16]

U.S. reactions abound. For labor leaders, the paramount question is whether the Japanese investment would save American jobs—and if so, whether they would be union jobs. The business leaders are primarily concerned about the immediate threat posed by Japanese competition for domestic sales. Economists, for their part, have a more long-term concern: that U.S. industry will be deprived of capital as the Japanese take home the profits from their American investment—something the Japanese have not done yet in significant amounts. For the most part, however, the growing Japanese investments in American business have been welcomed. Indeed, state and local government officials have been stumbling over each other trying to attract Japanese investment to their own local areas. Yet there are those who see the Japanese investment as a possible trap, fearing a concentration of power in a viable separate interest group. The Reagan administration does not seem to have a clear policy on the matter, and in fact, officials are rather reluctant to discuss such an emotional issue.

Japanese investment in the United States is not, of course, new. Sony's fourteen-year-old assembly line in San Diego produced by May 1984 the five millionth TV set. Matsushita's Quasar TV plant in suburban Chicago celebrated its tenth anniversary in 1984. In February 1983 Toyota and General Motors announced a $230 million joint venture to manufacture subcompact cars at an idle GM plant in Fremont, California. In April 1984 Nippon Kokkan announced an agreement to buy 50 percent of the National Steel Corporation for $292 million.[17] What appears new, however, is the suddenly increasing size of Japan's U.S. investment. Of late, aggressive Japanese companies, frustrated by stagnant domestic markets and eager to find a way around the increasing import controls that have stifled their American sales, have been pouring accumulated yen—somewhat undervalued—into American businesses.[18]

Japan's direct investment is also related to U.S. security arguments. The desirability of safeguarding American technology—particularly security-related technology—is often advanced as a reason to control Japanese investment. This was mentioned in 1978 when U.S. Boeing took in Japanese (a consortium of Fuji, Kawasaki, and Mitsubishi) and Italian partners to build the 767 wide-body jet. Panels for the fuselage are made in Tokyo and shipped to Seattle for assembly. "If they want to develop a commercial airplane they can do it with or without us," admitted a Boeing spokesman. The deal, he said, allowed Boeing to spread the costs around and to reduce its risks. For its next generation of commercial aircraft, Boeing promised its partners stakes of 25 percent instead of the present 15 percent. At a weekly luncheon of the Commonwealth Club in April 1984, U.S. CIA Director William Casey expressed a serious concern over the cooperative agreements—such as those between Hitachi and National Semiconductor and between Amdahl and Fujitsu—under which American computer companies rely heavily on their Japanese partners for design and component parts for the large mainframe computers they sell. Small U.S. computer companies' skepticism notwithstanding, Casey argued, "We view this as a dangerous course in a national security context as well as in a commercial context."[19]

Japan's participation in the Strategic Defense Initiative (SDI) will be discussed later, but despite national security risks, U.S. business as a whole has welcomed Japanese investment for now. It seems necessary and inevitable that American business accept the change graciously. Technological leadership seems to be as much a characteristic of the Japanese companies coming into the United States as the management techniques that have attracted so much attention. Japanese companies are known for their no-nonsense attitude toward featherbedding and restrictive work rules. Over the long haul, the Japanese can be expected to be much tougher on labor than American managers.

In brief, highly charged, increasing U.S.-Japanese trade frictions are a source of special concern for the entire Pacific Basin. In all probability, Japan would continue to run a large bilateral trade surplus with the United States even if it completely eliminated all the existing trade barriers to satisfy U.S. demands and made a substantial adjustment in the dollar-yen exchange rate. For Japan has few natural resources and is dependent on imports for her supply of primary products, particularly oil and other mineral fuels. It must earn the foreign exchange to pay for the oil by exporting other goods. Were the U.S. willing to sell enough Alaskan oil to Japan, for instance, the bilateral trade imbalance would be somewhat reduced. The important point, as indicated by the 1984 *Economic Report of the President*, is that

it is neither necessary nor desirable that any two countries' trade be in balance, any more than it is necessary or desirable for an auto manufacturer to be in bilateral balance with its steel supplier, or a household with its plumber. One looks at the overall balances of a household, company, or country, not a bilateral balance, to see if it is earning more—from all its trading partners together—than it is paying out.[20]

It is generally assumed, especially in the United States, that Japanese trade policy is responsible for the U.S. trade deficit. The Japanese, on the other hand, maintain a number of non-tariff barriers against imports that are sources of friction with the United States. These include import quotas for some agricultural products, particularly beef and citrus products. While Japan is the largest customer for U.S. agricultural products, these products still face restricted Japanese markets. To be sure, it would be in the Japanese interest, economically, to reduce the agricultural barriers, because they can import these products far more cheaply than it costs to produce them domestically, and it would reduce trade friction with the United States, as it would be in the interest of the U.S. farmers.

Viewed from Tokyo, however, there are geographical, historical, cultural, and political reasons for Japanese agricultural protectionism. These are limited arable land on the mountainous archipelago, the land redistribution program carried out by the American occupation that prohibited large land holdings, the cultural tradition of family-centered small-scale farming, and most of all, the agricultural lobby, which is a key source of support for the ruling Liberal Democratic party (LDP). The political strength of Japan's farmers comes from the over-representation of rural areas in the Diet because the postwar urbanization of Japan has not been reflected in the redrawing of voting districts. Consequently, there are four or five times as many voters for each parliamentary seat in some urban districts as there are for a seat in some rural areas.

Most of the ruling LDP members since 1955 have come from the conservative agricultural regions. Given this political reality, the high cost of Japanese agricultural subsidies paid to farmers is hardly surprising. In the fiscal year ending in March 1981, for instance, these payments amounted to $10.4 billion—54 percent of Japan's total farm income for the year.[21] These LDP members, while championing agricultural protectionism—for their own political survival—are also Japan's most pro-U.S. politicians and strong supporters of Japan's increased military spending, a goal sought by a United States eager to share global military expenses. Agricultural imports from the United States also cause other Japanese concerns as well. Being less than 50 percent self-sufficient in food, Japan is naturally anxious about how to maintain its security. Japan is America's single largest export market for agricultural products—a market worth about $5.6 billion in 1982. Yet the Japanese have reason to worry about America's reliability. They painfully remember the U.S. embargo of soybean exports in 1973 during the Nixon administration. Soybeans, in one form or another, are consumed in almost every Japanese meal; America's soybeans account for 94 percent of those consumed in Japan.[22]

How to resolve trade frictions? Saburo Okita, a former Japanese foreign minister, considers the U.S. trade deficit a natural aspect of the free market system. Japan, he argues, cannot be blamed for poor U.S. domestic economic performances. Nor can the Japanese market be considered restrictive toward American products. Japanese import quotas and non-tariff barriers, he insists, are more liberal than those of the European Community. The real problem, Okita suggests, springs from high U.S. interest rates, inflation, and the overvaluation of the dollar. These factors, he admits, have made Japanese exports advantageously competitive and hindered U.S. exports, but these trade frictions require joint solutions rather than mutual recrimination.[23] It is readily recognized in the United States that the cause of the decline in the exchange value of the yen against the dollar, at least since 1980, is the flow of capital out of Japan and into the United States. A primary cause for this capital outflow is the high real U.S. interest rates, but it has also been suggested that Japanese restrictions on the international flow of capital may be a factor.[24]

What, then, causes dollar-yen exchange rate misalignment? Fred Bergsten, a former assistant secretary of the treasury for international affairs, 1977–81, argues that the present exchange rate problem arises from five fundamentals: (1) a U.S. policy mix which creates huge budget deficits, (2) a Japanese policy which stresses the reduction of budget deficits, (3) international political uncertainties, (4) Japan's manipulation of its capital account, which adds to capital outflow from Japan, and (5) the U.S. government's reluctance to intervene in the exchange markets. In order to rectify these imbalances, he suggests, the United States and Japan must cooperate in bringing fiscal policy into alignment with monetary policy, and they must resume active intervention in the exchange markets.[25]

Naturally, trade frictions cause political tensions. As the Group of Wisemen observed in its January 1981 report, Japanese-U.S. bilateral economic disputes jeopardize cooperation in non-economic as well as economic fields as they become "visible and embittered."[26] They could very well create an overload effect, exacerbating physically and psychologically U.S. and Japanese senior officials through frequent and prolonged encounters without satisfactory outcomes. Most of all, trade conflicts have had a lingering unfavorable aftereffect on overall U.S.-Japanese relations. Given these bilateral economic conflicts, could the U.S. and Japan possibly provide leadership in establishing a Pacific Basin Community? Before taking up this question, let us turn our attention to U.S.-Japanese security relations.

U.S.-JAPANESE SECURITY RELATIONS

The U.S.-Japanese security relationship is based neither on common history nor cultural affinity. Unlike European-U.S. relations, it primarily depends on mutually perceived national self-interests. Moreover, a serious gap in perception and expectation appears to exist in the Japanese-U.S. security relationship.[27] Essentially, the U.S.-Japanese security arrangement is endangered by (1) Japanese ambivalence about its nature and reluctance to commit itself to an explicitly military relationship linking Japanese security with that of the United States, particularly that of the Indian Ocean and the Persian Gulf; (2) Japanese concern about the erratic, unpredictable nature of post-Vietnam U.S. foreign policy, wherein decisions affecting Japan have been sometimes unilaterally made with no prior consultation; and (3) the consensual character of Japanese decision-making and the possible emergence of extreme left pacifism or radical right militarism as Japanese public discontent with their security relations with the United States grows.[28] Of course, how these three fundamental problems will be handled by Tokyo and Washington will inevitably affect the prospects for establishing a Pacific Basin Community. Considering the changing U.S.-Soviet global balance of power, particularly in the Pacific, Hisahiko Okazaki, director-general of the Research and Planning Department of the Ministry of Foreign Affairs, suggests that Japanese policy must now be centered around Japan's own geostrategic importance to the U.S. and the Soviet Union. Japan could be, he argues, the site of an East-West military balance because its geography is more conducive to defense than that of Europe or the Middle East and because of its strong economy. Moreover, the Japanese public, he suggests, is beginning to perceive the need for these policy shifts.[29]

In a Japan buried in the radioactive ashes of Hiroshima and Nagasaki and humbled by the American occupation, but now confronted with an uncertain international environment, the rearmament question is destined to become one of the key national issues of the 1980's under the forceful leadership of Prime Minister Yasuhiro Nakasone. How Japan's rearmament question will be handled will affect not only U.S.-Japanese bilateral relations but inevitably the prospect for a Pacific Basin Community.

Today, Japan searches for her own security. This is largely in response to what she perceives to be the steadily expanding Soviet military power in the Pacific, lingering doubt about America's defense commitment, and most of all, Japan's increasing vulnerability to external circumstance, particularly in the Persian Gulf region. Given the fact that about 65 percent of Japan's oil comes from the Gulf, against an estimated 4 percent for the United States, Japan's uneasiness with the continuing Iran-Iraq conflict is readily understandable.[30]

Much more fundamental, however, is increasing Soviet military involvement in the Pacific. In 1978 and 1979 the Soviets armed the disputed islands of Etorofu and Kunashiri in the so-called Northern Territory, deployed some 70 to 90 Backfire bombers and 120 medium-range SS-20 missiles in eastern Siberia, acquired the use of naval and air facilities in Vietnam, and brought the aircraft carrier *Minsk* to Vladivostok. While Japan considers the Soviet Union a major source of threat, how imminent is that threat and what constitutes "threat" are intensely debated within Japan. In fact, Japan has thus far avoided regarding the Soviet Union as an "actual" threat as opposed to a "potential" threat on the ground that while the Soviets' capability to attack Japan is clear, their intention to do so is not.[31]

Reflecting changing public mood in Japan, Japanese political leaders have been maintaining lately that the Soviet military threat is real and serious. Prime Minister Suzuki stated, during his May 1981 Washington visit, that Japan, on its own initiative and in accordance with its Constitution and basic defense policy, would seek to make even greater efforts for improving its defense capabilities in Japanese territory and its surrounding sea and air space out to one thousand miles. Suzuki's successor, Nakasone, has been even more forthright in expressing, during his 1983 Washington visit, Japan's willingness to become an "unsinkable aircraft carrier" in the Pacific against the increasing Soviet military forces.

While these Japanese commitments have been welcomed by the United States, the two nations have fundamentally different geostrategic perceptions. Naturally, Washington considers the importance of Japan and U.S. forward basing in Japan in the context of global geostrategic considerations, whereas Japan tends to regard its own security from regional strategic perspectives. While agreeing, at least in rhetoric, on the necessity of a united Western security system and joining in the 1980 Moscow Olympics boycott, Japan at the same time attempts to avoid causing the Soviet Union to regard Japan as either a weak or a threatening country, and to have relatively normal relations with the Soviet Union in a self-confident but correct manner.[32] In fact, if for some reason the global balance of power tilted decisively in favor of the Soviet Union, it is by no means inconceivable that Japan would increasingly identify its interests with those of the Soviet Union. After all, Japan has traditionally operated under the principle of *nagai mono ni makareru* (do not offend the powerful).

In a most fundamental sense, Japan's search for her own strategy, has been caused by the present predicament of what U.S. Secretary of Defense Caspar Weinberger calls the U.S.-Japanese "defense partnership."[33] While the perceived mutuality of U.S.-Japanese security interests still far outweighs their differences, the partnership does appear to be undergoing a profound adjustment period, with the ultimate outcome far less clear than the resounding affirmation of Weinberger's "defense partnership" idea might suggest. A major transformation in the global balance of power, the positions of both the United States and Japan in the international system, the nature of their links with each other, their interaction with other societies, the character of their internal politics—most of which we have already touched on—have all very radically altered since the 1950's. Increasingly powerful interest groups in both countries have now come to view the partnership as leaving much to be desired. In spite of the apparent efforts by both governments to sustain and strengthen the partnership under Nakasone and Reagan (Yasu-Ron relationship), it appears by no means impossible that the present mutual security ties—similar to the Anglo-Japanese alliance during and after World War I—could very well become less and less intimate, and the two nations could gradually drift apart, even if that would not eventuate into conflict.

Meanwhile, the idea of "defense partnership" seems to move along. Tokyo, for instance, gave its long-awaited approval in September 1986 to the Reagan administration's SDI. Still, the Nakasone government stopped short of guaranteeing Japanese full participation, claiming that important details—including the commercial benefits Japan could expect—still had to be negotiated with Washington. Apparently, the Japanese are concerned that if they do not join the project they will miss out on new technologies that may emerge. They also worry about "one-sided contracts" that would effectively leave patents in American hands, depriving them of a chance to make commercial use of new technology. At the same time, American defense industry officials expressed serious doubt as to whether Japan's electronics giants would contribute their most advanced technologies to the project. They are also skeptical of entrusting key classified elements of the SDI development to Japanese industry, which is reportedly closely monitored by the Soviet Union. Washington previously signed agreements allowing companies in Britain, West Germany, and Israel to conduct SDI research.[34]

The other aspect of Weinberger's "defense partnership" involves joint military exercises. Japanese military forces, after years of caution and relative isolation, have sharply increased the level and sophistication of their joint military training with the United States, Australia, Canada, and other Pacific nations. This increase stems from a 1978 agreement that set guidelines for broad military cooperation. Japan first sent ships to the "Rimpac" multilateral exercise—known as "Rimpaku" in Japan—in 1980 and was the most active participant in February 1986, deploying eight destroyers and eight P3 aircraft.[35] Tokyo also reported in August 1986 that Japan and the United States would hold their first full-fledged military drill involving air, sea, and land forces in Hokkaido for five days in October 1986. General Shigehiro Mori of the Joint Staff Council of the Self-Defense Force stated that ten thousand men would be included in the drills, which are reportedly designed to repel an invader "from the north."[36] Masayoshi Ito—chairman of the LDP's policy board and former foreign minister—claimed that these joint military maneuvers were necessary for Japan "so as not to drive the United States into abandoning its defense commitment to Japan."[37] American pressure on Japan to increase military power and Japan's reluctant compliance to rearm—for political and economic reasons—may indeed prove to be counterproductive to U.S.-Japanese "defense partnership." For American capability to direct the "partnership" will be inevitably reduced as Japan increases its share in it.

Already a glimpse of the initial drift can be observed in the substantially different assessments of William Colby and William Casey—both former directors of the U.S. Central Intelligence Agency. Writing for the *Japan Times* in February 1979, Colby expressed the fear that America's past leadership in free-world political and strategic matters might be replaced by a Japan strong in economic and social issues, which would dominate the future. The strength of the Japanese economy, he suspected, could transfer world financial leadership to the yen at the expense of the dollar as the international medium of exchange. Anticipating these eventualities, Colby suggested that Japan and the United States develop a common political framework and permit full operation of their economies within a common framework instead of within two separate political frameworks. As long as two separate political frameworks exist, he predicted, competition in the economic field would be reflected in the political field, and the temptation would arise to use political tools to suppress economic competition.[38] As mentioned earlier, Casey in April 1984 denounced Japan's big stake in American computer industries as "Trojan horses" and warned that the excessive dependence on Japanese high technology was extremely dangerous for national security as well as for U.S. trade.[39]

Historically, there have been three stages in post-occupation U.S.-Japanese security relations: (1) the Yoshida strategy in the 1950's, (2) the National Defense Program Outline (NDPO) in 1976, and (3) the present military "realism" under Nakasone.[40] Japan's first post-occupation prime minister, Shigeru Yoshida, who had worked hard but in vain to avoid confrontation with the United States in the prewar period, advocated, after Japan's defeat in 1945, relying on the United States for Japan's security but declined U.S. requests for Japanese rearmament. Despite his general sympathy for Anglo-American democratic institutions, Yoshida—known as the "Adenauer of Japan"—reportedly regarded the U.S.-Japanese security system, which he negotiated with John Foster Dulles for the San Francisco Treaty in 1951, as nothing more than a transient association of convenience, the unavoidable result of the defeat, the U.S. military occupation of Japan, and the cold war. Yoshida believed that Japan—a small, resource-poor, maritime, trading nation, dependent for its economic survival on the import of raw materials and the export of finished products—had no choice but to maintain friendly relations with the United States, the world's great naval power in his time. Yet, given a favorable international environment and dynamic leadership, he was confident that Japan would be able to reemerge as a great power in its own right. The treaty relinquished jurisdiction over the U.S. forces stationed in Japan, permitted them to act against domestic unrest, and finally, lacked an expiration date.[41] The San Francisco Treaty was eventually replaced by the 1960 treaty of mutual cooperation and security. Since then, the United States has been fully committed to defend Japan (Article 5), but Japanese consent is required for the use of the Japanese facilities by American forces in Japan for the purpose of defending it and maintaining international security in East Asia (Article 6). Japan has no corresponding treaty obligation to defend the United States, thus making the 1960 treaty, in essence, an unequal treaty.[42]

The 1976 National Defense Program Outline initiated the recent Japanese security strategy. Conceived by the National Defense Council and the cabinet—both chaired by the prime minister—the NDPO's basic thrust was for Japan to possess its own minimum peacetime force to take care of small-scale aggression while assuming nuclear superpower equilibrium. What was gradually perceived in Japan as a decline of American security strength in the Pacific, evidenced by the Nixon Doctrine, the fall of Vietnam, and the subsequent relative decline of U.S. military superiority over the Soviet Union, aroused serious misgivings about the future reliability of the American commitment to the security of Japan.

No Japanese leader referred to defense matters in his keynote policy statements until 1978, when Takeo Fukuda broke the tradition in the National Diet. Still another unprecedented event was Director-General of the Defense Agency Shin Kanemaru's official NATO visit. Since then, the government of Japan has officially and publicly expressed serious doubt about U.S. capability to protect Japan, claiming that the U.S. can no longer unilaterally provide protection for its Western allies, given a marked expansion of Soviet forces in striking contrast to a previously overwhelming U.S. force posture. For the first time in the postwar period, in June 1979 Kanemaru's successor, Ganri Yamashita, officially visited Seoul to discuss a common security program. In October, Prime Minister Ohira decided, for the first time, to participate in the U.S.-sponsored "Rim Pacific" multinational naval exercise along with Canada, Australia, New Zealand, and South Korea, which took place off Hawaii in March 1980.[43]

Prime Minister Ohira also commissioned a study group headed by Professor Masamichi Inoki, former president of the National Defense Academy, whose report, in July 1980, emphatically stated that the "Pax Americana" is over and called for Japan's self-reliant efforts to cope with military threats. In April 1982 Prime Minister Suzuki reportedly stated that the USSR had achieved nuclear superiority over the United States.[44] The Japanese Defense Agency's 1982 Defense White Paper claimed that the Soviet Union already had an advantage over the United States in the area of intermediate-range ballistic missiles (IRBMs) and TU-22M Backfire bombers, and that the Soviet Union showed no sign of easing its large-scale military buildup. In September 1982, apparently under heavy U.S. pressure, Suzuki accepted the U.S. plan to deploy some forty to fifty F-16 fighter-bombers in the Misawa Airbase, quite close to Hokkaido and Vladivostok, after 1985.

Today, however, Prime Minister Nakasone appears to advocate what Mike Mochizuki calls "military realism." Primarily because of what Japan perceives to be the increased military threat to itself resulting from the shifting U.S.-Soviet strategic nuclear balance, Nakasone advocates a stronger military alliance with the United States, particularly for political and economic purposes. As the primary U.S. military concerns have been shifting to European and Middle East regions, the "military realists" feel the necessity to be responsible conventionally for the vulnerable Northeast Asia–western Pacific theater. They see closer U.S.-Japan defense cooperation as an affirmation of Japan's membership in the community of free and democratic nations. For this and other possible reasons, Nakasone in January 1983 visited Seoul—the first official visit to Seoul by a Japanese prime minister in 37 years—and offered $4 billion in economic aid over seven years.

This was applauded by Washington. Prime Minister Nakasone reportedly emphasized, at the May 1983 Williamsburg economic summit, the indivisibility of Western security. What appears to be emerging, in brief, is a much more equal and assertive Japan than the previously subservient and unequal Japan in the U.S.-Japanese alliance. While most American defense planners, who have been pressuring Japan to do more militarily, should welcome the security posture of the military realists, they somehow seem to be rather ambivalent. Many on both sides of the Pacific are, in fact, increasingly apprehensive about the uncertain future of "military realism" and whether such a strategy for a larger military establishment would be politically agreeable domestically. Japan's external environment, in all probability, would be even less tolerant of such a program. Even the United States in urging Japan to rearm, does not seem to be certain what it wants with a rearmed Japan, much less how to influence a Japanese rearmament program.[45]

What appears to be certain, however, is the probability that Japanese security strategy will be different from that of the United States. The fundamental difference is, as clearly indicated above, attributable not only to variations in geopolitics but also to the differences in historical, cultural, and ethnic backgrounds. Even Japan's January 1987 termination of a military spending cap of 1 percent which had been established in 1976, (the actual amount for a five-year plan (1987–91) called for $120 billion—1.04 percent of Japan's projected GNP) has not changed the situation. This is still the lowest military budget among the industrialized countries and may not completely satisfy the U.S. demand.[46]

CONCLUSION

Given these prevailing economic and strategic contradictions, U.S. and Japanese political leaders are less likely to press for PEC. On a semi-governmental level, however, the Pacific Community Movement has become much more active, as was clearly indicated at the Fifth PECC, Vancouver, Canada, in November 1986. Not only Beijing and Taipei formally joined the PECC but even Moscow sent an observer. Soviet interest may be part of Gorbachev's active economic diplomacy. Yet how successful the "privatized" PECC will be and for how long remains to be seen. It appears less certain whether Ronald Reagan and Yasuhiro Nakasone can exercise their leadership to activate PECC. The U.S. president has two more years in office, but the Japanese prime minister's term expires in October 1987. The United States and Japan, the two prime potential leaders for the Pacific community, seem, more often than not, to be overpowered by non-rational human frailties—ambition, status-seeking, face saving, illusions, self-delusions, fixed prejudices—inevitably blinding them from confronting realities and reasoning together for their mutual benefit. In all probability, a "privatized" PECC will muddle through while political leaders will fade away. For this reason, visions in history, however grandiose they may be, appear to have remained more often unrealized than otherwise.

NOTES

1. "California's Economic Survey," *Economist* (May 19, 1984), p. 3.

2. The complete text of Ambassador Mansfield's January 6, 1982, speech is found in *Japan Times*, January 7, 1982.

3. I. M. Destler and Hideo Sato, eds., *Coping with U.S.-Japanese Economic Conflict* (Lexington, Mass.: Lexington Books, 1982), pp. 2–10.

4. *Economic Report to the Congress, 1983* (Washington, D.C.: U.S. Government Printing Office, 1983), p. 61.

5. *Economic Report to the Congress, 1984* (Washington, D.C.: U.S. Government Printing Office, 1984), p. 5.

6. *Christian Science Monitor*, April 25, 1984.

7. Ibid.

8. Theodore White, *America in Search of Itself* (New York: Harper & Row, 1982), p. 424.

9. Michio Morishima, *Why Has Japan 'Succeeded'?* (Cambridge, England: Cambridge University Press, 1982).

10. *New York Times*, February 23, 1983.

11. Ibid.

12. *Wall Street Journal*, July 12, 1984.

13. *Christian Science Monitor*, July 13, 1984.

14. Felicity Marsh, *Japanese Overseas Investment: The New Challenge*, Special Report no. 142 (London: The Economist Intelligence Unit Unlimited, 1983), p. 50.

15. *New York Times*, May 6, 1984.

16. Ibid.

17. Ibid.

18. Ibid.

19. Ibid.

20. *Economic Report to the Congress, 1984*, p. 65.

21. *New York Times*, February 23, 1983.

22. Ibid.

23. Saburo Okita, "Japanese-American Economic Troubles: Lowering the Temperature," *International Security* (Fall 1982), pp. 192–203.

24. Ibid.

25. Fred Bergsten, "What to Do about the U.S. Economic Conflict," *Foreign Affairs* (Summer 1982), pp. 1059–1075.

26. The Japan-United States Economic Relations Group, *Supplemental Report of the Japan-United States Economic Relations Group* (Tokyo: Japan Center for International Exchange, 1981), p. 42.

27. Sadato Osata, "Some Japanese Views on United States–Japan Relations in the 1980s," *Asian Survey* (July 1980), pp. 694–706.

28. Taketsusu Tsurutani, "Old Habits, New Times: Challenges to Japanese-American Security Relations," *International Security* (Fall 1982), pp. 175–187.

29. Hisahiko Okazaki, "Japanese Security Policy: A Time for Strategy," *International Security* (Fall 1982), pp. 188–192.

30. *Christian Science Monitor*, May 25, 1984.

31. Mashashi Nishihara, "Expanding Japan's Credible Defense Role," *International Security* (Winter 1983–1984), pp. 180–205.

32. Comprehensive National Security Study Group, *Report on Comprehensive National Security* (Tokyo, 1980). This is perhaps one of the most comprehensive researches on the subject in recent times in Japan.

33. *Annual Report to the Congress, Fiscal Year 1985* (Washington, D.C.: U.S. Government Printing Office, 1984), p. 218.

34. U.S. Secretary of Defense Caspar Weinberger invited Japan, along with other Western allies, to participate in the SDI research in a letter in March 1985. For the background, see Defense Agency (Japan), *Summary of "Defense of Japan"* (Tokyo: Foreign Press Center, 1986), p. 87. For U.S. official analysis of Japan's defense contribution, see Caspar Weinberger, *Report on Allied Contribution to the Common Defense: A Report to the United States Congress* (Washington, D.C.: Department of Defense, 1986), pp. 67–69. The Japanese announcement and its analyses are found in the *Wall Street Journal*, September 9, 1986, p. 33; *New York Times*, September 10, 1986, p. 6.

35. *Summary of "Defense of Japan,"* p. 86; Fred Hiatt, "Where Rimpac Meets Rimpaku," *Washington Post National Weekly Edition* (September 15, 1986), p. 19. I am grateful to William M. Arkin, Institute for Policy Study of Washington, D.C., for providing me a copy of a document detailing these military exercises that he obtained under the Freedom of Information Act from the Pacific Command in Honolulu.

36. Edward Neilan, "Navy to Manuever on Soviet Doorstep," *Washington Times*, September 1, 1986. I am grateful to Stewart Goldman, Congressional Research Service, for this information.

37. Masayoshi Ito, cited in ibid.

38. "Japan and U.S.: An Intelligence Projection," *Japan Times*, February 13, 1979.

39. *New York Times*, May 6, 1984.

40. Mike M. Mochizuki, "Japan's Search for Strategy," *International Security* (Winter 1983–1984), pp. 152–179.

41. Nakasone allegedly opposed the San Francisco Treaty largely

because its contents were not disclosed either to the Japanese people or to the Diet until the day of the signing. Yasuhiro Nakasone, *My Life in Politics* (Tokyo?, 1983?), p. 5. This is an 86-page typewritten manuscript that became available from the Japanese Embassy in Washington, D.C., just prior to Nakasone's visit to the United States in January 1983.

42. Ibid. While admitting that it was a much improved treaty, serving the interest of both countries, Nakasone reportedly stated that "a people that have become used to the protection of another country soon lose the will to defend themselves. They degenerate into weak and selfish materialists who put the pursuit of economic prosperity above all else.

43. Nishihara, "Expanding Japan's Credible Defense Role," p. 203.

44. *Report on Comprehensive National Security.*

45. In comparison, U.S. military spending for 1987 reached 6.1 percent of GNP, and in 1985 figures were 5.4 percent for Britain, 4.1 percent for France, and 3.3 percent for West Germany. *New York Times*, January 25, 1987.

46. Ibid.

Conclusion

HILARY CONROY
with ROY KIM

As we have seen in the last chapter, the Japanese-American relationship, which was from early on presumed to be the keystone of Pacific Community, appears in disarray. However, it may also be said that as long as the Japanese-American relationship was one of full partnership, whether viewed as an alliance or as a client-sponsor relationship, there was little likelihood that "Pacific Community" would go much beyond the confines of that relationship; certainly it would not encompass the USSR and the People's Republic of China, unless it should be stabilized as a modus vivendi between two rival alliances.

With the "deterioration" of American-Japanese relations, as indeed, with the "Sino-Soviet split" of the 1960's, the international politics of the Pacific-East Asian area have become more "normal." I almost said "returned to normal," but that might bring to mind too many remembrances of the failures of the Washington Conference era of "normalcy" of the 1920's, when the Pacific was "frozen," though only on the surface. "Freezing the Pacific" was the chapter heading for the discussion of the Washington Conference settlements in A. Whitney Griswold's widely used textbook, *The Far Eastern Policy of the United States*. These settlements constituted the best hope for easing tensions and promoting trade and prosperity among the various powers with spheres of interest in the western Pacific and China in the pre–Pacific War era, but they proved to be unsatisfactory to Ja-

pan, which was treated as a junior partner by Britain and the
United States—a situation which provided sparks for the fires
of Japanese nationalism and militarism in the 1930's. Nor was
China satisfied, even though it was, according to the settlements, to enjoy an "unembarrassed opportunity" to establish a
stable government. Chinese nationalism was seeking an end to
the various unequal treaties upon which its foreign trade structure was based. And the Soviet Union was completely left out
of the conference and its settlements, as though it were not a
Pacific power and had no valid interests in the region.

In addition, and perhaps most important, overreacting to Wil-
sonianism, the United States had entered an era of increasing
isolationism in foreign affairs and protectionism in trade, and in
the later 1920's and early 1930's when the future viability of the
Washington settlements was at issue and cooperation with the
League of Nations was increasingly vital, the Coolidge, Hoover,
and early Roosevelt administrations were all isolationist.

Admittedly there are some similarities in the situation today.
There is a tendency for Japan to be too aggressive for its trade
interests, for the USSR to be neglected or deliberately kept out
of Pacific Community considerations and discussions, for China's interests to be considered only in terms of her free enterprise zone links to the market economy, with little or no attention to her needs and problems as a third-world country, and for
the United States to indulge in edgy avoidance of difficult problems whether at the United Nations, where at least some of the
pertinent Pacific issues might be discussed, or at Canberra, Tokyo, Beijing, or Moscow, where the Pacific may be considered
off limits as an American lake.

However, today, despite these tendencies to repeat the mis-
takes of the 1920's, the fact that both the Washington-Tokyo
and Moscow-Beijing relationships are in disequilibrium provides
opportunity for movement, especially when economic advantages for all four parties might result from cooperation among
them. Hence, from the "negative"—that is, the breakdown of
the previous alliance systems—a "positive" Pacific Community
system may be born. The opportunity is there if statesmen and
business leaders are wise enough to seize it. The one hearten-
ing aspect of the KAL 007 incident was the strange sea-search

aftermath, which found Soviet, U.S., and Japanese vessels almost side by side in the Sea of Okhotsk finding bits and pieces of the Korean Air Lines plane and its people and exchanging information on them.

The leadership of Yasuhiro Nakasone, whose administration began in November 1982 and is now extended until October 1987, marked the beginning of a new era in Japanese foreign policy. Seizing the opportunity, he invited the Soviet foreign minister to Japan. If Moscow would indeed be willing to go back to a 1956 formula to return two of the disputed northern islands (Habomai and Shikotan) to Japan to settle the controversial territorial issue—as reportedly hinted by Academician Primakov in December in Moscow and suggested by the Soviet Foreign Minister Eduard Shevardnadze during his visit to Tokyo in January 1986—this could very well bring about a substantial improvement of relations with Japan.

Not since the ill-starred visit of Tsar-to-be Nicholas in 1891 has a Russian leader been to Japan, but both Gorbachev and Nakasone have shown that they like to travel, and there is mounting evidence that they will exchange visits to Tokyo and Moscow respectively.

As for the Korean Air Lines 007 disaster in 1983, Moscow, Tokyo, and Washington apparently negotiated an arrangement to avoid such an incident in the future, and this was prominently mentioned at the end of the Geneva summit in November 1985. Moreover, Japan and the USSR have been quietly discussing a number of regional problems, including the Korean situation, to facilitate and enhance the prospects for reducing tensions between the two Koreas and having a successful Olympics in Korea in 1988. Perhaps most encouraging of all are the Reagan administration's serious efforts to defuse the rising protectionist tides in the U.S. Congress and the willingness of China and (perhaps) the USSR to experiment with the market economy in the Pacific, with hints even that Vladivostok may become an "open port."

In fact, there appear to be, as we approach the twenty-first century, slow but significant trends toward a symmetrical relationship among the four major powers in the Pacific. U.S.-Japan relations—whether strategic or economic—can no longer be characterized as a client-sponsor relationship. Nor can Soviet-Chinese relations be regarded as a client-sponsor relationship nor even as a "fraternal alliance." The two major powers have relied heavily on military power, whereas China and Japan rely more on economic strength. This gradually emerging four-power parity—while relative, to be sure—appears to be a major stabilizing catalyst.

How this emerging four-power stability will facilitate the formation of the "Pacific Community" is not clear. But what appears to be crystal clear is the emerging centrality of the Pacific region in the four powers' foreign policy. Despite the threat of protectionism in the United States, the Pacific region today is the most economically successful region in the world. The rising economies of the entire region have stimulated an awareness of its importance to overall global development.

Indeed, the potential for "Pacific Community" is real enough and timely enough that Pacific Community activists can no longer be put down or aside simply as dreamers. Certainly the literature is building up, and a brief discussion of this follows. Since Helen Ester's "Slow Start in the Pacific," *Far Eastern Economic Review*, no. 26 (September 1980), discovered with other items by Lily Lee for the U.S. Congressional Research Service, not only has the International Studies Association devoted several sessions to the topic at its annual meetings, but the journal *Asian Survey* edited by Robert Scalapino and Leo E. Rose at the University of California, Berkeley, has devoted large parts of several issues to various aspects of the Pacific Community theme (e.g., May 1981, June 1983, December 1983, and April 1986). See in addition, Scalapino, S. Sato, and Jusut Wanndi, *Asian Economic Development* (Berkeley: Institute of East Asian Studies, University of California, 1985). In addition, the Center for Strategic and International Studies at Georgetown University has published a dozen titles which it advertises as being "on the Pacific Basin," including one called *The Emerging Pacific Community Concept: An American Perspective* (1983).

In 1980 the Aspen Institute for Humanistic Studies and the University of Minnesota's Hubert H. Humphrey Institute of Public Affairs formed a joint non-governmental venture to explore the question of Pacific Community "not through political advocacy but by examining the functional needs for consultation, cooperation, parallel national action, and common action among and between the nations of the Pacific Basin," according to Harlan Cleveland, director of the institute. Under this program Westview Press, Boulder, Colorado, has published *The Industrial Future of the Pacific Basin*, edited by Roger Benjamin and Harlan Cleveland (1984). Westview also published *The Emerging Pacific Community*, edited by Robert L. Downen and Bruce J. Dickson (1984), and *United States Foreign Policy and Asian-Pacific Security*, edited by William T. Tow and William R. Feeney (1982).

Beginning in 1980, the Brookings Institution entered the "Pacific Community Movement" with *Economic Interaction in the Pacific Basin*, a 268-page collection of addresses, essays and lectures edited by Lawrence B. Krause and Sueo Sekiguchi and co-sponsored by the Japan Economic Council. In 1981 a "Pan Pacific Community Association" under the chairmanship of former Senator Hugh Scott was established in Washington, D.C., and this organization has been publishing a newsletter, *Pacific Economic Cooperation*.

The Hoover Institution has also been stressing Pacific Community awareness with an important analysis of the "Pacific Basin" problem by Ramon H. Myers in *To Promote Peace*, edited by Dennis L. Bark (1984); Claude A. Buss, ed., *National Security Interests in the Pacific Basin* (1985), and Staffan Linder, *The Pacific Century* (1986).

The British Economist Intelligence Unit has published a 99-page special report by Stuart Kirby entitled *Towards the Pacific Community* (London, 1983). While this somewhat overlooks the problem of the Soviet Union, it has a great deal to say about the smaller countries of East and Southeast Asia and is therefore a particularly good supplement to our *New Tides in the Pacific*.

PHP INTERSECT, published in Tokyo, which tries hard to anticipate future trends and potentials, especially positive ones, devoted its August 1985 issue to "Pacific Community," which its editor, J. J. Wargo, called "moving in the right direction."

Soviet-American Horizons on the Pacific, edited by John Stephan and V. P. Chichkanov (Honolulu: University of Hawaii Press, 1986), has been called a "pioneering work in US-USSR relations." It is indeed that, and much more, perhaps a "milestone," or a breakthrough in that it represents a genuine effort, perhaps the first, by Soviet and American scholars to present in the same book with mutual respect and minimal propaganda their respective views of the history and present condition of the Pacific relationships of the United States and the USSR. Significantly, there is no concluding chapter drawing things together, and indeed there are separate introductions by the American and Soviet editors also. However, and this may be the most significant of all, the last two chapters are very optimistic. The Soviet author of "Soviet-American Trade in the Pacific" sees great potential for increasing not only trade per se but tourism. And the American authors of "Soviet-American Scientific Cooperation in the Pacific" show that despite "the inhibiting influence of bureaucracy in both nations" much has already been accomplished, and the future potential is great.

Finally, to return to our launching pad and James Morley's chapter detailing the early development of the Pacific Community concept, beginning with Saburo Okita's efforts, it is gratifying to find Morley's own Columbia University co-sponsoring a major conference on "The Pacific Basin: New Challenges for the United States" in November 1985. A volume based on the proceedings of that conference, which included Okita himself on the agenda, was published early in 1986 as volume 36, no. 1 of the *Proceedings of the Academy of Political Science*. Its contributors include, besides Okita, such leading students and advocates of Pacific Community as Hugh Patrick, Evelyn Colbert, Donald Zagoria, William H. Overholt, Robert Ross, Peter Drysdale, Peter Stanley, Richard Sneider, John Bresnan, N. T. Wang, Kishore Mahbubani, and Lawrence Krause.

Despite the buildup of literature and interest in favor of the idea or at least the ideal of some form of large-scale and long-range thought and action toward a twenty-first century of new and mutually cooperative ties in the Pacific, the United States government has played a less than active role, leaving the private sector, the Japanese, and perhaps the general economic developments of the region to bring them about. Even though the word "initiative" has been a big word in the Reagan administration, from Caribbean Initiatives to SDI, there has been no real Pacific initiative from Washington as yet.

In all probability this will have to change, and rapidly, if the United States is not to be outmaneuvered by the Soviet Union. Gorbachev's Vladivostok initiatives, July 28, 1986, should not be underestimated. In fact, the speech may open the door not only to Vladivostok as he proposed, but to the new tides discussed in this volume, if the opportunities it pretends to offer are to be fulfilled. A careful analysis of the speech shows Gorbachev to be seeking (1) an end to Sino-Soviet estrangement, (2) a "summit" meeting with Japanese Prime Minister Yasuhiro Nakasone to rechart Soviet-Japanese relations in a positive direction, and (3) a somewhat backhanded appeal to the United States to facilitate rather than to hinder a process toward what he calls "Pacific Basin Economic Cooperation."

It works like this. The USSR will move toward withdrawal of troops from Mongolia, reduce Soviet-backed Vietnamese involvement in Cambodia, and slowly but steadily reduce Soviet forces in Afghanistan. All of these are largely directed at reducing tensions with China. He also offered three specific projects to the Chinese: an Amur River joint project, a Xinjiang-Uygur railroad project, and an invitation to participate in the Soviet space program. Even before his Vladivostok initiatives, he had already sent Shevardnadze to Japan in January 1986, and Nakasone dispatched his foreign minister to Moscow in May 1986 to improve the much troubled Japanese-Soviet relations. Gorbachev's reconciling overture toward Nakasone is largely based on his realistic assessment of Japan's emergence as a world economic power. Nakasone, for his part, clearly intends to make new friends and influence more people with Japan's steadily increasing global economic power. A Japanese-Soviet summit at any time to break the protracted deadlock between Moscow and Tokyo will certainly warrant a place in our history books.

Toward the United States, Gorbachev takes a tough line at first. He denounces "Pacific Community" and Washington's attempt to establish a militarized "Washington-Tokyo-Seoul triangle," but he declares Soviet willingness to discuss "the idea of Pacific Basin Economic Cooperation" without bias and "readiness to join in the deliberations on the possible foundations of such cooperation—provided, of course, it is conceived not in accordance with a bloc-oriented, anti-socialist pattern imposed from the outside."

And he continues, "If a change for the better in the Pacific is really achieved, Vladivostok could become one of the major international centres, a commercial, and cultural centre, a city of festivals, sports events, congresses, and scientific symopsia. We would like it to be a wide open window to the East. And then in the words of the great Pushkin, 'the ships of every flag and nation will hail our shores' will then apply also to Vladivostok."

To be sure, there are some flies in Gorbachev's ointment. The USSR still holds, well fortified, four islands which the Japanese contend are theirs: the aforementioned Habomai and Shikotan, plus Etorofu and Kunashiri, of the southern Kuril Islands north of Hokkaido. And China supports Prince Sihanouk in Kampuchea, regarding the Soviet-backed Vietnamese intrusion there as intolerable. Resolving such matters will not be easy, but such problems afford Washington the opportunity to play a problem-solving role in the coming of New Tides in the Pacific.

Selected Bibliography

Abegglen, James C. and George Stalk, Jr. *Kaisha: The Japanese Corporation*. New York: Basic Books, 1985.

Balassa, Bela, et al. *Development Strategies in Semi-Industrial Economics*. Baltimore, Md.: Johns Hopkins University Press for World Bank Research Publication, 1982.

Cheung, Stephen N. S. *Will China Go Capitalist?* London: Institute of Economic Affairs, 1982.

Connoly, David M. *Progress and Prospects for a Pacific Basin Community*. Philadelphia: Foreign Policy Research Institute, 1980.

Corbert, Hugh, ed. *Trade Strategy in the Asian-Pacific Region*. London: Allen and Unwin, 1970.

Foreign Press Center. *Statements and Opinions on Pacific Cooperation*. Tokyo, 1985.

Garnaut, Ross, ed. *ASEAN in a Changing Pacific and World Economy*. Canberra: Australian National University Press, 1980.

Hansen, Kermit O. and Thomas W. Roehl, eds. *The United States and the Pacific Economy in the 1980s*. Indianapolis, Indiana: Bobbs-Merrill Education Publication, 1980.

Hersch, Seymour M. *The Target is Destroyed*. New York: Random House, 1986.

Hoffman, Arthur S., ed. *Japan and the Pacific Basin*. Paris: Atlantic Institute for International Affairs, 1980.

Hofheinz, Roy, Jr. and Kent E. Calder. *The Eastasia Edge*. New York: Basic Books, 1982.

Hong, Wontack, and Lawrence B. Krause, eds. *Trade and Growth of the Advanced Developing Countries in the Pacific Basin.* Seoul: Korea Development Institute, 1981.

Ivanov, V. I. and K. B. Malakhovskii. *Tikhookeanskii Regionalism* (Regionalism in the Pacific). Moscow: Izdatel'stvo Nauka, 1983.

Kojima, Kiyoshi. *Japan and a Pacific Free Trade Area.* Berkeley: University of California Press, 1971.

Korea Development Institute. *Pacific Economic Cooperation: Report of the Fourth Pacific Economic Cooperation Conference, Seoul, April 29–May 1, 1985.* Seoul: Korea Development Institute, 1985.

Kovrigin, E. B. *Protivorechiya i Perespektivy formirovaniya "Tikhookeanskogo Soobshestva"* (Contradictions and prospects of the "Pacific community"). Moscow Mezhdunarodnye otnosheniya, 1986.

Lawrence, Robert Z. *Can America Compete?* Washington, D.C.: Brookings Institution, 1984.

Linder, Staffan Burenstam. *The Pacific Century: Economic and Political Consequences of Asian Pacific Dynamism.* Stanford: Stanford University Press, 1986.

Morishima, Michio. *Why Has Japan 'Succeeded'?* Cambridge, England: Cambridge University Press, 1982.

Myers, Ramon H. "The Future of Communist China and the Implications for U.S. Technological Transfer to China" (unpub. ms.). Stanford: Hoover Institution.

Okimoto, Daniel I., ed. *Japan's Economy: Coping with Change in the International Environment.* Boulder, Colo.: Westview Press, 1982.

Osborne, Michael. *Pacific Basin Economic Cooperation.* Paris: OECD, 1983.

Ouchi, William. *Theory Z: How American Business Can Meet the Japanese Challenge.* Reading, Mass.: Addison-Wesley, 1981.

Pacific Basin Cooperation Study Group. Tokyo, 1980.

Patrick, Hugh and Henry Rosovsky, eds. *Asia's New Giant: How the Japanese Economy Works.* Washington, D.C.: Brookings Institution, 1976.

Pepper, Thomas, et al. *The Competition: Dealing with Japan.* New York: Praeger, 1985.

Pye, Lucian. *Asian Power and Politics.* Cambridge: Harvard University Press, 1986.

Scalapino, Robert A. and Chen Qimao. *Pacific-Asian Issues: American and Chinese Views* Berkeley: University of California Press, 1986.

Segal, Gerald, ed. *The Soviet Union in East Asia.* Boulder, Colo.: Westview Press, 1983.

Shibusawa, Masahide. *Japan and the Asian Pacific Region*. London: Royal Institute of International Affairs, 1984.

Solomon, Richard and Masataka Kosaka, eds. *The Soviet Far East Military Buildup*. Dover, Mass.: Auburn House Publishing Company, 1986.

Stephan, John and V. P. Chichkanov, eds. *Soviet-American Horizons on the Pacific*. Honolulu: University of Hawaii Press, 1986.

Tasca, Diane, ed. *U.S.-Japanese Economic Relations: Cooperation, Competition, and Confrontation*. New York: Pergamon, 1980.

U.S. Congress. House of Representatives. Committee on Energy and Commerce. *The Soviet Role in the Pacific Rim: U.S.-Soviet Environmental Cooperation*. 99th Cong., 1st sess., 1985.

Vasey, Lloyd R. and George J. Viksnins, eds. *The Economic and Political Growth Pattern of Asia-Pacific*. Honolulu: University of Hawaii Press, 1976.

Vogel, Ezra F. *Comeback*. New York: Simon and Schuster, 1985.

Whiting, Allen S. *Siberian Development and East Asia: Threat or Promise?* Stanford: Stanford University Press, 1981.

Zagoria, Donald S., ed. *Soviet Policy in East Asia*. New Haven and London: Yale University Press, 1982.

Index

About the Contributors

MARK BORTHWICK is the Executive Director of the United States National Committee for Pacific Economic Cooperation. He is also responsible for coordinating the Japan-Thailand-U.S. project on foreign investment policies and the Korea-U.S. project on GATT trade negotiations. He was a Science and Technology Fellow at Duke University and also a staff consultant to the Chairman of the House Subcommittee on Asian and Pacific Affairs. He has traveled extensively in the Pacific area. After his undergraduate training at Northwestern University, he received a Ph.D. in social anthropology from the University of Iowa.

FRANCE H. CONROY, a Danforth Fellow at Yale University and the Union Graduate School from 1970–1975, wrote his doctoral dissertation on individualism and collectivism in comparative Chinese and Western contexts. Since then he has taught at St. Joseph's University, Punahou School, and Burlington County College and traveled in both China and the Soviet Union. His articles have appeared in the journal *Peace and Change*, and he is working on a study of Confucianism in the modern context.

HILARY CONROY, is Professor of Far Eastern History at the University of Pennsylvania, where he has taught since 1951. His first book was *The Japanese Frontier in Hawaii* (University of California Press, 1953, reprinted in 1974); other works he has written or edited include studies of Japanese relations with Korea, China, and the United States, and most recently *Japan in Transition* (Associated University Presses, 1984). He has been a Fulbright scholar at Tokyo University and a Senior Specialist at the East-West Center (Honolulu) and is past president of the Conference on Peace Research in History.

VLADIMIR I. IVANOV is a senior researcher on Oceanic economics at the Institute of World Economy and International Relations, Academy of Sciences of the USSR. He served as the Academic Secretary at the Institute of Oriental Studies, USSR Academy of Sciences. Thereafter he joined the Soviet foreign service. He wrote, along with Professor Kim B. Malakhovskii, *Tikhookeanskii Regionalism (Regionalism in the Pacific)*.

ROY KIM has taught Political Science at Drexel University since 1969. He is the co-author of *Calendar of Diplomatic Affairs of the Democratic People's Republic of Korea*, contracted by the Social Science Research Council. He received research grants from the Ford Foundation, the International Research and Exchanges Board, and the Social Science Research Council. He has been nominated as a Fulbright scholar to Korea and the Soviet Union. His published works have appeared in the *Christian Science Monitor, Problemii D'lanego Vostoka* (Far Eastern Affairs, Moscow), and the *Washington Quarterly*. He served as a Scholar-Diplomat at the U.S. Department of State in 1971. He has made a dozen trips to lecture at various institutes of the USSR Academy of Sciences. He is the chairman, in 1985–87, of the Committee on Korean Studies, Association for Asian Studies.

HIROSHI KIMURA is a Professor and Director of the Slavic Research Center at Hokkaido University and a Vice President of the International Committee for Soviet and East European Studies. A graduate of Kyoto University and Columbia University (Ph.D., International Relations), he was a Fulbright-Hays Visiting Professor at the Institute for Sino-Soviet Studies of George Washington University in 1977–78 and at Stanford University in 1982–83. Previously he served as a Special Research Fellow at the Japanese embassies in Vienna (1972–73) and Moscow (1973–75). He has written extensively on Japanese-Soviet relations. His publications include "Japan-Soviet Relations: Framework, Developments, Prospects" (1980), "Arms Control in East Asia" in *Global Perspective on Arms Control,* ed. Adam M. Garfinkle and "Soviet Policies in the Asian Pacific Region," in *Soviet International Behavior and U.S. Policy Options,* ed. Dan Caldwell, (1985). Most recently, he wrote, along with William G. Hyland and Karl Kaiser, Trilateral Commission's Triangle Papers no. 31: *Prospects for East-West Relations.* His other works were widely published in Japan and in the United States, including articles in *Orbis* and the *Washington Quarterly.*

JAMES WILLIAM MORLEY is a Professor of Government and Director of the East Asian Institute at Columbia University. He is past president of the Association of Asian Studies and the author of many books on East Asian–Pacific matters, including, among others, *The Japanese Thrust Into Siberia* (1957), *Japan and the United States in the 1970's (1971), Japan's Foreign Policy, 1868–1941* (1974), *Deterrent Diplomacy* (1975), *China Quagmire* (1983), *Japan Erupts* (1984), and most recently *Security Interdependence in the Asia Pacific Region* (1986) and *The Pacific Basin: New Challenges for the United States* (1986).

NORMAN D. PALMER is a Professor Emeritus of Political Science at the University of Pennsylvania, where he taught international relations and Asian politics for more than thirty years. He is the author of many important books and articles, including, among others, *International Relations: World Community in Transition* (1953), *The Indian Political System* (1971), *Indo-American Relations in the Seventies* (1972), *United States and India: Dimensions of Influence* (1984), *Major Governments of Asia, Changing Patterns of Security and Stability,* and his latest volume, *Westward Watch: US Security Policies in the Western Pacific.*

YEVGENY M. PRIMAKOV is an Academician of the USSR Academy of Sciences and Director of the Institute of World Economy and International Relations. He was previously the

Director of the Institute of Oriental Studies, USSR Academy of Sciences. He has written many scholarly books.

JOHN J. STEPHAN is a Professor of History and Director of the Soviet Union in the Pacific and Asian Region (SUPAR) at the University of Hawaii. He has made two dozen trips to Siberia, has lectured extensively in Russian at various institutes of the USSR Academy of Sciences, and has written among others, *Sakhalin, The Kuril Islands, The Russian Fascists,* and *Hawaii under the Rising Sun.* Most recently he co-edited with Dr. V. P. Chichkanov, *Soviet-American Horizons on the Pacific.* He lectured in 1986 on Siberia at Stanford University.